CU00695830

)5

)6

007

7

7

ARAB WOMEN: UNEQUAL PARTNERS IN DEVELOPMENT

To the memory of my late parents

Arab Women: Unequal Partners in Development

SHIRIN J.A. SHUKRI
University of Bristol

Avebury

Aldershot • Brookfield USA • Hong Kong • Singapore • Sydney

Published by
Avebury
Ashgate Publishing Limited
Gower House
Croft Road
Aldershot
Hants GU11 3HR
England

Ashgate Publishing Company
Old Post Road
Brookfield
Vermont 05036
USA

British Library Cataloguing in Publication Data

Shukri, Shirin J.A.
   Arab Women: Unequal Partners in Development
   I. Title
   305.42091742927
ISBN 1 85972 165 6

Library of Congress Catalog Card Number: 95-83281

Typeset by Breeze Limited, Manchester
Printed in Great Britain by Ipswich Book Co. Ltd., Ipswich, Suffolk.

Contents

BOOk IS VERY BIASED ✓

vi

List of tables

Acknowledgements

The purpose of analysing women's inequalities in rural Jordan is to me of value in its own right. I am indebted to a great number of people, far too many to mention individually, who have directly and indirectly helped me to accomplish this task.

To the president, board members, members and staff of the Al-Nahda Philanthropic Society for Women, I owe you my gratitude and respect for a very enriching working experience and the most privileged education.

To Pervaiz Nazir, my supervisor, I shall always appreciate your method as I carry out my research. A good supervisor makes a PhD or breaks it, and you let me make it. I will always owe a particular debt of gratitude for your support and valuable assistance in augmenting my research and your guidance throughout my writing up of this work.

To Nuha Hegelan, I am greatly indebted to your spiritual and intellectual encouragement to persevere and maintain a broader perspective on life and living. Your inspiration made me think in original and unconventional ways.

To Rashid and Pervin Shukri, your moral support sustained me through the hard work and will always be valued.

Shirin Shukri
Bristol
January 1995

Abstract

This book seeks to elaborate on the problem of gender inequality, in the process of development, in a rural village in Jordan. The purpose of the study is important for me in its own right. I want to examine in detail and analyse the reasons behind the inequalities in a social and economic context. This village differs in two important respects from other villages in the region. Firstly, men have to travel much further to find waged work and communications are poorer, so they really have to choose between being full-time wage earners or full-time farmers. Secondly, land in the foothills is not productive enough to make it worthwhile investing large sums of cash earned in employment.

The examination of the roles in production does indeed explain the social roles women experience and the inequality they face and encounter in the rural setting. The analysis of rural Jordanian women determines their priorities and identifies some of the pivotal issues which limit their options. The concept of honour (*sharaf*) sanctions their conduct. Honour is what makes life of value for them, while shame is a living death. The gender inequality revolves around this concept.

An overview of women's roles and status in the Middle East will seek to elaborate the various theoretical and empirical studies on women and development and their relevance for the present book. I shall proceed to examine the question of land and its importance in inheritance, and how women's inequality in the development process is revealed in their domestic roles in land and property ownership. The interaction between economic and other variables within the social system of the village will shed light on the process of increasing economic differentiation which has taken place in the village during the last fifteen years. The wealthiest farmers became wealthier and the poor poorer. The position of women in the household economy and their roles in the diversified economic activities of agricultural and domestic work will have a bearing on the cooperation that takes place between men and women in the household, in which women can translate their incomes into decision-making and control over their budgeting.

Some of the inequalities between men and women had their basis in the period of Mandate rule. Although before this time social relations between men and women, as between other groups, were by no means egalitarian, there is no doubt that the Mandate period and the introduction of exploitative labour regimes led to a marked deterioration in the social and economic status of women relative to that of men. The development of an international economy and the spread of wage labour in both agricultural and industrial production demanded very different roles for women and men in the economy, sometimes excluding women from wage employment while relying on their unpaid work on family farms or on their low-paid work within the informal sector.

To further my analysis of the inequalities women face as partners in the development process in the village, I shall attempt to elaborate and explore their social and political position in the marriage, kinship and female roles which they play, both inside the household and outside the household, with other women and neighbours.

This study of women's inequalities as partners in the development process in a rural village in Jordan will conclude that there are various factors which perpetuate the position of women in the ideological and legal processes that persist in the village, and that economic and social advancement hinders their own empowerment for a better future. My own contribution to the subject of gender and development is that, while I elaborate on economic and social issues, the new emphasis is on the legal aspect of divorce and widowhood, which has not been researched by others. However, I hope my attempt will lead others to carry this point further.

1 Introduction

My interest in the social role of Jordanian women is to try to concentrate on areas not covered by other researchers, especially the economic life of rural Jordanian women and their inequality in the development process, as well as neglected aspects of kinship and household organisation, dealing only summarily with aspects which have been thoroughly discussed by others. My ultimate aim is to develop the discussion of Jordanian women at a more theoretical level. The theme of Jordanian women and their role in production will be elaborated thoroughly in this book. The understanding is not just how Jordanian women are expected to act but why institutions like honour (*sharaf*) sanction their conduct. Honour is what makes life worthwhile: shame is a living death, not to be endured. Honour involves recognition, the openly acknowledged esteem of others which renders a person secure and important in his or her own eyes and in front of everone else. Honour closely defines the roles of men and women and all transactions between them, validating and dramatising them indelibly and at all times. This concept of honour still prevails in Shayfoun village and limits women's activities. One of the most important transactions is arranged marriages and how they function in rural areas. However, I must start trying to present my findings in a more rigorous way. In the following section I shall try to identify some of the inadequacies in our present knowledge of gender roles in Jordan, explain why I decided to concentrate on women's role in production and elaborate on the theme of this book: Arab women as unequal partners in development.

1.1 Women in Jordan: the theme of rural research

The efflorescence of research by foreign researchers on rural society in the Middle East in the 1960s–1990s yielded a wealth of ethnographic material and much sound descriptive generalisation, but it seldom trod boldly enough beyond the terms of reference provided by that society's own ideologies. Categories like 'rural' were given substance before they had even been studied. Trapped within this frame of reference, it was difficult to develop any thoroughgoing and independent theory about the underlying structure of that society. There was also a general obsession with the distinctive nature of rural women which precluded the asking of significant questions about many other aspects of Jordanian society, in particular the social relations between the sexes.

From village studies we do obtain a fairly detailed view of the domestic roles of women and even of the way in which the norms governing women's roles as wives and daughters-in-law vary with economic status. Mernissi notes that the dynamics between men and women vary: women of lower socioeconomic class may be less submissive and may appear to be less strictly integrated into the authority system of their husbands' households. They are less secluded and in economic terms are less dependent upon their men than are women of high socioeconomic class (Mernissi 1975, p.48). And we learn indirectly from the literature that many lower-status women do participate in agricultural production either as family labourers or as paid labourers, whilst high-status women do not work out of doors (Kandiyoti 1991). But all this can be said of men, so we still have no idea of the specific role of women in production.

However, other writers who provide detailed accounts of the daily activities of women of different social groups (Tinker 1990) concentrate upon the sexual division of labour in the household. Hence, although we get a clear picture of the division of labour within the family group for different social classes, we do not have an adequate conception of the division of labour between the sexes in the community in general. Gender divisions vary not only between different households but within households and are crucially affected by access to productive resources.

1.2 The problem of *sharaf*: how to progress beyond the descriptive

Women in Jordan bear a special responsibility for family honour (*ird*), insofar as so long as a woman conforms to certain standards of modest feminine conduct her family's status is maintained or even improved, whereas unwomanly conduct is a blot not just on her personal reputation but on the reputation of the whole family. The ultimate sanction for indiscreet behaviour on the part of a woman is the possibility that no man will wish to marry her and she will bring further disgrace upon her family. Correct feminine conduct means, among other things, being as inconspicuous in public as possible. Especially in a Muslim community, public invisibility is common in rural areas.

Men also carry responsibility for family honour, of course, but less precariously than their sisters. All aspects of a woman's behaviour outside the home are a matter of concern to her kin, and this concern affects all possible activities beyond the domestic sphere.

But the practice of honour has effects upon women's economic roles. The sexual division of labour has been considered a key variable in the analysis of women's subordination, although the conceptual relationship between the two remains a source of contention. Are the roots of the sexual division of labour and the subordination of women located in the sphere of production, in cultural institutions, in familial structures, in the unequal distribution of resources, income and power between women and men, or in a mutually supportive and interrelated system of institutions which perpetuate the subordination of women? Does the sexual division of labour form the basis of women's subordination, or is it only a manifestation of women's subordination? This is one of the questions that I shall address in this work.

Scholars differ widely on the origins of the male-favoured sexual division of labour. Some claim that its origins are biologically based and rooted in prehistoric cultures; but the heterogeneity of the sexual division of labour across time and space, cultures, regions and classes within the same society refutes the case for biological determinism. Others argue that the subordination of women by men is the basis on which early civilisation was formed and that the sexual division of labour has maintained a reciprocal state of dependency between the sexes (Levi-Strauss 1969). Marxists attribute the origins of women's subordination to the emergence of social differentiation and patriarchy caused by shifts in mode of production. Papanek, quite correctly, notes that 'female seclusion is integral to such other aspects of society as the evaluation of status, the ownership and inheritance of property, the organization of marriages, the division of labour and impulse control' (Papanek 1973, p.290). But she is not prepared to allocate determinant priority to any of these factors. Jacobson, more blandly, asserts that:

> Although it is true that, in general, women's status is lower than men's, it is not as low as these outward signs might indicate . . . men and women are actors in a complex social and ecological system which functions reasonably smoothly and provides benefits to both sexes . . . It is really a mistake to see women as competing with and being restricted by men; rather, male and female roles are clearly distinguished, and the sexes are seen as complementary to each other. (Jacobson 1977, p.60)

The demonstrations of deference which are demanded of women in the home, especially the de-emphasis of the husband's attachment to his wife, are

3

seen as promoting harmony and role congruence in the domestic group. Al Torki (1986) writes that these restrictions 'are to avoid jealousy and conflict and to ensure that the extended family takes precedence over the nuclear family'. Mernissi in similar vein notes that veiling from male affines is:

> An aid to harmony in the joint family, since it emphasizes the subordinate relationship of the woman to those in the family and de-emphasizes her tie to her husband. Veiling and seclusion in her conjugal home constantly remind her she must quietly subjugate her individual wishes to those of the group. (Mernissi 1975, p.64)

The function of honour as status indicator has also been dealt with extensively (Abu Lughod 1984; Fernea 1985; Krieger 1986). The women value their status as well-cared-for ladies of relative leisure. But this is only to say that those who have greatest wealth and rank can afford the closest conformity to whatever ideals society values as having worth and dignity. Poor rural women cannot afford to observe the seclusion and other forms of ritual taboo which preserve the purity of the household, nor can they afford fine clothes or jewellery. The lives of the poor are so structured that the moral riches of their society are as far out of their reach as the material riches.

A more important limitation of this essentially functionalist approach is that it leaves us with the honour ideology as a cultural 'given' related to other institutions but not accounted for: the only kind of viewpoint that is adopted is an historical one.

I would argue that it is logical to consider together all those norms and practices which limit women's behaviour and appearances in public places, whatever we choose to call them. Women in practically all societies observe honour in some degree, Western women simply standing at the weaker end of the spectrum or expressing it in different forms. If my broader usage of the term reveals this, I would regard this as a recommendation rather than a disadvantage, for then the strict definition employed by some loses its exotic and remote peculiarity.

However, to elaborate on very fine grounds, I have to discuss the role of women in production next.

1.3 Women's role in production and ideology

This is still speaking in terms of the effects of honour norms and prescriptions, when we need to ask what produces this ideology. By 'ideology' I mean the social role and its interaction with economic production. Feminist studies in the West gathered momentum when they turned from the scrutiny of gender role ideology to the interaction between this ideology and women's position in the capitalist mode of production (Maher 1974; Mernissi 1975). This relationship has been discussed from a number of different points of view. One line of exploration has been to study the development of the housewife's role as an historical product of changes in the economic function of the household and of the physical and conceptual separation of domestic work from other kinds of work (Ember 1983). From another point of view, women constitute a 'labour reserve', being defined first and foremost as domestic workers; women may be drawn into the industrial workforce or excluded from it according to the needs of capitalist production and the state (Mernissi 1975). The definition of women as primarily domestic workers enabled their work outside the home to be undervalued and hence underpaid. Their domestic work is nevertheless essential to the smooth running of the capital economy, even though they are not paid for this work at all. The domestic labour of women as housewives and mothers contributes both to the renewal of the labour power of the workers and also to the production of a new generation of workers.

In this fruitful phase of feminist research, starting in the late 1960s, the ideological culture of gender roles and the demands of capitalist production and property relations were seen as interacting with each other.

Feminist researchers did not deny the role of ideology in controlling the behaviour and expectations of individual men and women, especially through the pressure of familial roles, but they did deny that the complex norms which define women's role in Western capitalist societies as primarily domestic and maternal can be seen as some kind of independent historical variable.

Feminist researchers have also realised that women's social position in non-capitalist societies and in societies which are still undergoing transformation into capitalist societies cannot be explained solely by appeal to the force of norms and values. Among feminists engaged in comparative research, Engels's *Origin of the Family, Private Property and the State* has been particularly influential, since Engels was concerned with the original subordination of women which quite evidently pre-dated the development of industrial capitalism (Engels 1972, p.121). Engels's speculation on what may have happened in prehistory has been discredited, but the central question which he posed is still regarded as a valid one (Engels 1972, p.123). Engels rejected the idea that women's subordination could be treated simply as given by nature. But equally he dismissed the idea that it could be explained by reference to legal rules and social custom; these codes are not, so to speak, plucked out of the air but are themselves closely related to prevailing economic and political conditions. He located the original subordination of women – the 'world historical defeat of the female sex' – at the point when the domestication of animals created a new kind of property, herds of cattle, which could be accumulated and transmitted. This led to the overthrow of mother-right or matrilineal inheritance which had hitherto constituted an adequate principle for the assignation of children to lineage groups and for the transmission of the insignificant forms of possessions already in existence (Engels 1972, p.126). Mother-right was replaced by father-right, that is, patrilineal inheritance, as men gained control over the new forms of wealth, and women were consequently dispossessed and devalued. This transformation laid the foundations for the subordination of women in all subsequent modes of production, in which quite different forms of private property were to become important. The ultimate restoration of the female sex to its rightful status could only take place with the total abolition of all private property. Engels urges that 'the first premise for the emancipation of women is the reintroduction of the entire female sex into public industry' (Engels 1972, p.137). If private property enabled them to be enslaved, full participation in wage labour would enable them to begin to set themselves free.

Some feminist writers (Abu Lughod 1985; Afshar 1985; Lim 1983; Mernissi 1975) have taken seriously Engels's concern to locate the basis of women's subordination in the structure of material production and much empirical research activity has been directed to this problem, yet there has been considerable confusion about which aspects of material production need to be studied in order to yield general explanations of women's status or position in a given society.

Should we attend to the kinds and amount of productive labour which women perform? Or is it more important to examine their capacity to control resources and regulate consumption? Or should we study their property rights and the kinds of property they can inherit or hold, relating this to other aspects of their situation? I argue that production is only a general activity; the specific aspects of production which underpin the relationship between the sexes can only be identified within a particular mode of production. We cannot predict that, say, property rights, or women's role in the labour process, or any other particular aspect of production, will provide some kind of universal key to women's position in all societies.

Essentially there are four areas of female activity in the village family that relate to female consciousness or the way they perceive themselves. The social label 'mother' encompasses the bearing and raising of children and allows women to see themselves as 'caregivers' who anticipate and cater to the material and emotional needs of other family members. The social label 'wife' calls for women to provide services that lead to their own self-perception and to acknowledgement by other women. The social label 'love' includes all those activities that provide emotional comfort to family members; it leads women to see themselves as providers of sympathy who emotionally cushion everyone. Finally, the social label 'housewife' incorporates all the domestic chores vital to the smooth functioning of a home (Sacks 1979).

In sum, women in Shayfoun are controlled labour because the socialisation and sanctioning systems ensure that women's consciousness is intricately focused on what they do. Failure to comply with the social activities of work can result in financial and social difficulties.

1.4 Women, work and property

Using work which rural women do as my starting point was still a useful priority, but those women who work do not control the resources. Clearly it is necessary to look at the specific nature of the relationship which women bear to property, especially their effective position in regard to the inheritance of land, which is largely the basis of their dependence upon men in the villages and which may also be the basis of their symbolic devaluation.

What are the forms of property which it is most relevant to consider here? Land is without doubt the most important category of wealth-generating property in an agrarian society. But land cannot be cultivated without certain tools and equipment, and so we must also consider cattle and farm machinery. Nor must we forget forms of property which can be converted into land or agricultural equipment, for example gold, jewellery or accumulated cash savings.

Land cannot be farmed without labour. The rights which men have in the reproductive powers of women will be important where children are also a resource – that is, where their productive labour can be controlled or appropriated in some way. This is the case in most of the households studied. However, all these forms of invisible property take their identity from the specific nature of landed property in the village and cannot be understood without reference to it. Land is usually vested in males, and in most villages of the region is concentrated in the hands of males of particular families and clans. Rights in the earnings of others are closely related to the form and distribution of land rights. Therefore I shall concentrate on the latter, paying particular attention to the manner in which women are largely excluded from the possession and control of land.

The actuarial advantage of women who belonged to the rural élite contributed more than any other factor to their prominence as custodians of estates built up by male relatives. Their greater life expectancy after marriage, due in part to their youth upon entering into betrothal, rendered women ideal choices as supervisor. In the registers of the village courts vast estates presided over by women who had inherited from fathers or husbands could be subject to confiscation. In 1992 (H12) demanded an 'obligatory gift' of 2 000 JD from a woman to help defray the expenses of paving the courtyard. The woman demurred, 'claiming that she had nothing to pay'. But the man insisted that her father would enable her to meet this figure, and he placed all her assets under sequestration with no private transactions permitted. He subsequently arranged for the auctioning of enough property to yield up the required sum. The woman was then honoured in the court and allowed to resume her life as before.

Some relevant ideas concerning the relationship between property, production and women's roles in rural societies have recently been developed by Goody (1976). He builds on the distinction made by Boserup (1970) and others between social structures based on hoe agriculture and those based on plough agriculture, of which Shayfoun is an obvious example. Goody's line of argument is that plough cultivation makes the production of a surplus possible and facilitates a complex division of labour. Land becomes a scarce and valuable resource, the basis of class stratification. Plough cultivation is associated with male farming systems in which men play the dominant role in agricultural production; women are valued as producers of heirs rather than as producers of food. I move that this general argument should be borne in mind. It has the virtue of providing new ways of linking gender roles with production, and suggests an ordered structure of explanation, so that one can make connections between honour, work, property and marriage without begging the question of how they are connected.

Property is important, and we must not ignore the different kinds of property. Hence, although land is considered as generating new wealth, other kinds of property, such as jewellery or domestic goods, are more likely to be controlled by women and can be considered as forms of wealth, although they cannot generate new wealth. We may also need to identify the senses in which a woman's own labour power becomes a form of familial property which can only be alienated with the consent of the family group.

This investigation of women's role in the process of production therefore has to include more than just a description of the kinds of work which women do. It must include an account of familial authority relations derived from economic power – which this book discusses – and of the property relations which realise and maintain it. Although it could be argued that production is generally household-based and that the production process is controlled by men, the resources available to households are highly variable and depend upon their place in the class hierarchy.

1.5 Women's status in modernisation

The impact of socioeconomic changes and the overall process of modernisation on the status of Arab women is still problematic and not fully understood. The concept of modernisation itself has come under fire from scholars, both Arab and non-Arab. Apart from the fact that it tends to be both vague and descriptive, 'modernisation' is often applied from a Eurocentric perspective, in which it is equated with 'Westernisation' (Afshar 1985).

Modernisation is thus contrasted with its presumed polar opposite, traditionalisation, the two being viewed as being mutually exclusive economic and cultural systems. Women are thus urged to strive for 'modernity', which is taken to represent an ideal, yet they are aware of the various forms of inequality which persist in the West and the severe social and political problems that plague Western nations. Arab women aspire to a more genuine form of liberation than that promised by current forms of Western-style modernity.

Arab researchers have in general tended to emphasise the coexistence of modernity and tradition in their society, insisting that the challenge is to determine their exact expression in any given context. Writing of Saudi Arabia, Al Torki (1986) says that modernisation does not necessarily entail destruction of traditional structure, but rather it allows for wide margins of coexistence between traditional and modern forms. On the other hand, tradition does not constitute a uniform, static system antagonistic to modernity. Tradition was found to have sufficient a degree of flexibility and diversity to accommodate modern patterns. Modernisation is thus a continuing process in which the cultural and historical experience and the national goals of the country concerned intervene to set their 'choice' of the margins of coexistence between tradition and modernity (Mernissi 1975).

One area where traditional attitudes have persisted in the face of modern structural changes is that of women and fertility. In fact, this is a good example which illustrates the complexity of the issue especially as it relates to women's status. In an important article on status and fertility patterns, Nadia Youssef, an Egyptian sociologist, attempts to understand the high fertility rates of Muslim women (Youssef 1972, p.53). She seeks the answer in the specifics of women's status in Muslim society: 'The critical point is to relate the fertility levels of Muslim populations to women's status and position. This latter is measured in terms of five indicators: female literacy rates, sex differential in literacy rates, female income-earning activities, and the timing and incidence of marriage.' What emerges from her analysis of these variables is an interesting assessment of women's status and a clear indication of how it relates to reproductive behaviour. Youssef argues that women who occupy a clearly subordinate position in the social, political and legal domains nonetheless derive great respect and a measure of power from their marriage- and maternal-related roles. It follows, then, that women will not easily risk giving up the one role where their status is high, namely, that of mother. 'Muslim women are fully cognisant of the need to attain marital position and motherhood for commanding respect and status in their own kin group and community. They are not about to de-emphasize willingly the only role that now gives them a bargaining position in the social structure' (Youssef 1972, pp.66–100).

Youssef acknowledges that highly educated Muslim women may be ready to explore alternative sources of prestige and status besides motherhood, and that the increased participation of women in the labour force may have its impact on the reproductive behaviour of women and their perception of their role within and outside the family.

Critical appraisal of conceptions of women's work in the Third World has prompted researchers to note the failure of development policies to recognise the value of women's contribution to production in both rural and urban societies. It is argued that:

The apparent invisibility of women's worth, as well as their work, is widespread and persistent. Women's work has, on the whole, been severely devalued by a universal ideological framework that regards them as inferior bearers of labour . . . This perception appears to be at its strongest in many rural areas in under-developed countries, where a coincidence of interests between capital and male policy makers has resulted in the creation of a female domain in subsistence agriculture responsible for reproducing and nurturing a large reserve army of cheap labour. (Afshar 1985, p.ix)

This selective overview of the major theoretical approaches utilised to study the status of women makes it clear that the understanding of the position of women seeks the most effective means for change, improvement and development. It is not that researchers raise problems and criticism rather than offer the solution. Dramatic changes in the status of Arab women will no doubt provoke strong reactions, especially from the increasingly vocal and powerful Islamic Fundamentalist movement. Given the political and economic realities of the Arab world today, it is likely that women will continue to be the hostages in the conflict between security and tradition, and the aspirations for full human dignity and respect.

1.6 Women and economic development

There is one other area of debate relevant to my consideration of women's role in production. This is the debate as to whether economic development actually benefits women, relative to men, that is. Boserup has pointed out that economic development may be accompanied by the actual closure of traditional opportunities for women to gain wealth or control resources, without the substitution of new ones (Boserup 1970). This observation is useful to counter the bland optimism characteristic of many public pronouncements about development. But no useful theoretical account of why this should be so has yet been offered. Obviously, one facet may be the exportation of Western models of gender roles along with the know-how and the hardware as part of an aid package. But whether such cultural diffusion is a contingent or a necessary effect of the aid relationship is unclear; partly the problem is difficult to resolve because it has been formulated in terms of the effects of 'development' rather than as, say, the effects of capitalist expansion or the effects of aid programmes or industrialisation of the Jordanian economy.

In the Jordanian context, it has been noticed that women's use of economic opportunities has not increased relative to that of men in spite of legislation designed to improve women's status in the economic sphere (Masri and Abu Jaber 1983). Their participation in the labour force has not increased in relation to that of men, if this is understood as an indication of opportunity (see Table 1.1). On the other hand, we have to remember that in an area such as Shayfoun, the withdrawal of women from outdoor agricultural labour or any other labour should be interpreted as reflecting the withdrawal that women experience in a period of economic difficulty and structural adjustment policies. However, the general relationship between the ideological definition of women's roles and their position in the process of production should be studied and investigated. The changing nature of the production process increases women's workload in the domestic sphere. Nevertheless, my original thesis that women's role in production does indeed explain much else about their social roles and the inequalities they experience as partners in the development process will still be defended. My work in this area will contribute to an overall understanding of women's development in rural areas.

Table 1.1 Women's presence in the labour force

1984		1994	
Men's %	Women's %	Men's %	Women's %
72	28	74	26

Source: Jordanian Statistics Bureau, 1994.

Note: The data were compiled in 1994 by the Statistics Bureau to study the involvement of women's presence in the labour force.

The process of economic and social development is a gradual shift from a stage at which people use all their time to produce goods and services for family use to a stage when they produce for others, either as self-employed or as employees. Most often, men are the first to take the step from production for family use to production for others, while women continue to spend most of their time working for their own families. If this difference in the work pattern of the sexes becomes an important part of the traditional culture, as is the case in rural Jordan, the possibilities for development may become severely restricted.

In countries with *sharaf* systems women lose status if they perform work which requires them to leave the confines of their own household. Therefore, they cannot make a rational choice between different types of money-earning activities nor can they decide how to allocate their time between income-earning and domestic work. For lack of acceptable alternatives, they are forced to continue low-productivity domestic activities and production within the household – that is, activities which have long ago been replaced by the purchase of goods and services in societies in which women have more freedom of choice. In Jordan the degree of self-sufficiency of rural households is still so high that rural women must perform hard work for long hours every day, although they confine their work exclusively or mainly to activities for the benefit of the family. Because of this lack of specialisation and the consequently low productivity of female work, the rural households remain poor and unable to purchase either industrial goods or specialised food or artisan products. Thus, the market for agricultural and non-agricultural products remains too small to provide sufficient encouragement to either industrial or rural development.

To break this vicious circle of rural self-sufficiency and lack of market outlets for specialised production is a complicated matter. Of course, both men and women in such countries want to raise family incomes, but if rigid segregation of the sexes is the generally accepted ideal, at least in rural areas, neither women nor men want to raise family incomes by means which imply a radical break with the accepted status system. Therefore, the primary goal for women's projects in such areas is to create opportunities for rural women to contribute to family income by means which are acceptable both to themselves and to the male villagers on whom they depend.

The present study describes and analyses rural Jordanian women and how such women determine their priorities, and identifies some of the pivotal issues which limit their options. The marriage process and divorce affects their lives also. Chapter 1 has described the reasons for women's role in production, the ideology of *sharaf* and women's status in economic development. Chapter 2 is a literature perspective of women in the Middle East and North Africa. Large-scale studies of women and rural production put the study in relative perspective. Chapter 3 explains the setting of Shayfoun village and its socioeconomic structure. How land tenure is structured and the means of production are explained extensively. Chapter 4 explains the roles of women in where they are allowed to go and in property. Chapter 5 is a thorough analysis of the economic development and change in the standards of living in the village. Chapter 6 explains the roles of women and the household economy as an economic unit and multiple source of income. Chapter 7 sheds light on women's work in agriculture and domestic areas and on women's perceptions of and relationships between agricultural and domestic work. Chapter 8 analyses women's economic and political position in marriage, the importance of dowry and the role of women in marriage, divorce and widowhood. Chapter 9 explains women's relations with other women in the neighbourhood and outside the family. Chapter 10 consists of a final discussion and conclusions. There are many lessons which development researchers and rural women themselves can and should draw from the study.

2 Literature perspective

This chapter provides an overview of women's roles and status in the Middle East and North Africa. It seeks to elaborate the various theoretical and empirical studies on women and development and their relevance for us. The aim also is to contextualise the present study. I will deal with the inequalities women face in their daily lives pertinent to my book. By 'roles' I refer to the manifold activities carried out by rural women, such as child care, housework, subsistence farming, remunerated employment and health care. By 'status' I refer to the value and meaning given to these activities by wider society, which in turn both reflect and influence the general rubric of gender relations. Barbara Rogers (1980) points out that the phrase 'status of women' often carries a rather 'pejorative tone', and suggests that 'judgements made by anthropologists and sociologists alike about the "status of women" in other societies may tell us more about who are making these judgements than about their subjects' (*ibid.*, p.33). However, I use the term with no derogatory overtones and recognise that 'status' should be construed as a dynamic concept, with the implication of change over time.[1]

The conclusion is that women in the Middle East and North Africa are forced not only to conform to the roles of wife and mother, but also to bear additional burdens such as obligatory deference to their mothers-in-law and restrictions on their freedom of movement and association.

---

1 The measurement of women's status is confined to women's general standing in the context of the countries to which they belong and makes few attempts at cross-cultural comparisons.

2.1 Women in the Middle East and North Africa

The reason for dealing with Middle Eastern and North African countries in one section is that they cover a relatively contiguous geographical area bordering the southern and eastern Mediterranean, and display considerable social and cultural similarities as a result of common historical experiences, in particular the imprint of Islam. This is not to suggest that Islam has the same aspect in all areas. Indeed, there are two main doctrinal schools, Sunni and Shia, of which Sunni, the 'orthodox' form, has more adherents and is predominant throughout the region except in Iran, Syria, Iraq and Afghanistan (Kabeer 1993). Nevertheless, the basic beliefs and practices are similar, especially as they affect women. I have also included three countries of the eastern Sahelian belt of Africa in this section, namely the Sudan, Somalia and Ethiopia; the populations of the former two are predominantly Muslim, and the latter has pockets of Islam interspersed with Christianity. In Sudan, 82 per cent of the people are Moslem, 18 per cent Christian (UNDP 1994).

Many Middle Eastern countries are dependent on the export of oil and are very wealthy; however, despite high per capita GNPs (US $7 900 per annum in Saudi Arabia and US $7 170 in Kuwait (UNDP 1994)), inequality is rife and widespread poverty exists. Corresponding per capita GNPs in poorer North African states are US $1 030 in Morocco and US $610 in Egypt (UNDP 1994). The oil-rich industrial economies of the Middle East and North Africa have supported generally higher levels of urbanisation than those countries in the region where people depend primarily on agriculture. For example, 67 per cent of Saudi Arabia's population and 72 per cent of Iraqis were urban in 1980, compared with only 41 per cent in Morocco and under 10 per cent in the Yemen Arab Republic (Gilbert and Gugler 1982, pp.6–7). Population growth in North Africa in 1980–85 was projected at 2.6 per cent per annum, and in the Middle East (defined by the UN as 'Arab countries') at 3.3 per cent (UN 1991).

Women in the Middle East and North Africa have the lowest rates of labour force participation (Townsend and Momsen 1987). Usually less than one-quarter of women aged 15 or more are engaged in waged work or trade, and in many countries, notably Syria, Algeria, Saudi Arabia, Libya and Egypt, this figure is below 10 per cent; on average less than 15 per cent of the total labour force in the region is made up of women (*ibid.*, p.32).

In much of the Middle East and North Africa men far outnumber women and the sex ratio may therefore be described as highly masculine-biased (Hariss and Watson 1987). Female life expectancy is between 60 and 69 years across most of the area, and between 50 and 69 in Saudi Arabia, Sudan and Oman (Townsend and Momsen 1987). Given that, other things being equal, women should expect to live longer than men on account of inherent biological hardiness, male-dominant sex ratios indicate the degree to which the cultural under-valuation of women results in a disproportionate number of female deaths, especially during infancy and childbirth.

The division of gender roles is extremely pronounced in most Islamic countries of North Africa and the Middle East. Women are not only segregated from men, but are also frequently subject to seclusion or *purdah*. Fatima Mernissi (1975) suggests that this rigid control of Muslim women stems from a conception of women that is markedly different from that of the West. In the West, women's 'inferiority' has been tied to an idea that they are sexually passive, physically weak and in need of protection from men. While these ideas are also found in Islamic society, Mernissi suggests that the fundamental rationale behind female subordination is that *men* are seen to need protection from *women*. Muslim women are regarded as extremely powerful, capable of making men lose their reason through *fitna* (disorder or chaos provoked by sexual attraction) and threatening in terms of their potential to divert men's devotion from Allah. Women in North Africa and the Middle East are thus possibly subject to greater constraints than their counterparts in many other developing societies.

Despite the fact that the *Quran* (the holy book containing the word of Allah as told to the Prophet Mohammed) and the *Hadiths* (interpretive moral codes based on the sayings of Mohammed) contain numerous references to gender equality (Ingrams 1983), and despite women being required to submit to the will of Allah just as much as men and to observe Muslim teachings, they are rarely allowed to attend religious gatherings, enter a mosque, or assist at public meetings and festivities. The *umma*, or community of believers, is an all-male community (Mernissi 1975).

According to Islamic faith, marriage is compulsory. Polygamy (up to four wives) is permitted and practised in many Muslim societies, albeit with the proviso that a man treats his wives equally (Afshar 1987; Ingrams 1983). Polygamy is an extremely significant variable in the equation of female subordination and male privilege: married women often see their co-wives as rivals, thus preventing the development of any genuine female solidarity. Polygamy also allows a man to fulfil his sexual appetite, at the same time detracting from the formation of strong conjugal bonds with individual women (Mernissi, 1975).

Inequality within Islamic marriage is institutionalised by law. In the Moroccan Family Code, for example, there are separate articles for a man's rights *vis-à-vis* his wife and a wife's rights *vis-à-vis* her husband. This point will be discussed further in my book. On marriage a man has the right to total fidelity from his wife, obedience, the performance of domestic labour, breastfeeding of children and the right to command his wife's deference towards his parents and close relatives. A wife, on the other hand, cannot expect her husband to be faithful, obedient or to show respect to her own relatives, even though she can legitimately demand financial support, the right to be treated equally with other wives, permission to visit her parents and the prerogative of disposing freely of her possessions (Mernissi 1975, p.110). As Mernissi notes, Moroccan husbands owe no moral duties to their wives and the alleged

NOT TRUE

15

'rights' of women are in fact restrictions on their freedom. The clause on female deference towards her husband's immediate relatives opens a door onto one of the key characteristics of the Islamic family – the importance of a woman's *hma* (mother-in-law).

Muslim mothers-in-law usually play a significant part in arranging the marriage of their sons, particularly in the selection of a bride, and thereafter exercise a major influence over the nature of the couple's relationship. Wives often go to live with their husbands in their family homes (Mernissi 1975, Chapter 2). This continued close contact with the husband's mother inhibits the couple's potential for intimacy and thus drives a wedge between them. As Magida Salman (1987, p.8) points out: 'The mother of a male child will often interfere to prevent the appearance and growth of love and companionship between her son and daughter-in-law.' Filial bonds take precedence over conjugal bonds and reduce scope for the development of joint interests between husbands and wives, thereby exacerbating women's oppression. Men's mothers act as moral watchdogs and often burden their daughters-in-law with a huge range of ethical demands, exhorting them to look forward to the future when, if they bear sons, they in turn will achieve seniority and status. Age is also associated with greater spatial and social freedom; post-menopausal women are no longer an object of sexual desire and as such cannot bring shame upon their families by appearing in public places (Mernissi 1975; Salman 1987).

Between 25 and 50 per cent of women aged 15 to 19 years in the Middle East and North Africa are or have been officially married (Seager and Olson 1986). Only a very few remain unmarried by the age of 30 (Minces 1982). Youthful marriages ensure that women's sexual behaviour is controlled and therefore that they do not bring dishonour upon their male kin. However, as much as marriage is an almost inevitable event in Muslim women's lives, the spectre of involuntary divorce is never far away. Although women themselves have increasingly obtained the courage and/or right to divorce their husbands in many Islamic countries, they remain extremely vulnerable to the threat of repudiation. One of the most common forms this takes is the *talaq al bid 'a*, or 'innovatory divorce', where the husband merely repeats a repudiation statement three times before a witness (Minces 1982). Infertility, or failure to bear sons, both of which are blamed on women, frequently provide grounds for men to divorce their wives. Nevertheless, if a husband so decides, he can take his wife back within the first three months following the divorce, during which time she legally remains his property (Youssef 1972).

The fate of divorced women is hard; it is difficult for a 'used' (non-virginal) woman to remarry, and the family's need to protect her honour while unattached means that she will probably have to return to live as an appendage in her paternal or fraternal home (Youssef 1972). Children from a broken marriage eventually come under the guardianship of their legal father, defined as the man to whom the woman was married at the time of the birth, irrespect-

16

ive of whether or not he is the natural parent (Minces 1982). Even where children stay with their mother because the father is deemed 'unfit', as is sometimes the case in Qatar, it remains the man's duty to make financial provision for the food, clothing, shelter and education of his offspring (Abu Saud 1984). The issue of divorce will be extensively analysed later in my book.

Given the pressure on women to bear sons, fertility is high in Islamic countries, although birth control is not expressly forbidden by the *Quran* and certain countries such as Egypt, Algeria, Tunisia and South Lebanon have instigated family planning programmes (Minces 1982; Salman 1987). On average, women in North Africa and the Middle East give birth to at least six children (Seager and Olson 1986), and crude birth-rates were projected at between 41 and 44.5 per 1 000 in the period 1985–90 (UN 1989).

Apart from general considerations of women's vulnerability and subordinate position within the family, there are two further aspects of gender inequality in Islamic societies which have been interpreted as reinforcing male control and women's secondary status: seclusion and 'circumcision'. It is important to note that, although they occur in Islamic societies, they should not be construed as Islamic customs. They are by no means known in all Muslim countries either. Nevertheless, they are most common in the Middle East and North Africa where Islam is the religion of rule.

Apart from restricting women's mobility, as we observed earlier, seclusion (*purdah*) involves the wearing of long concealing garments and/or a veil. The degree to which Muslim women are covered varies considerably from place to place (Minces 1982). In eastern areas of Algeria, for example, a long cloak and black veil cover the entire face and body except for one eye, whereas in Tunisia women may go unveiled. Qatari women have traditionally worn a *batula*, a kind of face mask with two slits for the eyes, although this is now dying out among the younger generation (Abu Saud 1984). The primary function of the veil is to ensure modesty and to limit women's contact with all men other than their own husbands or male kin (Youssef 1972). The veil also symbolises the invisibility of women in 'male spaces', such as the street or public places (Mernissi 1975). In some cases *purdah* can also signify social status: some argue that only rich men can afford to seclude their wives. Nevertheless, there are also pragmatic reasons why women wear *purdah*. In Iraq, for example, Doreen Ingrams (1983) points out that the *abaya* (a voluminous black garment covering everything except the face and hands) is sometimes worn by poor women who put it on to enter the mosque, as a sign of decorum and respect.

The concept of space will be elaborated later in my book, and how some women believe in the privacy and intimacy of their homes will be examined.

The other practice which has become equated in the West with Islam, but which is by no means a Muslim institution, is female 'circumcision' (Thiam 1986). Termed by some 'genital mutilation', circumcision is often defended as reducing women's sexual desires, thereby ensuring pre-marital chastity and conjugal fidelity. However, there are severe doubts about its effectiveness.

One of the few countries in the region which has attempted to 'raise the status' of women is Tunisia, which, after independence in 1956 and under President Habib Bourguiba, introduced a Personal Status Code to replace *Quranic* law in the fields of marriage, divorce and children's rights. The Code forbade polygamy, instigated court proceedings for divorce, granted universal suffrage and established a minimum age for marriage (15 for girls, 18 for boys) (Durrani 1976; Huston 1979; Tessler *et al.* 1978). However, in the late 1960s and early 1970s, partly due to Bourguiba's repeated bouts of illness, and partly due to the rise of Islamic fundamentalism, the position of women once again showed signs of becoming more constrained (Tessler *et al.* 1978).

Another country in which Muslim women have undergone dramatic and fluctuating changes in terms of their legal and social position is Iran, where in 1936 women were compulsorily unveiled, making it one of the first countries officially to outlaw the veiling of women (Jayawardena 1986; Pakizegi 1978). The Shah felt that the seclusion of women resulted in a waste of half the country's productive resources and called for the participation of women in wider social and economic life; this began a long process of relaxation of some of the major constraints and restrictions placed on Iranian women (Jayawardena 1986). For example, the Family Protection Law of 1967 prohibited men from taking multiple wives, and stipulated that they had to obtain permission from a court of law if they wished to take a second wife. The court was obliged to consult the first wife for evidence of her husband's economic capacity to support another woman; the law also granted women the right to ask for a divorce in the event of their husbands bringing another woman into the home (Pakizegi 1978). However, the social position of Iranian women consistently lagged behind changes in their legal status, and women could still, for example, be prevented from working by their husbands if their employment threatened to disrupt the smooth running of the family home (Pakizegi 1978). Furthermore, as the London Iranian Women's Liberation Group (1983) (*ibid.*, p.63) stated, women's emancipation under the Shah was foisted upon them 'top-down' to suit the needs of the regime and not out of any genuine concern for women *per se*.

Gender inequalities have intensified since the revolution of 1978–79, where emphasis on Islamic fundamentalism has meant that women have returned to wearing the veil (*chador*) and given up a number of freedoms. In addition, under Khomeini some women have been executed for adultery and prostitution. As Haleh Afshar (1987:83) points out:

> The Islamic Republic in Iran has created two classes of citizen: the male who benefits from the provisions of Islamic law and justice, and the female who does not. With the sole exception of the right to vote, Iranian women are in all other respects formally recognised as second-class citizens who have no place in the public arena

18

and no security in the domestic sphere. The husband has become an absolute ruler, entitled to exercise the power of life and death in his own home . . . Iranian women have little to lose and everything to gain by opposing the regime and its dicta concerning women.

To summarise, women in the Middle East and North Africa are forced not only to conform to the roles of wife and mother, but also to bear additional burdens such as obligatory deference to their mothers-in-law and restrictions on their freedom of movement and association. Women's place in the extended or joint household renders them particularly vulnerable to control and domination. While in other societies the nuclear family may give women little freedom and autonomy, several writers on the Islamic world see it as an important vehicle for female emancipation.

2.2 Large-scale studies of women and rural production: the problem of statistics

Ester Boserup's (1970) *Women's Role in Economic Development* was the first attempt to provide a serious and comprehensive analysis of the issue of women's productive roles. Boserup argues that women's status varies with the nature of productive activity and their involvement in it, and further, that with economic development, women's status declines. Her work was germinal in exposing women's vital contributions to agricultural production. Despite the fact that anthropologists had written of women's labour in farming, the most common assumption had been that because male labour was central to agricultural systems in Europe, it was *ipso facto* central to farming in all parts of the world, another example of a totally misappropriate transfer of academic technology! This kind of assumption has often been incorporated wholesale into rural development policies, and in turn has led to a decline in women's status and, in some cases, to a drop in the overall levels of production.

Very generally, Boserup's thesis is that where shifting cultivation is the norm, women do most of the agricultural work; where the plough is used, men do more work than women; and where land is irrigated and farming is intensive, such as in parts of Southeast Asia, then both men and women are highly involved in agricultural production. Boserup concludes that women's status is high where their involvement in production is high, that is, in shifting cultivation systems or systems of irrigated agriculture. However, she notes that with economic development, broadly understood as the mechanisation of agriculture, and increasing specialisation and differentiation of non-agricultural tasks, women tend to become separate from production and their status correspondingly declines. Boserup's prescriptions for improving the lot of women focus on increasing their access to education, thereby improving their chances of competing on an equal basis with men in the labour market.

While the empirical statistical associations (drawn from official national census and survey data) between types of farming systems and women's status remain broadly true, Boserup's theoretical overview (or perhaps lack of it) has been criticised. Lourdes Beneria and Gita Sen (1981), for example, while praising the empirical range of Boserup's work, point out the drawbacks of relying to such an extent on empirical material in what is, or, according to them, should be, a predominantly theoretical work; they see Boserup as falling into the empiricist trap of bringing in ideas/ideology in idiosyncratic ways as 'filler' to block in areas of her thesis. Beneria and Sen's criticisms can be divided into two: those directed at Boserup's reliance on models drawn from neo-classical economics and on assumptions of modernisation, and, secondly, her failure to provide an adequate theoretical analysis of women's subordination, in spite of her overt concern with women.

These two lines of criticism are not mutually exclusive: Boserup's over-concentration on productive work outside the home (remunerated work) at the expense of domestic (reproductive work), together with her failure to show the systematic nature of women's subordination under the imposition of capitalist methods of production (the hegemony of capitalist patriarchy), mean that her prescription for the future improvement of women's condition – 'education' – is totally inadequate. Until we have a satisfactory theoretical analysis of the significance of reproductive work in different modes of production and with different cultural patterns of gender relations then such prescriptions must remain deficient; that is, any analysis of women's status must draw upon both economic and cultural/ideological factors.

Whyte and Whyte (1978), in discussing the applicability of Boserup's categories to women in rural Asia, come to similar conclusions, but add the proviso that in Southeast Asia where intensive irrigated agriculture predominates, other 'cultural' factors mitigate the association between 'type of agriculture' and women's status, including religion, forms of marriage payments and residence. However, women's involvement in agricultural work remains the key factor in the ascription of their status, and other factors are only brought into play to explain deviations from the expected pattern.

In northern India, for example, where plough agriculture is dominant, women's status is lower than in other parts of Asia because of their exclusion from critical aspects of production – what we should expect from Boserup's predictions – and Whyte and Whyte (1978) show that for these areas major religions (Islam and Hinduism), types of marriage payment and so on have acted to reinforce women's low status. In parts of Southeast Asia where irrigated rice is grown, for example, Thailand, the Philippines and Java, women have relatively equal status to men, whereas in other irrigated rice areas, such as Bengal or Bangladesh, women's participation in production is frowned upon and their status is lower. Whyte and Whyte explain these differences by pointing to the fact that Islam is dominant in the latter countries, and this imposes far greater restrictions on women than in the former states, where Buddhism is prevalent.

20

Carmen Diana Deere and Magdalena Leon de Leal (1981, 1982) critically analyse material from the Andean regions of South America with respect to women and their productive activities. In Boserup's classification, the Latin American region is classed as a 'male' farming system, that is, one with settled farming, use of the plough, and so on. However, their conclusions indicate that the term 'male' farming system is perhaps a misnomer: 'family' farming system would be more appropriate. Andean women do, in fact, participate in agricultural activities, even if men do the majority of field work. But their study also shows the different influence of ideological/cultural factors on women's relations to production and on women's status. Boserup's thesis, they argue, is only directly applicable to rural producers who have access to land, grow cash crops and are relatively wealthy, that is, the middle and élite farmer groups.

Among the vast majority of farmers, however, land is not sufficient to support a family group and some members have to become involved in wage labour in one form or another. Although in theory land can be owned by both men and women in all groups, in practice it is only among the poorer farmers, where women have to work in the fields and for other people, that they have a significant 'say' in major agricultural and other decisions which affect the family. Here the interrelationship between class and production is singled out as a significant factor influencing women's status in ways not predicted in Boserup's work.

According to my work in this book, the inequalities in land ownership and the social aspects of women's role do indeed affect their role in production. We will look at housework as part of a subordinate mode of production that gives us a new angle of vision that transforms that old debate about its productive or class character.

Both Whyte and Whyte and Deere and Leon de Leal provide specific tests of Boserup's ideas, as well as stressing other factors in their analyses of women's status and their involvement in production. In particular, Deere and Leon de Leal (1981, 1982) point out defects in the statistics used by Boserup: the usual design of surveys and censuses does not allow for accurate categorisation and enumeration/evaluation of women's activities (see also Rechini de Lattes and Wainermann 1986). Ruth Dixon-Mueller's (1985) review of women in agriculture is positively directed at the problems of finding out about women's work in rural areas of the Third World. Her book is part of one of several series of monographs (in this case, *Women, Work and Development*) published by the International Labour Office (ILO) with the sponsorship of other aid agencies. The ILO has been extremely active, especially since the inauguration of the UN Decade for Women in 1975, in promoting women's visibility in Third World states, both in rural and in urban areas. Dixon-Mueller's work in this case is a methodological text, but it complements and highlights some of the problems singled out by other writers on the quality of official data on rural women (Deere and Leon de Leal 1981, 1982, for example).

Different sets of official statistics can also be interpreted in varying ways. For example, according to Seager and Olson (1986), less than 10 per cent of the total agricultural labour force in Angola is composed of women. According to the Organisation of Angolan Women (1984), however, women's participation in agriculture is 25 per cent (based on 1978 figures), but they do stress that their figures do not include '. . . the vast majority of working women' (*ibid.*, p.41). The discrepancy noted by Ruth Dixon (1983) between the ILO revised estimate (27 per cent) and her 'predicted' estimate (42 per cent) of women's participation in the agricultural labour force in Angola is one of the largest in sub-Saharan Africa, which probably indicates shortcomings in the basic statistics rather than a fault in the ILO's methodology (see also OAW 1984).

In Guyana, according to Seager and Olson (1986), under 10 per cent of the agricultural labour force is female. However, Stella Odie-Ali (1986), working under the auspices of the Women in the Caribbean Project, suggests, on the basis of her survey of four government-designated development areas, that women are involved in agricultural work to much the same extent as men and that their ownership of productive resources, particularly land and housing, is increasing. Ruth Dixon (1983), using ILO revised figures, suggests that women's participation in the agricultural labour force in Guyana is 32 per cent (the predicted figure in this case is 37 per cent).

These two examples illustrate the care which must be exercised in using official statistics uncritically. Even within her samples, Odie-Ali shows the extent to which factors of race and culture (East Indian, Negro, Mixed or Amerindian) influence women's participation in agriculture. Rather than relying on 'official' statistics to any great extent, Dixon-Mueller (1985) suggests ways in which information on women has been and can be obtained, depending on budgetary and time constraints.

Bearing in mind the fact that we must be cautious in using figures, it is generally accepted that there is a huge global variation both in the proportion of women living in rural areas and in rural women's involvement in production. Overall, in sub-Saharan Africa women's agricultural employment rates are high and their urban employment rates low. In Latin America and the Caribbean the reverse is the case: rural employment rates are low for women and those in urban areas high. In the Middle East, North Africa and South Asia, women's employment rates are low both in the cities and in the countryside, and in Southeast Asia women's participation rates are high irrespective of location (Townsend and Momsen 1987). In sub-Saharan Africa, where, overall, a relatively small percentage of the population is urbanised, women make up at least 30 per cent of the non-subsistence agricultural labour force (Seager and Olson 1986). According to Dixon (1983), in most of the sub-Saharan African states women in fact form well over 30 per cent of the agricultural labour force, and in many areas over 40 per cent. It could be the case that women constitute a high proportion of the agricultural labour force simply because they form the bulk of the rural population: in Zimbabwe, for example, women make up 75 per cent of rural inhabitants (Chimedza 1987). Nevertheless, proportional activity rates for women living in rural areas in Africa are far higher than those of women in towns: in Malawi, 23 per cent of women between 15 and 69 are employed in urban areas while the corresponding figure for rural areas is 58 per cent (UNCHS 1985).

Latin America has a higher proportion of its people living in cities than in any other regions: 62 per cent of the population lives in settlements of 20 000 or more inhabitants (Gilbert and Gugler 1982). Since women predominate in urban migration, they are often outnumbered by men in rural areas, which could, in part, account for the low rates of female labour force participation here compared with cities (Butterworth and Chance 1981). However, women's proportional activity rates, allowing for the fact of their reduced numbers, are low in rural areas. In Brazil, for example, 31 per cent of all urban women between 15 and 69 were classified as employed, compared with only 17 per cent in the countryside (UNCHS 1985). This, combined with a relatively small rural female population plus systematic under-recording of women's work (discussed above), means that there appears to be a very low rate of female agricultural labour force participation in Latin America.

In Southeast Asia, women's labour force participation is high in both rural and urban areas. In the Republic of Korea, for example, in 1975, 31 per cent of all urban women and 61 per cent of rural women aged between 15 and 69 were employed (UNCHS 1985). In Islamic areas (the Middle East and North Africa and also Pakistan and Bangladesh) female participation rates tend to be low: for Morocco, the figures are 15 per cent of urban women employed compared with 9 per cent of rural women, while in Pakistan the figures are 9 per cent in both rural and urban areas (UNCHS 1985). In India the ILO revised estimate for women's participation in the agricultural labour force is 47 per cent. Obviously there are huge regional disparities and severe problems in synthesising from widely divergent data sources, and in all of these areas labour force participation is strongly influenced by both cultural and economic factors, which sometimes reinforce and at other times work against each other: these variations are discussed in detail in the second half of the chapter.

2.3 Rural production in the Middle East and North Africa

It is convenient to deal with the Middle East and North Africa in one section because religious and cultural patterns in the area (primarily Islam and Hinduism) confine women largely to the home or to domestic production activities. Male farming systems and the use of the plough are widespread in South Asia; rice is also grown, along with other grains (maize and wheat, for example) in the Middle East and North Africa.

When we examine rural women's productive roles in these areas we have to consider not only variations in the division of labour, but also the question of women's status in relation to work in the fields in many areas. Where women's work is effectively confined to the household, as in the case of many Muslim women, the division between 'productive' and 'reproductive' work is even more entangled than for other rural women. In my study of Shayfoun village I will elaborate on this point and discuss the issues involved.

Among rural women in Bangladesh or among the women of the Delhi shrine (Abdullah and Zeidenstein 1982), being in *purdah* does not mean that women are confined to the women's quarters (*zenana*) of large houses. They occupy their own rooms within the house, but their work is carried out in the courtyard spaces onto which the rooms face. Abdullah and Zeidenstein also suggest that women may leave their compounds provided they remain within the neighbourhood; such is the construction of their social and physical environment: houses are separated by secluded paths and people in the same locality tend to be kin because of prevailing marriage patterns.

Even where women are not involved in field work their role in subsistence may nevertheless be crucial. In Bangladesh, rural women are responsible for overseeing the initial germination of seed rice, as well as for the processing and storage of rice for consumption and seed (Abdullah and Zeidenstein 1982). In addition, it is women who have the responsibility for the care of the cattle, which are not only draught animals but also give milk and are a source of prestige in the community: this involves feeding and watering them, cleaning out their sheds (and storing the dung fertilisers), taking them to bathe and making sure that if any do fall ill, they are able to cure the illness from a range of traditional and modern remedies. Women are further indirectly involved in rice production in that it is they who cook food for communal (male) work parties. As in other areas where women are members of an extended family group, a women's position and roles in the household depend to some extent on her age and status: as a newly married wife she must work hard and do as her elders tell her; as she gets older, and particularly if she produces sons for the family, then she may eventually be able to delegate some of her duties to daughters-in-law of her own (*ibid.*).

Vanessa Maher's (1978) and Susan Davis's (1978) descriptions of rural women's work and options in Morocco give very similar instances. In the Moroccan case, the restrictions on women are not so severe: for example, women may market agricultural produce in the absence of their husbands or sons, something which is not possible in Bangladesh; from my field work it shows it is also possible to market agricultural produce in Shayfoun village.

Berny Horowitz and Madhu Kishwar (1984) describe women's lives in the Punjab in a village mainly occupied by a middle-ranking peasant caste of Sikhs, the Jats; the remaining inhabitants are mostly from the 'scheduled' castes (low-status groups). In spite of the differences in economic status between the Jat and other women (Jat women tend to be married to men who own land), there are similarities in their lives. Both groups of women work anything up to 15- or 16-hour days, in the fields and at home. Women's work here, as elsewhere, includes the care of cattle. The opportunities for landless women to work for money are fewer than those for men. Women are not involved at all in weeding, for example, and the only reliable work that women have is during the cotton harvest and, occasionally, during the wheat harvest. Some work in gleaning is also available. Women are never taken on by landlords as permanent labourers, but are always hired and fired as the need is perceived. Again we see similarities between rural and urban women's employment conditions. Maria Mies *et al.*'s (1986) study of rural Hindu women's work in Andhra Pradesh supports these findings, and focuses particularly on changes in women's lives, work and status in recent years. Many Indian landowners are not mechanising their farms since the labour of women is cheaper. The relatively low cost of women's labour is likely to continue, she argues, as more and more women compete for what agricultural work there is and as village craft specialisation is swamped by urban mass-produced goods and mechanised services. Whatever their actual tasks, these women perceive their lives as hard: although they put in so many hours' work, they receive less food than the men and less general health care, and are denied access to medical care. This account by Horowitz and Kishwar, together with the other articles in the same collection (Kishwar and Vanita 1984), have the more general underlying theme of emphasising women's continuing disadvantages and oppression in rural Indian society.

However, we cannot assume that such exploitation of women is universal in India: Manipur in northeast India is a small state whose population is divided between the Hindu Meiteis of the valley areas and the tribal peoples of the hills. Women are very visible in production in this area (Jain 1980), both in the markets of villages and small towns and in the state capital, Imphal. While men are largely responsible for rice cultivation, women have charge over the production of vegetables and mustard seeds, which are inter-cropped with the rice. What occurs in Manipur is completely the opposite to what I analysed in Shayfoun; here women of lower socioeconomic class are openly seen in the markets selling their products of milk, garments and honey. Women in Manipur have economic security by virtue of their access to productive work, and they have a public political presence, mainly through market networks, which act as a focus for the spreading of news and the planning of possible collective action.

However, here, as in other areas, in spite of their enjoying economic and political autonomy, social security and status are conferred on women only through marriage, that is, through their relationship to men. This point is also emphasised by Abdullah and Zeidenstein (1982) in their study of rural Bangladesh. They stress that the quality of the male support is irrelevant and that the male may be father, husband or son (depending on the stage in the woman's life cycle). Male support is more than economic: 'it is a matter of acting for women in "male space", the public world they are not supposed to enter' (*ibid.*, p.89; see also Sharma 1978).

This ultimate reliance on men to mediate with the public world is also a key issue where rural women are involved in non-agricultural productive work, and is dealt with both by Maria Mies (1980, 1982) in her discussion of the lace-makers of Nasapur and by Haleh Afshar (1985) in her discussion of carpet-weavers in rural Iran. In both of these cases women produce for the world market, but in both cases also, it is men who mediate the sale of their produce, and, hence, any relation they have to the public domain. Money made from lace-making or carpet-weaving does not become the property of the women responsible, but goes to enrich the family coffers. In the Indian case, it is the coffers of a woman's husband's family, and because this is also true to some extent in the Iranian example, wily fathers are now delaying their daughters' marriages in order to prolong their control of such valuable assets.

2.4 Gender and rural development policy

Two themes of particular relevance to women and rural development policy have figured prominently in our discussion so far: one is the problem-ridden conceptualisation of women's work in rural environments and, in particular, the failure (by census-takers, gender-blind researchers, and so on) to recognise the importance of their reproductive labour (however that is defined) as a vital component of agricultural production. When these underestimations and undervaluations of rural women's work slide, as they so often do, into the sphere of development planning, the consequences are even more serious. Failure to acknowledge the importance of women's multiple contributions to rural survival means that practical policy interventions are frequently not only detrimental to women themselves, but also to the rest of their communities. This will show in my critical analysis of the economic development in Shayfoun.

The second theme is that of the generally negative consequences of 'external influences' (colonialism, entry into the world capitalist system, the effects of world religions, and so on) on the lives of Third World women (see, for example, Abu-Saud 1984). Given that development planning also represents an intrusion of outside influences and ideologies into rural communities, it is highly likely (unless those responsible for designing and implementing rural development projects are particularly concerned with improving women's situation) that the outcomes will also be unfavourable. As such, both the above issues are critical to our discussion here.

Thus, we are concerned, on the one hand, with changes that have been introduced, 'successfully' or otherwise, from outside, either by Third World governments or their agencies, or by international development organisations, including various offices of the United Nations, The European Union (EU), the International Labour Office (ILO), the World Bank (International Bank for Reconstruction and Development: IRBD), and non-governmental organisations such as Save the Children and Oxfam. This takes in not only discussion of the design and consequences of specific 'development projects', but also of the implications of governmental decrees on such issues as land reform or resettlement. On the other hand, we also look at the changes that have been initiated from within, often by women themselves ('bottom-up' approaches to development), and assess their merits and demerits in comparison with externally-introduced initiatives in rural areas.

The 'inclusion' of women in development ideology at the formal planning level is a relatively recent phenomenon and is one focus of Barbara Rogers' (1980) book. We take 1970 as a convenient watershed for a change in attitudes towards women, and, in addition, the UN Decade for Women (1975–85) had a major impact on the visibility of women and their viable incorporation into development planning.

2.5 The design and methodology of rural development

Many of the assumptions underlying the design of development schemes and projects, certainly up to the early 1970s, were those we have already criticised as being of the 'modernisation' approach. If women were considered in rural development programmes at all, it was, at best, as adjuncts to their husbands, or as daughters or mothers. It was assumed that women's 'position' would improve as did the economic prosperity of their husbands (see also Cubitt 1988). However, this assumption 'denies the unequal power relationships which exist between people of different castes, races and classes and between men and women' (IBG 1984, p.107). Furthermore, it takes for granted the notions of male–head–breadwinner and female–housewife: an ILO report discussing the design of such programmes severely criticises this model stating:

> Among the rural poor in most countries it is quite ridiculous to presume a male head of household who provides for the family's needs and a dependent wife who looks after the house, the children, the elderly and the sick. Yet this (urban, middle class) model underlies the approach that has generally been taken to assisting women in developing countries. (Ahmad and Loutfi 1985, p.5)

Zubeida Ahmad and Martha Loutfi also go on to criticise more generally projects designed by outsiders for rural women, which do not take into account the latters' views, attitudes and abilities, or the constraints upon them. The authors advocate a 'bottom-up' approach and stress the importance of initiating change through a more positive evaluation of the work that women already do. This, they argue, will lead 'naturally' to a more equitable distribution of resources within the household and community and have the effect of raising the status of women.

As part and parcel of a 'bottom-up' approach, Ahmad and Loutfi urge the active participation of women in the design and implementation of rural development projects and cite several examples in which women, through their own initiatives, have successfully organised to improve both their economic power and their status in rural communities. Although they recognise that women face several obstacles to participation, on account of various cultural prejudices, they feel that the active involvement of women in development programmes is the only way forward. Nevertheless, the section on 'Violence' in Madhu Kishwar and Ruth Vanita's (1984) collection of articles from *Manushi* (an Indian magazine) highlights the extremely formidable nature of the obstacles to the improvement of women's standing in society: landlords, police and bureaucrats often collude in denying women their rights under the law (see also the section on 'Violence against Women' in Davies 1983). Thus, while I support the general idea of female participation as a means of improving the status of women, I also stress how difficult it is to implement such schemes, quite apart from the fact that they in no way guarantee change for the better.

Until the early 1970s, programmes devised to improve productivity, basic amenities and living conditions in rural areas tended to have two major design faults. In the first place they took little or no account of local knowledge or the environment and cultivation methods, and secondly, they tended to be addressed to household heads, using the type of model criticised above. Almost invariably, these schemes resulted in failure in the sense that, although productivity may have been improved for a short time (usually only as long as the inputs from the aid agency lasted), once this initial phase had passed, the transfers to local control were fraught with problems of both supply and distribution. Bureaucratic inertia, national balance of payments problems and (in some cases) corruption meant that supply inputs, such as 'hard' (foreign) currency to buy fertiliser, spare parts for machinery, fuel and lubricants, and seed for new crops – either HYVs (high-yielding varieties) of crops already cultivated or new crops grown for export – became increasingly scarce. At the same time the distribution of inputs (if and when they came) and of profits and/or payments owed to the participants in the scheme were subject to delay and often did not materialise at all.

The second problem in the design of rural (and urban) development schemes up to the early 1970s, that of channelling initiatives to (male) household heads, resulted from a failure (and, perhaps, unwillingness) to recognise the work done by women. It was generally assumed that women worked as part of their wifely duties, as something natural, as part of the marriage contract, which was therefore not open to discussion and negotiation or seen as having the potential for change in its own right. These assumptions owe much to sociological theories which see the family as a natural unit and one in which the elements of household production and reproduction are somehow separate from the elements of production in the wider society. Both Functionalists and Marxists are guilty here.

Several writers have criticised both the problems identified in the design of rural development projects and the early attempts to 'integrate' rural women into development. Some take as their starting point Hanna Papanek's (1977) assertion that 'a curious ambiguity in the concept of *integrating* women in the development process hampers the achievement of the goal from the start. For women are full participants in all processes of social change' (Papanek 1977, p.15; quoted in Roberts 1979, p.60). Pepe Roberts, from whose work this quote is drawn, criticises both the design of 'gender-blind' schemes and the earliest attempts to 'integrate' women into the development process. Her work draws on field experience in Niger evaluating government-sponsored programmes designed to increase rural Hausa women's economic production outside the home. The assumptions underlying the scheme were that, since under existing conditions women worked on family plots for some of the time as their husbands desired (the *gandu* system) but were also entitled to cultivate their own small plots when not working on the family farm, then the women's own plots could be 'developed'. The scheme aimed to increase women's productivity and personal income by giving them access to inputs of fertiliser and seed and to advice from the *Animation Feminine* extension workers. The planners also assumed that women had time to cultivate these smaller plots more intensively. However, when the women's plots became highly productive as a result of increased inputs they were promptly taken over by the men for *gandu* production. There was no compensation for the women: they were not given new plots, but the proportion of their time spent in *gandu* labour increased and they experienced more, rather than fewer, constraints on their productive activities. Further, since men in this rural Hausa society control access to resources, it was men who were most often given the fertiliser, leaving little or none for the women (Roberts 1979).

The 'neglect' of rural women, along with the problems of incorporating them into the design and implementation of development schemes, are discussed in detail for Asia by Nici Nelson (1979) and more generally by Ingrid Palmer (1979) and by Sue Ellen Charlton (1984). Nelson's review of the South Asian literature brings out the points we are concerned with here: the general failure of planners to appreciate what women do, whether in the household or outside; their totally false assumptions about women's existing responsibilities and their capacity for extra work; and their blindness to existing gender inequalities in control over resources, which hampers equitable development. Nelson (1979, p.45) also criticises the design of schemes based on 'the myth of the ever-present male head', when many rural households are at least *de facto* female-headed and when it is also frequently the case that resources directed to families through male heads do not end up in the hands of their wives and children.

Palmer and Charlton trace change in the design of development schemes to the early 1970s, and both recognise that there are major pitfalls to be overcome if women's status is to be improved, notably in the area of the cultural assumptions about women held by both rural populations and planners (see Barbara Rogers 1980, on the integration of women into development projects as both participants and policy-makers). Charlton sets out three 'levels' of development into which women have to be incorporated: the micro-level, integrated regional projects and the macro-level, although it is difficult to differentiate the micro-level from the integrated regional projects (Charlton 1984, pp.176ff). Macro-level change, according to Charlton, involves major shifts in state ideologies, such as the change to a socialist government or the introduction of large-scale land reform.

Our discussion thus points to the fact that it is all very well to talk about the 'integration' of women into development schemes, but we have to ask the question, on what basis? If women are to be reached and their incorporation made possible, we have to know what women do, the range of their activities, and what time they have at their disposal beyond that taken up by existing tasks. In a way, discussing how to improve women's chances in rural development schemes is jumping the gun: one of the most problematic areas in the design of projects is assessing both the nature and value of what work is done already. We have already hinted that 'Western' survey methodology is inadequate when it comes to trying to assess women's status, and it is equally ineffectual in shedding light on what rural women do, how much time they spend doing it or what value is placed on their 'work' (both productive *and* reproductive). In all areas, both in initial assessments and in roles for the future, women lose out.

Until the 1970s, the dominance of the positivist assumptions of the main body of social science meant that information on which development projects were based was derived either from existing national census figures or agricultural survey data, for example, or from data collected for the purposes of scientific projects, all of which were based on Western academic survey techniques. It is hardly surprising, therefore, that women were neglected in the information considered by planners as fundamental to designing rural development projects. Households were the study units, and the premise was that the 'ever-present' male head identified by Nelson (1979) was the person with whom the planners and their extension workers should communicate. The male head would act as the planners' agent within the community and distribute the ideas and profits from his participation in the development project among the various members of his household.

When the emphasis began to shift in the 1970s and planners increasingly recognised that women's contribution and participation were crucial if 'development' was to have permanent effects (see Charlton 1984; Nelson 1979; Palmer 1979; Rogers 1980), they also realised how difficult it was to design projects to incorporate women when they effectively knew nothing about what women did. (Although there were numerous highly specific ethnographic descriptions by anthropologists, these too tended to be gender-blind.) The task facing planners was twofold: firstly, to uncover the range of work that women did, in a qualitative sense, and secondly, to find a way in which this work could be 'operationalised', made usable for survey techniques so that women's contribution could be quantified. At this stage, the values placed on women's work in the cultures themselves were not apparently considered problematic: only later was this issue taken up.

Since the early 1970s there have been various suggestions on how to collect and organise information on women and their work for development planning. Carmen Diana Deere and Magdalena Leon de Leal (1982), in their study of women in Andean agriculture, show that, although official census data suggest that Andean women are scarcely involved in agricultural production, and that what involvement there is seems to be declining, this apparent trend is probably an artefact of data collection techniques: in recent years, women's contribution to production, rather than declining, has been systematically ignored (see also Deere 1977; Deere and Leon de Leal 1981; Rechini de Lattes and Wainermann 1986). The methodological problems of incorporating women in data collection are also discussed in Sondra Zeidenstein's (1979) *Learning about Rural Women*.

The ILO has also looked for ways to incorporate women into both data collection and the design of development projects. We have already discussed the critical evaluative work of Deere and Leon de Leal, and a survey of what has been done to date is provided by Ruth Dixon-Mueller (1985). She assesses in turn the sexual division of labour, time-use surveys, problems with the measurement of productivity, and the use of employment statistics in the assessment of women's labour force participation rates. Her overall conclusions, in terms of suggestions for research and policy formulation, give an indication both of the amount of work to be done and the kinds of questions that must be asked if valid evaluations of women's 'work' are to be made and, hence, effective and realistic policies designed (Dixon-Mueller, 1985). On another tack, in recent years Christine Oppong has been working out a model for understanding what women do in terms of seven roles and statuses often allocated to them. Although her material is based on empirical data from Ghana, her model is designed to be universally relevant (Oppong 1980; Oppong and Abu 1985, 1987).

The critical importance of making women visible in the design stages of development projects is also recognised by Joycelin Massiah (1986a) in her overview of the Women in the Caribbean Project. This project was given direct impetus by the inauguration of the UN Decade for Women in 1975. The UN Decade for Women is also more generally relevant here in that with its inauguration came a call for more female-centred research (Massiah 1986a, p.3). The Women in the Caribbean Project is seen as relevant for the Caribbean region as a whole and has five major objectives:

1   To find out more about women's subjective conditions and what objective realities women face.
2   To devise a theoretical framework for the study of changing aspects of women's roles (also implied here is an analysis of what women do).

31

3   To use the information generated for coherent policy formulation (and implementation).
4   To use the information generated directly in the planning of development programmes.
5   To produce a group of women who have skills in data collection, analysis and communication and dissemination of results to ensure continuation of the project.

(paraphrased from Massiah 1986a, pp.1–2).

All the examples we have discussed above deal specifically with the task of enabling women's incorporation into development schemes and projects. In more general terms, the 1970s saw at least a recognition of the problems arising from large-scale farming schemes, export-orientated programmes and initiatives deemed scientifically appropriate by expatriate experts, and a move towards development focused on recognising the needs and wants of the indigenous cultivators. The two formally labelled approaches relevant here are the 'Basic Needs' approach and 'Farm Systems' research. The Basic Needs approach (see Palmer 1979; Webster 1984), crudely speaking, is what it appears to be: its proponents set out to find out what rural people need and to help them fulfil those needs. However, there are several criticisms to be made here from the point of view of women (Palmer 1979). Firstly, there is no easy solution to the problem of how to go about identifying women's needs, and secondly, there is no provision, in theoretical terms, for the redistribution of resources and power between men and women.

Farm Systems research, which rose to prominence in the early 1980s, might also prove valuable to women (Charlton 1984; Moock 1986). In this approach rural households or other groups identified as production units by the scheme are regarded as systems within which there are sub-systems embracing different aspects of productive and reproductive work, but which are also integrated into wider community and regional systems. Such an approach allows for the recognition of women's contribution to all kinds of work and can incorporate cultural evaluative elements. Moreover, it seems to fit the requirements both of economically-minded social scientists and of cultural/socialist feminists, who stress the necessity of looking at relationships within the household. 'Participation' and a 'bottom-up' perspective are integral to both these approaches to development (see also Nelson 1981).

Although much valuable research on the neglect of rural women and ways in which their incorporation can be improved has come from those working at the ILO, at the same time gender-blind studies from within the organisation continue to be produced. On the one hand, the World Employment Programme of the ILO produced *Rural Development and Women in Africa* (1984) and *Rural Development and Women in Asia* (1982), which focus entirely on the problems of and for women and development. On the other hand, the same Programme produced *Poverty and Landlessness in Rural Asia*

(1977) and *Agrarian Policies and Rural Poverty in Africa* (Ghai and Radwan 1983), while the wider body of the ILO also produced *Studies in Rural Participation* (Bhaduri and Rahman 1982), all of which effectively ignore women in their analyses. It is as if 'real' studies, about whole countries, need not be concerned with women at all, let alone especially focused on women, and only those concentrating on particular sectors, or written largely by women, may single out questions of gender as of specific importance (see also Robertson 1987, for similar criticisms). The continuity of gender blindness in the literature is not confined to the ILO; Hirashima's (1977) *Hired Labour in Rural Asia* – among many other such studies – is also guilty. Just as serious a distorting device as problems with the enumeration and evaluation of women's work and status is 'a set of cultural assumptions about the secondary importance of anything women do' (Elise Boulding, quoted in Charlton 1984, p.40).

The widespread undervaluation of women's work on the part of governments, planners, academics and others has been one of the major obstacles to change, and even though some positive trends in gender-aware rural development policy may now be identified, there is still a very long way to go. In the words of the Women and Geography Study Group of the Institute of British Geographers, 'Discussions about the impact of development policies on women see them as *objects* rather than *agents* of change' (IBG 1984, p.107).

However, I proceed in my discussion to describe how I organised my field research, and the methodology which I used.

2.6 Organising field research – methodology

What is the general relationship between the ideological definition of women's roles and their position in the process of production? As soon as I had decided to address the matter of identifying the inequalities women encounter as partners in the development process, I was faced with the problem of *how* to identify them. What was the unit of Jordanian rural society appropriate for such an investigation? Is it the clan (*hamula*), or the village or the household? Some researchers (Abu Lughod 1986; Afshar 1987; Sharma 1986) have treated the village as the microcosm of the wider society: the villages are 'blocks' from which society is built, so that we can comprehend society if only we study enough of them. The village can be treated as the basic unit of Jordanian society, because any search for a 'basic unit' in a substantial or empirical sense is fruitful. A second approach, which is more important from the point of view of the theme of this study, is from a feminist perspective. I suggest that the concentration on the village as the unit for study arises from a specifically researcher-orientated perspective on Jordanian society.

In Shayfoun, the village under investigation, which I name in my book for research ethics and purposes, the women of the village enter the village at marriage and their daughters will leave it when they marry to live elsewhere for a better quality of life. A woman conceives her social world as a dichotomy between the village where she was born and that where she presently lives. At the conceptual level, the main opposition is not between the internal and external life of any particular village, but between the two villages to which a woman belongs and in which she has different kinds of membership. But for men, who do not often move (because of their land ownership they remain members of the same political and social community), for men the village is where part of the kinship relations are worked out. The sense of belonging to two places is not central to their social experience – the vital relationship for a male villager is that between co-members of his own village and the outside world in general. From the point of view of the male villager, the continuity of the village as a social unit is provided by the succession of men to positions, titles, property roles and offices. Although women concur with this view, which constitutes the dominant ideology, this is not the only way in which they structure their social experience. For them, the social ramifications of the village beyond its boundaries through the family ties of its members are as striking as the unity of its male members. The more 'female' view of the village is that of a location where a number of extensive female kinship networks overlap or converge. Women are less inclined to view the tract of countryside in which their village is located as having their own village as its 'natural' centre; they are more inclined to regard it as a region scattered with their own kin and relatives of their kin. Insofar as researchers tended to study the village as a bounded entity opposed to an external society, they have actually favoured the male villagers' view. The consequence of this, not surprisingly, is that women's activities are often relegated to the 'background'; they belong to the domestic sphere and are kept private while publicly men proclaim their own activities as having real social and political significance. For women to achieve status or access to differing resources would bring about changes in the social life of the village.

So how did I resolve the problem of defining a study area for my field study of women and production?

In the end I decided to gather data along two different dimensions. From what I knew of Jordanian rural society, the household would be an important crucial unit for study in an investigation of the role of women in production. I sought to locate different types of family groups – man, women, no children; man, wife, one child, and so on – and to conduct intensive studies of this limited sample of 46 households. I wanted to include different compositions of household. The sample was systematically compiled by taking a full census of the number of households living in the village at the time of the field research in July 1993. Thus my first enquiry covered the entire spectrum of the village.

To investigate and analyse the source of data I collected and calculated the averages per consumption unit of the sample households I studied. I had to compile data from the Ministry of Agriculture in Jordan based on the price index of 1975 for the calculation of the average budgets in that year for rich, middle and poor household farmers.

2.6.1 Land and property

On the subject of land, a map was drawn to explain the distribution of land among men and women and what inequalities women experience in the village of Shayfoun. Having thus covered a complete picture of land property I had to turn round and check the list of possible items that a village household might possess. I had to collect property details for each of my sample households and therefore included households of different composition, size, age and sex. For purposes of comparison, I had to utilise the concept of the consumption unit and divide the total property of each household by the number of its consumption units. Thus the figures will show the non-productive property all based on consumption units.

Many of my informants were keen to find out the value of their property and, apart from those few who were eager to brag of their riches or to impress their poverty upon me, they were on the whole honest about the number of items they possessed.

But in each case I tried to cross-check informants' data by personal observation as well as by enquiry from their relatives and neighbours. The interest of my informants in having an idea of the total value of their own non-productive property, and my extensive cross-checking of the data they had supplied, led me to believe that the error factor in my basic data on property was only small. The use of participant observation, rather than formal interviews and long questionnaires, reduced any problems associated with respondents changing their behaviour when studied. Shayfoun village is approximately 2 460 square metres in area. The number of households in the survey is 46 households. The types of households are shown in Table 2.1.

2.6.2 Household budgets

On the basis of households grouped according to their economic status I selected a third from each composition type completely at random. Thus my sample was random insofar as the actual households in the sample were selected at random, but was at the same time stratified inasmuch as households had previously been put into economic categories on the basis of landholding and the size and age composition of the household. My Shayfoun sample was made up of 46 of the 268 village households. Each of the sample households was subjected to intensive enquiry. From each I collected details of the major crops and of property as well as of income and expenditure. In the compilation of household budgets I encountered much greater difficulties

Table 2.1 Typologies of household structure in Shayfoun

Typology	Household structure	Number of households	Total number of households %
1	Man, wife, 0 children	3	6.5%
2	Man, wife, 1 child	7	15.2%
3	Man, wife, 2 children	6	13.0%
4	Man, wife, 3 children	4	8.7%
5	Man, wife, 4 children	3	6.5%
6	Man, wife, 5 children	4	8.7%
7	Man, wife, 6 children	1	2.2%
8	Man, wife, 7 children	1	2.2%
9	Man, 2 wives, 6 children	1	2.2%
10	Man, 2 wives, 8 children	1	2.2%
11	Man, wife, middle-aged	2	4.3%
12	Man, wife, elderly	6	13.0%
13	Widow	1	2.2%
14	Widower	1	2.2%
15	Man, child	1	2.2%
16	Man, wife, 1 child, wife's younger sister and eldest sister's child	1	2.2%
17	Man, wife, 3 children, wife's mother	1	2.2%
18	Man, wife, 2 mothers	1	2.2%
19	Man, wife, 3 children, 2 aunts	1	2.2%
Total		**46**	**100%**

Source: Village Survey, 1993.

than in the collection of data on property. Here the villagers in Shayfoun were torn between two conflicting interests: they wanted to impress me with their great expenditure while at the same time they were keen to show their extreme poverty by underestimating their incomes. In the first instance many budgets showed a considerable deficit. However, I collected three separate monthly budgets so as to cover variations between households. In this way, I managed to get a more accurate picture of household income and expenditure. Usually I got husband and wife to act jointly as informants on their household's expenditure: for all items of regular consumption, such as food, I noted how much they used of each item during the unit of time the villager himself indicated; thus, for example, for rice it was so much per meal, for vegetables and other items they bought it was so much per week. I carefully checked the prices and compiled a price list for all items of villagers' expenditure. There was only slight divergence between prices stated by informants and those I found ruling at the market. On the basis of all this information I calculated monthly totals of expenditure for the sample households.

The collection of income details was even more difficult than that of expenditure. I could not very well expect the farmer to state his monthly income when his subsistence and cash income was derived from his crop harvests once or twice a year. It was relatively easy to gather details of the household's subsistence income by enquiring for each item of consumption whether it was self-produced, bartered, received as a gift or bought with cash. But to arrive at the household's cash income I had to fall back on some statistics and records from an olive oil factory which enabled me to establish what money farmers received from the sale of their olives. By these means I worked out fairly accurately the major source of cash income of the sample households. It was much more difficult to collect details about the income of women from the sale of milk and butter or carpet-weaving products. But by checking the income of each sample household more than once during my stay in the village, I think I fairly well covered all sources of income and items of expenditure, and if I failed to collect all the details correctly, I suspect the margin of error can only have been small. In order to balance income with expenditure I calculated income per consumption unit per household. The difference between household income and expenditure was either savings or net borrowing. However, this was not just a balancing item: I tried in each case to verify if the household actually saved or borrowed money. In most, details of savings and indebtedness bore out the budget data.

I presented the budget data in the form of monthly averages per consumption unit for all the sample households I studied. Moreover, I gave details of the distribution of the different items of income and expenditure in the sample households.

Considerable effort was expended on questionnaire design, both prior to commencing field work and in Shayfoun. I tried to design the questionnaire so as to be easy to use and to order the questions so that they followed a logical sequence. I also found pilot testing most helpful. Pilot testing made a huge difference, leading to substantial amendments and improvements to all parts of the questionnaire.

2.6.3 Qualitative data

As far as my research is concerned, I regarded the collection of quantitative data as constituting the skeleton of my material; the qualitative data provided the flesh. I found that only by combining numerical with behavioural data could I get full in-depth insight into the socioeconomic organisation and its change in Shayfoun. This is the second dimension I wanted to cover in my research. It was seldom necessary to conduct formal interviews, although my informants were quite aware that I was studying them and many of our conversations were tape-recorded. These household studies yielded valuable information on women's role in the domestic economy, family decision-making processes, women's standing in the kinship system and their role in arranging marriages.

To answer other kinds of questions, I had to locate a place where most women meet. I found a small market which performed both a social and commercial function for my study. This produced useful material on the political roles of women in the locality, the restrictions on women's use of public space, changes in land tenure and methods of agriculture. The two dimensions of the study – the 'household' dimension and the 'locality' dimension – yielded different kinds of information and were complementary to each other. Therefore Shayfoun represents the focus for the study of women and their economic roles in the locality rather than for a study of the village considered in terms of social groups.

However, my decision to concentrate on women's issues was influenced by two principal factors. At the personal level, I wanted to explore the gender aspects of my cultural identity as a Jordanian woman. Academically, since gender relations and female welfare in the rural areas of Jordan remain largely under-researched, their investigation seemed worthwhile. I chose to work with women rather than men, but this was not because I anticipated difficulties in establishing rapport with respondents of the opposite sex. In fact, I encountered no such problems during my field work. This may seem puzzling at first, for it could be argued that as a female researcher, it must be very difficult to enter the male realm of a strictly sex-segregated society. But this view ignores a subtle relationship between gender and other variables. Factors such as class and outsider status can interact positively with gender, thus reducing its constraining influence on the researcher's accessibility and freedom. I had not only a relatively privileged access to the female domain, but also an altogether unproblematic relationship with the village men. I had a particularly good rapport with older women and widows. This was partly because I wanted to hear their accounts of 'the old days', which did not interest other young people. The fact that the widows were household heads also meant that they had more freedom in deciding how they spent their time. In other households, especially if the women were younger, their time and attention would be taken up not just by their many children but also by their husbands, who expected tea and food when they came in from work. With older married women this was less of a problem, as their husbands seemed to place fewer demands on them.

It is worth reiterating that it was my class, education and researcher status that allowed me to talk to non-kinsmen at all. No other unmarried woman in the village could do so with such ease. These factors put me in a separate category. My female respondents often told me that my contact with the village men was acceptable because I had a reason for doing so; it was for my work and not for fun.

3 Land changes and means of production

3.1 New economic opportunities

Economic expansion in underdeveloped rural communities is normally the result of an interaction between external stimulus and internal response. There are few, if any, village economies where economic growth has been internally generated. Usually new opportunities for villagers are either the result of conscious planning by the government or other external authorities or they are the by-product of private enterprise activities in the wider economy. Rural residents may face one dominant type, or a combination of different types, of new economic opportunity. The whole community or a section thereof may respond positively to some new opening while rejecting or neglecting others for no obvious rational reason discernible by outsiders. It is therefore essential to examine the total range of variables which come within the reach of villagers to be able to analyse the regularities, if there are any, in their response.

This chapter seeks to discuss the composition of Shayfoun village taking into account the structure of the population, the climate and crops and the village economies. The second part will analyse the land structure and it will conclude that, due to the *mushaa* system and the presence of British Mandatory rule in the early twentieth century, land changes and means of production affected the structure of Shayfoun village. The chapter will conclude that the heritage of common political action and common economic control has had positive consequences for the roles of production and the inequalities in land ownership.

3.2 Shayfoun village

This section is descriptive, straightforward, summary and brief. It is designed to provide sufficient background socioeconomic material on the contemporary state of affairs to enable readers who may have no special knowledge of Jordanian rural areas, and of Shayfoun district in particular, to experience some sense of locality before embarking on the subsequent, detailed analysis of the role of women in production and the inequalities they experience in the process of development.

3.2.1 Population

Most of those who live in Shayfoun district are of Bedouin origin and belong to four big *hamulas* – Bani Sakr, Bani Ali, Bani Ibrahim, and Bani Hassan. They all speak Arabic and are Orthodox Muslims, worshipping as Sunnis. Most of the population live scattered over the farmland and depend almost entirely on cultivation and associated rural activities for their livelihood. The population density is very variable; the reasons for this are not always well understood, but sometimes have to do with such diverse factors as long-distance trade routes and the height of the water table. At one extreme there are vast tracts of quite lightly populated areas, some of which are proving attractive to farmers from more densely populated localities outside the district; at the other extreme, there are certain more densely populated rural zones of which by far the largest and most remarkable is an area of dispersed settlement. The high population densities are as much due to unusually high rates of national growth, either today or in the past, as to high rates of immigration from less densely populated localities in former times. The population of Shayfoun in 1992 was approximately 3 000 inhabitants.[2]

Reliable demographic statistics being altogether lacking for rural Jordan, we can do no more than presume that rural population growth rates are much higher than in urban areas. Infant mortality rates are still very high indeed, perhaps as high as 15–18 per cent for children under five years.[3] Rates of outward migration of men are rather high despite the proximity of the big cities. As for inward migration, the capacity of some localities in the region to continue to absorb strangers is quite notable, given the high population densities.

Jordan is one of the countries that have undergone rapid urbanisation during the last thirty years. Both compulsory and voluntary internal migration have led to the rapid growth of some cities, such as Amman or Zarga (Madi 1984).

The percentage of urban population has increased from 44 per cent of the

---

2 Jordanian Ministry of Agriculture, 1991.
3 Jordanian Ministry of Health Report, 1992.

41

total population in 1961 to 74 per cent in 1985. Three-quarters of the population of the Amman area are concentrated in the central part of Amman. However, if we consider the population structure with respect to its age–sex pattern, Jordan is not much different from neighbouring Arab states. The male to female ratio was 105:100 in 1992. A sizeable proportion of Jordan's population (50 per cent in 1992) is under 15 years of age. The group aged between 15 and 59 accounted for 46 per cent of the total population, while those of 60 years of age and above accounted for 4 per cent of the total population (Ministry of Planning 1992, p.96). One of the most important characteristics of the Jordanian labour force is the low crude participation rate. For the last twenty years, the participation rate has remained almost constant at 20 per cent. Several factors account for this state of affairs including the large proportion of people under 15 years of age, low female participation rates, and continued outflow of manpower, especially of the younger generation, to other countries.

3.2.2 Climate and crops

Although all matters of farming and economic development are left for later chapters, perhaps I cannot postpone a brief mention of climate and crops. The region is on a plateau in northern Amman and at an altitude of 1 500ft, and is consequently cold at some seasons. The climate is rather dry with average annual rainfalls not much exceeding 30 inches in Shayfoun. The cultivators are greatly troubled by the erratic monthly distribution of rain. Ordinary farm tools and cultivating equipment have remained basically unchanged for at least fifty years, still being made by local blacksmiths, carpenters and other craftsmen. Shayfoun cultivators depend almost entirely on a range of hoes designed for different operations. There are still not many agricultural machines other than two-wheeled wooden carts, drawn by a pair of cattle. All the main food crops are grown both for household consumption and for sale and any attempt to distinguish subsistence and cash crops or subsistence and cash farmers begs the very questions with which we are primarily concerned.

The degree of self-sufficiency, however, is measured by the ratio of domestic food production to domestic food consumption. The major determinants of food consumption are family size, family consumption, family income, or increase in both family size and per capita income level. Other factors of importance are price changes or variations in the level of income needed to survive, urban or rural residence, occupation, social status and a number of sociological, cultural, psychological and environmental factors.

The figures in the following table indicate that expenditure on food is strongly related to the size of the population and per capita income level. In 1992, Amman had the highest expenditure on food. This is mainly because it contained 56 per cent of the total population, in addition to enjoying high levels of per capita income.

**Table 3.1 Geographical distribution of expenditure on food
commodities 1992 (JD millions)**

Commodity	Amman	Irbid	Shayfoun
Cereals	22.7 JD	15.8 JD	1.6 JD
Meat	57.2 JD	27.6 JD	3.1 JD
Vegetables & fruit	40.7 JD	16.8 JD	2.3 JD
Eggs	41.4 JD	24.5 JD	2.2 JD
Dairy products	33.7 JD	19.7 JD	1.8 JD
Total	195.7 JD	104.4 JD	11.0 JD

Source: Department of Statistics, 1993.

Note: The data were compiled in 1993 by the Department of Statistics to
examine the distribution of expenditure on food commodities.

3.2.3 Village economies

Putting the matter absurdly briefly, the rural communities, as such, should be
thought of as assemblages of households, surrounded by cultivated farmland,
which mainly connect to the outside world by means of 'exporting' certain
types of farm produce, which enables them to pay for the 'import' of a great
variety of essential consumer goods, building materials and so forth which
they cannot make for themselves.

In Shayfoun the custom of producing rural craft goods continues to flour-
ish; there are no craft guilds and no restrictions on entry to any occupation.
The public amenities in the village are dominated by a primary school, a quite
outstandingly excellent and spaciously built establishment; in addition there
is a fairly large, recently built, Friday mosque. There are five concrete-lined
drinking-water wells with walled tops, which provide water to the ordinary
households. There is a tiny shop – most selling being done by women in their
houses, or by men sitting in the street. The postal service is poor, electricity
supplies are lacking and bus services are few.

Farmers from rich *hamulas* live in superior, spaciously built houses. The
quality and size of the houses occupied by Shayfoun's people vary according
to their means and the sizes of the households. There are separate cattle sheds.
Some of the streets are dirty, as well as congested, for there is a strong reluc-
tance to enlarge the built-up village site as population increases. There are no
outdoor granaries.

For those who enjoy the light of the day and the stars of the night sky, as
well as a certain minimum of privacy while sleeping, Shayfoun habitations

are in principle superior. But such a conclusion does not benefit the introductory section of this book, which is mainly concerned with demolishing the concept of averages which, in the words of Lenin,[4] 'obscure the differentiation and [are] therefore purely fictitious'.

I continue my discussion of Shayfoun village by analysing the important subject of land in the late nineteenth and early twentieth century under the Mandate period, examining the role of production and whether it explains the social roles of the inhabitants.

3.3 An historical sketch of Ajlun administrative boundaries in the late nineteenth and the twentieth century

Although Jordan was part of the Ottoman Empire and lay along the caravan route from Damascus to Medina, the Ottoman government paid little attention to the area in the nineteenth century. To be sure, the government paid the Bedouins a stipend to allow the caravans safe passage, but frequent defaults in payments were followed by the sacking of caravans. Villagers were forced to pay a tax on wheat or animals levied by the neighbouring tribes in return for protection and being allowed to till their soil (Madi 1984, pp.19–24).

In response to these depredations, villagers united under the leadership of the strongest family among them, to protect their crops and sheep. A leader (*Shaykh*) was appointed to handle important day-to-day functions and matters of arbitration. The role and authority of the *Shaykh* were essentially political. His authority extended beyond the acceptance of his decision in arbitration. The *Shaykh* made war and peace and collected taxes. The villagers in his district constituted a potential military following that could be called upon in any crisis. His principal political function was protection; it was offered in return for economic contributions on the occasion of the harvest and often in return for permanent land grants. He also constituted a redistribution point for economic surplus. He earned his reputation as a wise man by his skill in settling disputes and his reputation as a good man by slaughtering sheep for the guests who came to pay him homage or ask for advice or aid. The tribal custom demanded the sharing of every slaughter with as many men as possible. The circle of generosity was very wide indeed. The *Shaykh's* guest house was the political centre of the whole region.[5] The leader of this district network utilised the economic tribute (which was frequently in the form of sheep) to win political adherents and to achieve his own or his family's high standard of living.

The importance of the *Shaykh* was accentuated by the absence of any centralised administration in the area. No local police post existed. The Ottoman governor of the Ajlun district lived in Syria. Considering the con-

4 Lenin: *Collected Works*, 1967, Vol. 3, p.103.
5 This information is based on the account of an elderly villager.

ditions of communication and transportation in the late nineteenth century appeal to him against the rule of the *Shaykh* was out of the question. Moreover, Ottoman authorities found it easiest to deal with the single authority who could collect taxes and maintain some sort of order. The *Shaykh* became recognised as the political overlord of the area by his own followers, by the Bedouins who opposed him and by the Ottoman government who sought his aid. The elders of Shayfoun were overruled and bound by the *Shaykh* in all matters.

Before 1922, when Shayfoun was a refuge from the depredations of the Bedouins and from the arbitrary taxation and conscription policies of the Ottoman Turks, the need to defend it encouraged families to settle there. But with population increase and the establishment of centralised government in 1922 the very advantages which had made Shayfoun a political centre in a period of anarchy – its remoteness from administrative centres and its inaccessibility to attack – became disadvantageous. By settling in the village, peasants were not only able to care for their crops more efficiently, but also were able to attend markets, dispensaries, courts and land registry offices which had become so much a part of rural life with the spread of centralised government.

Nevertheless, as late as 1922, the *Shaykh* of Shayfoun refused to attach the subdistrict of Al Kura to Irbid under the new state of Transjordan being organised by Amir Abdullah. It was only with the bombing of Shayfoun by British aircraft in the service of Amir Abdullah in 1922 that the proud overlords of Shayfoun submitted to government control.

3.4 Land tenure: the *mushaa* system

There are five official classes of land tenure in the Kingdom of Jordan (Madi 1984, pp.66–69):

1 *Privately owned land* is land which the owners can dispose of as they like, whether to exploit, give as security, sell or bequeath. Nearly all the cultivated land in Shayfoun falls into this category.
2 *Land held as a religious endowment* is property set aside in perpetuity according to Islamic law and for religious or charitable purposes. In Shayfoun, 11 acres of land have been set aside as religious endowment. This land is tilled by various sharecroppers every year, the proceeds of the crop being used for the upkeep of the village mosque.
3 *State land* is land registered in the name of the state treasury. Its profit reverts to the government although it may be rented to the inhabitants of the area. It may also be sold to them for a price set by the government. Part of it is woodland which the government oversees and protects. One-third of the land in Shayfoun, being woodland, is held by the government as state land.

4   *Communal land* is land close to settlement left for the inhabitants as pasture or woodland. No single person may own it. It is preserved indefinitely for the general welfare. It includes woodland close to the area of settlement, pasture and barren rocky lands suitable for grazing.

5   *Wasteland* is desert land, unexploited, unclaimed and far from settled areas. In Shayfoun, the percentage of land in the above categories is shown in the following table.

Table 3.2 Official categories of land tenure in Shayfoun

Type of land	Approximate area (acres)	Percentage of land in village
Privately owned land	2 709	69.4%
Religious endowment	12	0.3%
State land	1037	27%
Communal land	132	3.3%
Wasteland	0	0%
Total	3 890	100%

Source: Ministry of Agriculture, 1989.

Until 1939, when the lands of the village were individually registered, Shayfoun held the greater part of its cultivated lands under an official category of land known as *mushaa*. Even during Ottoman times, however, at least one-fourth of the cultivated lands of the village were exempted from this. The *mushaa* system of tenure has been described by John Glubb in 1957 as follows:

> Under *mushaa* the properties of land are regarded as being owned by the community – but are in the actual possession of several owners each of whom has a certain share of the joint property, though his ownership on any special area is not fixed. Usually the fields are redistributed periodically among the members of the community according to some generally accepted plan. (Issawi 1966, p.31)

A number of contradictory explanations, none of them wholly satisfying, have been offered for the development of this type of land tenure in certain areas of the Fertile Crescent. Some have claimed that *mushaa* is associated with a former nomadic way of life which stresses common rights in property among the agnatic groups. But Grannot (1952) has pointed out that in the area of Palestine most susceptible to Bedouin influence – the Beersheba district – individual ownership holds sway. Others have suggested that more valuable lands tend to be developed for profit and registered individually while less valuable lands have remained under *mushaa* tenure. Weulersse (1946), noting the geographical incidence of *mushaa* in the arid inland steppes of the Levant, has associated it with the semi-cereal monoculture (wheat, barley and legumes) of relatively fertile plains.

Mushaa is generally found in infertile foothills. It is 'a system born of aridity and permanent menace of nomads and requiring a concentration of people while the necessities of rotation required strict communal discipline.' (Grannot 1952)

Shayfoun, though it does not lie in the valley itself, was open to sporadic depredations by Bedouins. Its two-crop cereal-growing regime required the discipline of communal organisation. Grannot's general statement regarding the agricultural regime associated with *mushaa* in Palestine is also applicable to Shayfoun:

> *Mushaa* tenure must not be regarded as simply a form of land ownership; it also necessitates a certain style of agricultural work. It demands from every co-owner no small measure of acquiescence in methods of cultivation, and in an order and timetable of field operations imposed from without. Every co-owner is obliged to follow a rotation of crops from the various fields which is fixed and uniform for all the co-owners, that is to say to grow the same crops, at the same periods, and by the same methods as all the rest of the co-owners. (Grannot 1952, p.231)

In Shayfoun, the introduction of fixed dates of planting and harvesting set by the council of elders and the biennial or triennial rotation required by *mushaa* did not allow the individual peasant to sell his share in the land of the village to strangers; he was not able to keep unused pasture or enclose his land. Furthermore, public or private paths or dwellings of any sort could not be kept on cultivated land, for in the redistribution of land they would be ploughed over.[6]

The *mushaa* system necessitated cooperative and consecutive harvesting. Villagers or kinsmen banded together to harvest the crops of each individual's plot; they would finish it and then move on to the adjoining plot. A cultivator was not allowed to anticipate and harvest his plot before his turn came. This prohibition was enforced in order to prevent depredation by plough animals and sheep if harvesting was individually carried out on a helter-skelter pattern. After the harvesting of the whole area, all the cultivators were permitted to turn their flocks onto the fields of the village. A crop watchman was hired by the village to protect the unharvested crops from thieves and animals. Depredation was quite likely, due to the fragmentation of each landholding into a number of widespread parcels.

I argue that, although the intrinsic complexity of *mushaa* does admittedly render it very difficult to analyse, it still seems to have been regularly misunderstood or misrepresented by the colonial officials who became the main source of information about it, most of whom saw it as an archaic system

6 This information was communicated to me by the land registry officer in Shayfoun.

destined soon to wither away. The unsatisfactory nature of their treatment provides few clues to such central questions as where did it begin.

According to both Weulersse (1946) and Firestone (1975) there were two basic types of *mushaa* system in the Mandate period in Syria and Palestine. In each, the village land subject to collective ownership, excluding orchards and gardens, was divided into sections of relatively homogeneous quality (usually three or four in number) and then periodically redistributed in such a way that every person or group of persons entitled to a share obtained a parcel or plot in every section. The principle according to which the land was allocated varied, however. According to the first system, which Weulersse calls the 'old' and Firestone the 'open-ended' system, plots were distributed to each family on the basis of the number of males or the number of ploughs it possessed – in other words according to some local definition of agricultural input, whether in terms of labour power or tools, or both. Any increase or decrease in the number of such units meant a corresponding increase or decrease in the number of shares.

Under the second system (which Firestone calls 'quantified shares') access to the land was not dependent on units of input, but rather was divided into a fixed number of shares which did not vary over time. As in the first system, each share entitled its owner or owners to plots in each of the village's three or four sections, but in this case future distribution of land took place only between shareholders, so that newcomers could no longer be accommodated. In addition, the shares themselves rapidly developed into something much more like a fixed title and could be bought and sold or transferred either among the villagers themselves or in transactions with outsiders. They could also be subdivided as a result of sale or inheritance. Gender relations are important for the distribution of lands in Shayfoun (Firestone 1975).

Lastly, to complete the list of major variations, it was possible for re-distribution under either system to come to an end, leaving the actual plots of land, or title to them, in the hands of whoever possessed them at that particular moment.

According to Weulersse, the second system just described was a natural development of the first; and it is easy to see why he should assert this (Weulersse 1946, p.30). To a researcher, change to a fixed or 'quantified' method of sharing – to use Firestone's word – might well seem to have been a response both to growing commercialisation and to those changes in local power relationships which tended to increase the role of merchants and notables. As already noted, this second system allowed the sale and purchase of title as a way of valorising an individual's or family's share in the communal land. It also permitted non-labouring outsiders, excluded under the first system, to obtain access to village land, something insurers, protectors and local strongmen must obviously have been anxious to do. To this list of factors, Firestone himself could add the growth of population pressure: as he rightly points out, the 'quantified share' system allowed out-migrants from over-populated areas outside the village to continue to hold either a title share or part of one without actually living there (Firestone 1975).

However, against this, it is important to note that Firestone himself, unlike Weulersse, is unwilling to allow that all villages passed inevitably from one system to the other, and this is certainly a useful caveat. Given the paucity of information, the enormous variation in local conditions and the different historical experience of different villages in different districts, it would be wise not to be too categoric (Firestone 1975). To make only a few of the most obvious points: although it is known that collective ownership was common in Syria and Palestine in the late nineteenth century almost all the data concerning it comes from a later period. Again, there is the obvious distinction to be made between those villages which may have held their fields in common for many decades and those new settlements established on recently secured land. To make matters even more complex, the number of variables which have to be taken into account when seeking to explain changes within the system are very large, and include the role of increasing monetisation and of rural power systems, which I am going to explore in detail, in the economic development that occurred and in the changes in the lifestyle of different households. To these, I argue, should be added the question of availability of labour, something which, when scarce, might well have encouraged a system in which newcomers, especially those with ploughs, were rapidly given access to village land (the 'open-ended' system) and, when plentiful, one in which surplus labourers could more easily be exported (the 'quantified share' system) (Firestone 1975).

Lastly, there is the vital question of the incidence of taxation and the way in which the tithe was actually collected. In Firestone's valuable argument, the open-ended system, with its built-in mechanism for dividing the available land into equal shares among all producers, can readily be seen as a natural response on the part of both cultivator and collector to a situation in which taxes were collected in one lump sum from whole villages at the highest possible rate. It follows logically that communities in which the burden of both agricultural production and tax payments were equally divided could manage to deliver a larger volume over a longer period than those in which an unequal distribution of land must inevitably mean that the weaker units were soon driven to the wall, leaving an even smaller number of cultivators to shoulder the total burden on their own. There is also Weulersse's (1946) observation that the *mushaa* system seems, historically, to have been closely associated with the dominant type of agricultural practice, dry farming of cereals.

Sadly, however, I argue that such an argument can constitute only a useful hypothesis so long as the data to prove it are unobtainable. The actual correlation between high taxes and redistribution of land in equal shares remains to be demonstrated. If and when it can be managed it will have to be done with reference to the fact that, in many districts, the tax-farmer and the man who controlled the land were the same person – or else closely in league – and that their joint interest in maximum taxes might well have been in conflict with their wider concern to personally appropriate more of the surplus via the additional roles of insurer, protector or even, if they could break into the village monopoly of land, owner.

When so little is known about the origins, development and geographical spread of the *mushaa* system in any of its variations, it is naturally just as difficult to say anything very much in general about its economic and social consequences. It has long been a commonplace among economists that systems of communal land ownership inhibit investment and changes in agricultural practice (Weulersse 1946, pp.32–36). But the argument is not as simple as it may at first seem. For one thing, the *mushaa* system, with its emphasis on communal solidarity, was almost certainly a useful mechanism for facilitating the colonisation of newly secured land. For another, if Weulersse is right about its connection with dry farming, it was associated with a type of agriculture for which no great improvement in productivity was possible anyway, short of large-scale mechanisation. Meanwhile, those key activities in the rural economy where improvement *was* possible – notably the cultivation of fruit, vines and vegetables – were carried out on privately owned land.

Having said all this, it also remains a fact that the *mushaa* system, as well as frustrating any initiative to stop the regular redistribution of village land, was a major contributor to that minute and inefficient subdivision, or parcelisation, of agricultural properties which was so widely remarked upon during the inter-war period. According to one survey of the Jordan valley, carried out in 1932, the number of separate parcels of land owned by each proprietor varied between 14 and 56 (Weulersse 1946, pp.50–61).

Since the law of inheritance, when enforced, also contributed to the continual break-up of larger plots, it is obvious that the *mushaa* system itself cannot be attacked as the only major cause of the phenomenon, but it was certainly an important one. Once the redistribution of land under the open-ended system came to an end, those in possession of what were already three or four separate parcels in the various sections of the village land were left free to dispose of them as they wished or as the law and economic circumstances dictated. Parcelisation was the obvious consequence. By the same token, it may well have been that one of the major reasons for switching systems was just to prevent the possibility of such a damaging subdivision. Under the quantified shares system, while the shares themselves could be endlessly subdivided, it was still possible, at least in theory, to keep the land to which they referred intact and to farm it as one unit.

The fragmentation of land parcels was a necessary part of the *mushaa* system. Every villager with a share in the land, for it was shares and not land that were held by the individual, received a parcel in every one of the categories into which the village lands were divided. Table 3.3 indicates the ownership and type of Shayfoun village lands. The division of land into categories was to ensure that every landowner had a portion in fertile as well as barren land, in level as well as sloping land, in near as well as distant land, in land accessible to springs as well as that not accessible, in woodland as well as cultivated land, and in land suitable for summer as well as winter crops. Each family was assigned the number of parcels corresponding to the number of shares in village land. In Shayfoun a landowner commonly held five or six parcels of land. In this situation no single landowner was in a position to guard his own crops or to ignore the field operations of his neighbour.

Extra-familial cooperation continued on the threshing ground: kinsmen and neighbours aided one another, particularly if the season had produced a bumper crop. The owner of the crop often staked a goat on the threshing ground. When the threshing was complete, the goat was slaughtered and all who had contributed in helping the owner and his family were invited to the feast, which often took place on the threshing ground itself. This helps to defend my thesis that the role in production also explains much else about the social roles (Madi 1984).

However, not all of the cultivated land in Shayfoun was held under *mushaa* tenure. At least a quarter of it had been exempted from periodical redistribution during Ottoman times. The express purpose of the Ottoman land law of 1858 had been to fix individual rights of ownership on all lands to which the state had residual title. This included most agricultural land. Although this law was never fully carried out, due to the corruption on the part of the officials who administered it and evasion on the part of the peasants to whom it was supposed to apply, a number of families in Shayfoun had been able to gain government recognition for their claims to certain areas in the village. The land so exempted seemed to be no better and no worse in quality than the other lands of the village. The Turks, then, albeit inefficiently, had attempted to breakdown the *mushaa* system as early as the middle of the nineteenth century (Grannot 1952, p.261).

Moreover, within the broad category of land tenure known as *mushaa*, several variations existed. Under one type, every man living in the community at the time of the biennial redistribution of land, including infants, received equal shares in the communal land. Under another, land was distributed according to ability to work it: that is, distribution was according to the number of draught animals held by each household. Families without draught animals did not receive shares in the land. Shayfoun represents neither of these types; rather, redistribution of land was in proportion to the number of shares in land held by the head of each household. Since the ownership of shares differed widely, the resulting redistribution of land between households was relatively unequal.

Whatever the consequences of these variations in the *mushaa* system for economic and social status, in every case, including Shayfoun, the village was regarded as the corporate owner of the land, and a villager could not alienate a share of land to strangers. In Shayfoun, however, it was the clan within

Table 3.3 Ownership and type of Shayfoun village lands

Type	Villagers				Outsiders				Government				Total			
	1955		1990		1955		1990		1955		1990		1955		1990	
	Acres	%	Acres	%	Acres	%	Acres	%	Acres	%	Acres	%	Acres	%	Acres	%
Irrigated	352	68	630	76	165	32	200	24	–	–	–	–	517	100	830	100
Dry	249	60	180	78	166	40	50	22	–	–	–	–	415	100	230	100
Waste	–	–	–	–	–	–	–	–	542	100	457	100	542	100	457	100
Housesites	42	65	42	65	–	–	–	–	23	35	23	35	65	100	65	100
Tanks	–	–	–	–	–	–	–	–	118	100	75	100	118	100	75	100
Total	643	39	852	52	331	20	250	15	683	41	555	33	1657	100	1652	100

Source: Shayfoun Village Land Records 1991, Vol(3), pp.32–33.

Note: The data were compiled in 1992 from Shayfoun municipal records in order to trace the figures of 1955 land owner-ship and check the ownership of land in 1990 for comparison analysis of land property.

which the actual redistribution of land took place. The village lands were divided into three equal parts corresponding to the three clans of the village. The three clans were of unequal size, however, and often families would join the smaller clans to even up the division. Each clan was assigned one of the three areas by lot. Then each clan would redivide the stretch allotted it among its component families. Thus 'every *hamula* (clan) or family received an area corresponding to the share which was originally assigned to it in the landed property in the village' (Madi 1984, p.13).

Stressing the right of every living male as a member of the village community and thereby entitled to land, the system of *mushaa* practised in Shayfoun was basically unegalitarian in permitting the holding of unequal shares in the village based on an initial historic division that was not responsive to population growth. The last historic settlement of shares in land in Shayfoun had probably been imposed by the Turks in the nineteenth century when they had registered a share of land for every able-bodied male who volunteered for military service. Thus land rights and military obligations were closely connected, so much so as to be covered by the same term. (See Table 3.4.)

Table 3.4 The distribution of shares in Shayfoun

Types of farmers	Shares in the year 1948	Shares in the year 1992
Rich farmers	26 acres	34 acres
Middle farmers	20 acres	19 acres
Small farmers	15 acres	12 acres
Poor farmers	10 acres	3 acres
Poorer farmers	3 acres	landless

Source: Ministry of Agriculture, 1993.

In 1929, registration of cultivated land was begun in Palestine and Transjordan. By 1943, 968 500 acres had been settled – 84 per cent of all cultivated land and nearly all land held under *mushaa* (Madi 1984, pp.81–83). Land settlement officers reached Shayfoun in 1939. It was not they, however, who carried out the actual partition of land. This task was left to the cultivators, who were in a better position to assess the quality of the soil and the numerous factors that affected its fertility. After the initial cadastral survey (which had never been carried out by the Turks, whose registration was by personal ownership and not cadastral) and the partition of lands formerly held in common, came the investigation of claims to land ownership and the registration of title. All lands of the village were registered in the names of individuals, and a land map was drawn up which demarcated individual boundaries and on which all subsequent sales were recorded. Each villager who possessed shares under *mushaa* now received two plots – one of cultivable land and another of woodland, instead of the five or six held before. Many plots of land were registered jointly in the names of brothers or patrilineal first cousins and still continue to be held in such manner today. With population increase and the division of household, however, such individual plots may be gradually reduced.

Although state land devolves on the death of a possessor 'in equal shares and without payment of any price, upon his children of both sexes whether residing on the spot or in another country' (Madi 1984, p.93), and although this rule has been extended to cover privately owned land, numerous local customs have operated to avoid the partition of the inheritance. Land is commonly registered in the name of a son or sons during the life of a father or it may be given as a gift to a single individual. Women are, in this manner, commonly excluded from inheritance. This is particularly true of women who marry out of their community or patrilineal group. The registration of land, then, has not had as revolutionary an effect in terms of land division and, conversely, land agglomeration as one might have expected from formal considerations. Frequently, 'the courts have held that such customs are valid when shown to be ancient and invariable in spite of the fact that they run counter to statute law' (Madi 1984, p.89).

The significance of the abolition of *mushaa* tenure for village and clan cooperation should not, however, be underestimated. The necessity of the scattering of the land parcels of a single cultivator to equalise the quality of his land prevented land agglomeration or cooperation among big landowners. A rich farmer under *mushaa* could not purchase land from his less fortunate fellows. He could only purchase shares in land – land whose quality would change at every distribution. With the registration of land in individual ownership purchase of land became not only possible but potentially profitable. A plot of land of known quality might now be bought, held over a number of years and developed by its owner.

Today Shayfoun cannot be regarded in any sense as a corporate village with control over economic resources. Land sales occur and may be to nonvillagers. However, the village has not yet passed from under the shadow of its corporate history despite the formal revolution in land tenure. Over the course of the last twenty years very little land has been alienated to nonvillagers. Owners of adjacent land plots are usually granted the privilege of prior purchase before a sale is made. Most sales are to neighbours on the land or to members of the same lineage and clan. A comparison of the distribution of land plots in terms of lineage and clan affiliation in 1939 and in 1993 shows very little change. Owners of abutting land plots tend to be affiliated with the same clans and lineages.

The *hamula* organisation at village level did not decline in the Mandate period, but it epitomises the process of Arab 'subsistence' farmers being gradually integrated into a 'modern' economy from 1920 onwards (Asad 1975, p.42).

Up to and including most of the nineteenth century, Palestine suffered from general insecurity, which was responsible for the decline of population and of agriculture. Under these conditions land was abundant and almost free. Groups and individuals established rights on unused land simply by settling on it and cultivating it. In the villages, all land was state land and was held by the village community in a form of joint ownership called *mushaa*, which I have already referred to. The village was divided into *hamulas*. Membership in the *hamula* determined rights to a share of the village lands. Thus the dominant cleavage in the village was on *hamula* lines. *Hamula* organisation provided the basis of political organisation. Law and order in the village was maintained by means of a balance of power between the *hamulas*, regulated by institutionalised forms of collective self-help. Politically and economically the villages remained isolated (Asad 1975).

During the latter half of the nineteenth century, and well down to the Mandate period, economic and political conditions changed drastically. The country became the centre of interest for European power, so a large number of missionaries came and established institutions of various sorts, spending a great deal of imported capital. The administration was reorganised and social order became more stable. A substantial increase in the population followed as a result of the natural increase from Arab immigration from the neighbouring Arab countries and of the settlement of Bedouin in permanent villages. These developments were associated with the break-up of the joint estate in many villages and the conversion of land to private property. In the process, a large proportion of peasants became landless and lived as tenants on the land of others.

Disparities within the village increased. The accumulation of wealth produced a leisured class who migrated to the towns and lived there, acquiring modern education and monopolising the élite occupations (professionals, businessmen and politicians). But there was also a flow of landless peasants into the towns, particularly as a result of the high birthrate in the rural population (Asad 1975).

During the Mandate period, the development of Arab nationalism proved an insurmountable obstacle. Communications facilitated the formation of nationalist organisations, and a pyramid of political alliances, culminating in the nationalist leadership of the towns, integrated the entire Arab population, urban and rural, into a unified political entity. In the course of political disturbances in the country during the 1920s and 1930s the Arabs developed their own armed, though mainly irregular, forces, their own banks and industry, labour and business establishments, youth associations, propaganda offices, and associations for aiding peasants and saving Arab lands from being sold to Jews. However, with the conversion of a great proportion of joint estates to private ownership, the *hamula* lost its economic basis. The new lines of stratification cut across *hamula* boundaries and tended to disrupt the *hamula*. The development of an Arab countrywide nationalist organisation weakened the *hamula* further by the creation of national associations that cut across particular patronymic and territorial groupings. The dominant cleavage in the village now ran on class lines.

After 1948–49 the Arab village lost its centuries-old economic autonomy. Land shortage was no longer so economically important. The Arab villager could concentrate on production for the market, produce for his own consumption, lease his land to a more enterprising peasant while he himself worked for wages or he could cultivate his land for part of the time and work for wages for rest of the time, leaving the care of the crops to his wife and children. Within the village itself, the new economy created a new egalitarianism. At the political level, a new system elected local councils connected with the central government departments. This revival of *hamula* organisation has thus provided a social mechanism for the preservation of Arab traditional values and for the maintenance of the political and social autonomy of the village (Asad 1975).

The object to be grasped is the developing class situation of Arab villagers within a specific historical social formation and it is to be explained by analysing the articulation of a capitalist with a non-capitalist mode of production which defines that social formation. In this context it is essential to defend my thesis that the rural population produced not only for themselves but also for the ruling classes: although most cultivators in general consumed what they themselves produced, much of what the cultivators produced was not consumed by them. This surplus was appropriated directly by the Ottoman State, through tax-farmers and later by landowners on whom the direct liability for tax rested. From at least the beginning of the nineteenth century, the involvement of the Ottoman Empire and in particular of geographical Syria with the market forces of European industrial capitalism increased the need for surplus extracted from the peasant population and served eventually to change the legal expression of the production systems which facilitated that flow. The increasing extraction of surplus, determined in the final analysis by the increasing dominance of the capitalist ethos, produced the increasing social disparities in the countryside. At its most abstract level, when the non-capitalist mode of production prevails the productive process is unmediated (the production of goods for immediate consumption) or mediated by simple circulation (production for the market in order to obtain other goods for consumption). In the capitalist mode of production the productive process is mediated by a compound circulation of production for the market in order to produce more goods for the market. But the capitalist productive process is also mediated by the negotiated exchange of tax on profits for state-provided services. These services or externalities were provided largely out of surplus extracted from a sector in which production was primarily non-capitalist, that is, capable of generating surplus but

56

not of accumulating it. Such accumulation as did occur remained largely in the sphere of circulation and was therefore unproductive. Growth in the capitalist mode of production inevitably meant increasing, though indirect, pressure on the non-capitalist mode – both at the point of circulation, the non-productive urban classes, and that of production, the cultivators and crafts-men. But as soon as the British Mandate, which helped to reconcile the differences between the two modes of production, gave place to the political dominance of the capitalist sector, and to the unforeseen unity of the social formation, the complete destruction of the non-capitalist mode of production was inevitable (Asad 1975).

The pattern of agricultural production is today changing in the major sector from intensive mixed farming to large-scale production of industrial crops. A discriminatory price structure for agricultural products, fewer loans, less assistance to farmers and legal expropriation of land discourage the residual sector of traditional agriculture. The new inability to control their means of social reproduction is expressed in the fact that for many farmers their labour power can only be productively applied to their own land after it has first passed through an exchange system, which is an integral feature not of Arab village organisation but of the capitalist mode of production which sustains the entire society. The key to any real understanding of the changing organisa-tion of villagers is their class-position within a developing non-capitalist mode of production in conjunction with an increasingly dominant capitalist mode. In this way the villagers' own land becomes an instrument in the hands of the capitalist for realising their labour power – at a rate of exploitation far greater than was possible when they were peasant owner-producers. This new 'egalitarianism' is the equality of a repressed and exploited working class, and a class situation which has become totally transformed since the Mandate. One can look at this process as a matter of families buying leisure for their women by relying more and more on bought goods. Alternatively, one can look at it in terms of women being pushed out of their traditional roles in production by the economics of mechanisation and capitalist manufacturing, much as women of a lower social class are being pushed out of processes like irrigation or threshing, which are being mechanised today.

3.5 Conclusion

In this chapter, I outlined the various ecological factors that establish the limiting conditions for the agricultural regime in Shayfoun. Its subsistence agriculture based on a two-crop rotation is a direct result of these factors. The random variation in soil, topography and rainfall, and the low incidence of the latter, prevent great economic differentiation within the agricultural sector of the village economy. This fact I shall demonstrate more clearly in the examination of incomes in the next chapters. On the basis of the information available, I have attempted to sketch certain historical events which are important for an understanding of life in the village today. The two most important events were the breakdown of the district political structure in 1922 and the termination of the communal system of land tenure and cultivation in 1939. The registration of land destroyed the corporate nature of the village, at least in its economic aspect, and in a sense freed individual households for enterprise within and mobility outside it. The remarkable fact is that, despite the revolution in land tenure and despite the increase of occupational mobility, so little change has occurred in the village, whether in the actual alienation of land to outsiders or the agglomeration of land in the hands of those within the village. What is important in the present context is that the heritage of common political action and common economic control has had positive consequences for village and clan solidarity. Despite basic economic, political and social changes and developments, the village and clan continue to function as a framework for political rivalry, social status and social control, and as the loci of kinship ties and land ownership. However, having investigated the *mushaa* system I will proceed to examine the relationship between women and property, especially land, in the coming chapter.

4 Women, territory and property in Shayfoun

I am continuing my discussion by analysing two aspects of women's general social roles in Jordan's rural areas which are very relevant if we wish to identify the part which women play in production, for they help to define women's position in relationship between themselves and territory (space considered as a social rather than a geographical reality). By 'social' I mean the role and status women have in decisions about where they are allowed to go, and the relationship between women and property, especially land. I refer to the previous chapter in linking the modes of production with gender analysis to carry further my analysis on the inequality women face in both freedom of movement and property.

Facing a challenge in my attempts to analyse the data from my respondents and informants in order to discover and reconstruct the female experience in the Jordanian rural culture, I explore what the villagers in Shayfoun do in their daily lives. What is the nature of interaction? Besides these important questions the concept of the opposition between the public and private domains is used to clarify our understanding of the female experience, and to show how far women abide by the restrictive rules of space. My conclusion in this chapter is that women's positions in Shayfoun community are severely limited by general standards of female behaviour in public which stress women's invisibility and passivity and which circumscribe their movements, especially their contacts with men.

4.1 Women and territory

Like other Asian cultures, Jordanian women villagers viewed their basic roles as lying within the boundaries of the household, caring for the family and managing household matters. Among the middle and upper-middle classes in urban areas this view was reinforced by an ideology of strict segregation where the female was asked not to overstep her spatial boundaries. Ibn Al-Hajj[7] was a strong protagonist of this view, as is evident in his bitter criticism of women who did not adhere strictly to these rules: women belonging to the lower, middle and upper-middle orders were often seen crossing the private boundaries of the home into the public world of men.[8] In this regard, Ibn Al-Hajj repeatedly admonishes the man, be it husband, father, brother or religious scholar, to prevent anarchic behaviour by women on the street; he explains to them the rules of going out (*adab al khuruj*) according to the *Sunna*. A woman should go out only for a necessity and if she does, she should go in long and unattractive garments. If women walk in the streets, they should walk close to the walls of the houses, in order to make way for men. Roads used by women should not be narrow. These norms have been neglected in modern days. Table 4.1 shows the number of times women go out. The table illustrates the correlation between age and time.

Heedless of such behaviour, Shayfoun women went to the markets to

Table 4.1 **Number of times women are out of house**

Age structure	Number of outings	Percentage
15–19	10	7.7
20–24	41	31.5
25–29	35	26.9
30–34	24	18.5
35–39	11	8.5
40–44	3	2.3
45–49	4	3.1
50–53	2	1.5
Total	130	100.0

Source: Village Survey, 1993.

Note: The data were compiled during field research work.

7 Ibn Al-Hajj's full name was Abu' Abdallah ibn Muhammad al Abdari al fasi. He was born in Fez, Morocco and died in Cairo, AH737/AD1336–37. He composed several religious treatises.
8 See Ibn Al-Hajj, *An Introduction to the Development of Deeds*, Cairo 1929, Vol 1, p.282.

purchase their needs and they seem to have done that regularly on two important market days: the *suq* (market) on Mondays and the *suq* on Thursdays. The favourite spots of women were the jeweller's shop, that of the cloth merchant and that of the shoemaker. Women sit in shops for several hours conversing and humouring, hoping for a good bargain. However, to secure their household needs, women also dealt with male pedlars who facilitate selling and buying transactions in their home environments away from the market. I argue that while the women in the village were protected from going out to the market, the pedlar phenomenon has created a dependent relationship. The bringing of such important items as water, milk and oil entailed regular visits to homes, which in turn must have led to the development of some degree of familiarity between the pedlar and his female client.

Nevertheless, for a village woman, the place where she feels most confident and relaxed is her own courtyard and house. Soon after I became fully familiar with Shayfoun one of my respondents, Fatima (H46), told me that she 'hardly ever stirred beyond these four walls'. I took this to be a comment on the circumscription of her life. Later I realised that it had been said in a spirit of pride. She did not need to stir beyond her own four walls. A good woman is one who stays at home as far as she can. She must have recognisable business to justify her free movement in public places. Just as there are 'no-go' areas for respectable women in some European cities, so the no-go area for village women is the purposeless wandering about that is condemned in practice. One's own land is regarded as a kind of extension of the home, and so women can move about in their own fields with confidence in their right to be seen there. Even some high-status women in Shayfoun who were otherwise very circumspect about being seen in public moved about freely and openly on their own fields. One well-to-do farmer's wife who seldom stepped into the streets of the market used to go to her field to watch the crop growing. She would be seen in public with some specific and ostensible purpose.

The rules are observed with differing degrees of rigour. Women of poor households do not have pedlars to knock on their doors and bring their household items, they have to go out themselves and obtain what they need. The wives of rich farmers, although they are most restricted in their local movements, often accompany their husbands to the farms. The style of interaction of village women who are obliged to cross public spaces informs us that they do not feel free to use these spaces in the casual manner permitted to men, for the exchange of information, for political discussion, or to make deals and strike bargains. As I shall discuss later, village women find alternative venues and alternative modes of tapping local information networks, but the constraint which they must exercise in their use of public space has important effects on their economic and political roles in the local community and shows inequalities of movement between women themselves and between men and women.

These principles regarding the mobility of women in public spaces have to be respected by all women. It could be argued that the rules in the village sit more lightly on some categories of women than on others. Women classified as aged women of the village have special respect and the status of not going out in the street of the village. Leila (H45) informed me that the two mothers-in-law who have lived in the same household with them for years rarely go out of the house. It was their seniority as much as their status as old women of the village which enables them to take liberties with the rules that restrict other women. In agricultural families where circumstances will not permit all the women staying at home, there is often an informal division of labour by which tasks which involve moving outside the home are done by junior women, so that the senior women stay at home.

What sanctions support this restriction of women to the public sphere and what does a woman risk by violating them? It could be argued that junior women must have full control of all aspects of their behaviour in public for the fear that they will be unacceptable as wives if they do anything which might possibly mar their reputations. For married women, it is still the 'honour' of the family which is at stake. It is the honour of the husband's family. What wife will wish to risk having to live with the disapproval of her husband and mother-in-law if they believe that her lack of circumspection in public has tarnished the reputation of their household?

However, as Ardener explains, 'societies have generated their own rules, culturally determined, for making boundaries on the ground, and have divided the social into spheres, levels and territories with invisible fences and platforms to be scaled by abstract ladders and crossed by intangible bridges'. (Ardener 1981, pp.11–12).

The passage I cite here encapsulates what I came to realise of the central significance of how people use space to express and act out basic Jordanian notions of self and society. The separation of men and women for much of the day, the privacy of the household when family members are together and hospitality to guests order how space is used in the household. This separation requires a careful coordination of movements on the part of household

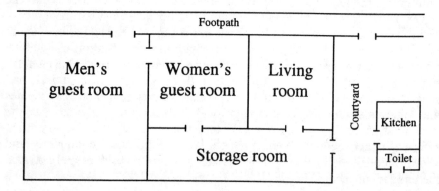

members in time and space, the implicit cooperation of other households, and careful attention to non-verbal clues indicating when a household desires privacy.

The above sketch is a map of the house I examined carefully. The men's guest room has a separate entrance and is never used by women. There is one small room used for sleeping and the storing of clothes, mattresses and blankets. The courtyard is used for drying clothes and olives.

The segregation of the sexes within the household for much of the day facilitates visiting by non-related males and females. People simply will not call if they know that a husband and wife are together in the house because this relationship is considered a very private one that bars all but the closest family members. The presence of a man in the house prevents visits by unrelated women and vice versa. If the outside gate is open more widely than usual, neighbours know that the household is expecting a formal visit, usually of family members. The structure of the men's room is usually larger in size than the women's rooms.

Tact and mutual coordination of movements allow the household to entertain guests of both sexes at separate times without feeling too cramped, and also to be alone together. While there are in general more female guests than male ones, nearly all households receive many male guests during holidays, marriages and periods of mourning. When there is intense visiting, the women use a mat outside their house to entertain guests (Abu Saud 1984).

Some households have two entrances, one to a men's guest room and a second one to the household proper. This second entrance is also used by female guests. In other large households there is one entrance and men and women immediately turn to separate sections of the house after passing the threshold.

These are the boundaries within which women operate and which define in advance the economic and political opportunities which are open to them. The rules and boundaries exist for all residents. The Shayfoun Muslim culture viewed the basic role of women as lying within the boundaries of the household, caring for the family and managing household matters: they safeguarded the rules of sexual segregation and the boundaries of female territory so valued by Muslim cultural norms. In the coming section the analysis will stress the norms regarding women's use of property. The main kind of property which is most central to this book about the inequalities of women in the development process is the question of their possession of land or rights in land.

4.2 Women and property

The norms regarding women's relationship to property are in some ways more difficult to study than the norms regarding women's use of territory, yet in other ways easier. They are simple to study to the extent that the basic rules

63

are more explicitly recognised and easier to identify. On the other hand, there is not one set of rules here but at least two – the statutory law and the customary law of the particular locality.

Differences in customary practices in class, place and time mean that there never was a uniform group of Muslim women operating under one set of rules. A variety of historical and anthropological works contribute to the following overall picture of different female statuses. In general rural and tribal women do not inherit as the urban and Muslim law says they should, although 'in return' they generally get permanent security from their natal family and in some cases their sons may get all or part of their share. Court records past and present suggest that urban women, however, usually do inherit and are willing and able to go to Islamic courts to protect rights, generally successfully. Sources also suggest that agriculturalist practices prevail, although the great freedoms and powers of nomadic tribal women are also noted, with ruling class and upper-class women in both tribes and towns often notable for their powers and independence whereas poorer women are more dependent. Hence the modern differences in styles of living between town, tribe and countryside and between classes in town originated in earlier times and in continuing functional differences (Mernissi 1975).

Muslim women's lives have varied greatly by class, mode of production, time and place. It could be argued that women could hold and manage any amount of property, although seclusion often made effective management difficult. Regarding the two-thirds or more of inheritance that followed fixed rules, women were supposed to receive half the share of men. In Shia law daughters without brothers inherited everything, whereas in Sunni law they generally got no more than half. In spite of the presumption of female inheritance by all schools, it was common for women not to inherit, especially land. This kept land from passing outside the parental family. Partial compensation in the form of gifts or sustenance in case of divorce or widowhood was some-

Table 4.2 Women possessing land in Shayfoun

Age Group	Acreage of Land	Percentage
30-34	2	1.5
35-39	29	21.6
40-44	5	3.7
45-49	92	68.7
50-53	6	4.5

Source: Village Survey, 1993.

Note: The data were compiled during field research work.

times given to a woman who renounced inheritance. In addition, the institution of *waqf*, inalienable endowment, was sometimes used to endow descendants in the male line, thus avoiding both property division and female inheritance. Some *waqfs*, however, benefited women particularly, both as recipients and as guardians (Mernissi 1975).

Although women customarily did not inherit land, and most of them still do not in spite of modern legislation which permits them to do so, many women will speak of land as though this discrimination did not exist. Table 4.2 shows the number of acres possessed by women. It is interesting to note that one woman is considered to be the richest person in Shayfoun.

A woman in the village will talk about 'my land' or 'our land' referring to land held in the name of her father or by her husband's family. Women do not speak as though they felt excluded from ownership. But land is not regarded as though it belonged to individuals *qua* individuals anyway. In fact no major form of property is regarded in this way, and this is perhaps why it is difficult to disentangle women's specific rights in items like jewellery and other goods given in dowry from the family's more general rights in them (Mernissi 1975).

It is generally argued that, since daughters have been given half the share in inheritance compared to their brothers, they are therefore considered inferior to men in worth. Many use this kind of argument. It is an erroneous one on many counts. Firstly, sexual equality is a quite distinct concept from inheritance. The former is a moral category while the latter is an economic one. If for some reason the share given in inheritance to one or the other sex is less or more it does not imply that the recipient of the lesser share is considered inferior. Inheritance depends very much on a social and economic structure and the function of a particular sex within it. Women had a role different from that of men in Arabian society. According to al Razi (1968), a great commentator, there are two criteria of inheritance: 1) relationship and 2) oath. According to the former criterion male relatives who took part in raids and captured loot were generally entitled to inherit property, while female relatives were excluded. In the latter category two persons would say 'your blood is my blood and your garment is my garment, you inherit me and I inherit you' and thus a mutual relationship on oath would be established.[9]

Thus it becomes clear that whereas women were not regularly as a rule given any share in inheritance, the *Quran* ensured they got it in their capacity as a daughter, wife and mother. The fact that they were given half of the share of male heirs is to be seen in its sociological and economic context. It is a well-known principle that a wife is to be looked after by her husband even if she possesses a great deal of wealth. She is not obliged to spend any of her wealth and it is her right to claim maintenance from her husband. Not only that: at the time of marriage she gets a dowry which is hers and hers alone,

9 See Eakhurddin al Razi, *Tafsir Kabir*, Beirut 1968, Vol. V, p.210.

whatever the amount, and she can demand whatever she wants, which husbands are obliged to pay with good grace. Thus, as a wife she adds to whatever she got by way of inheritance as a daughter, and that too without any obligation either to maintain herself or her children. The whole thing has to be seen in proper perspective taking both the present and future into account. In the immediate present the daughter might get half of the son's share, but taking the future into account it is the daughter who ultimately gets more and that too without any obligation to support herself. For this purpose one should bear in mind that the value of the dowry in most communities is usually quite high and puts a substantial amount into her hands. This dowry also acts as an insurance against divorce, which is relatively easy in village communities.[10]

However, here one may ask what about the woman who does not marry for certain reasons, maybe social or other reasons? She would have only what she inherits – half of her brothers' share. Moreover she may also have to look after herself and fall back upon her own resources to maintain herself, but nevertheless these resources are there and must be taken into account. I argue that society consistently violated the injunction to give women their due share in inheritance. The central argument of my study is that the critical factor in inequalities among women lies in the procedures of their owning land or their rights to land. Although there is no fixed rule for their deprivation of land ownership, it is the constraints of the social and cultural values that prevail in society that hinder their involvement in using land for their own prosperity. Women were especially generally deprived of their share in agricultural societies where land caused problems. It should be remembered that in Arabia, which was by and large a non-agricultural society, there was no danger of division of land if the women also inherited it. Thus its law of inheritance is quite liberal and favours women. In agricultural societies elsewhere, if a woman marries and goes to her marital home, there is a clear possibility of division of land. This possibility was very real, as generally women enjoyed no property rights and whatever belonged to them was vested either with their fathers or with their husbands after marriage. Because of this landed property could not be transferred to women (Tucker 1993).

However, there was no such consideration in Arabian society, which was chiefly a non-agricultural one. Secondly, and this is quite important to note, Islam recognises the woman's right to property and that whatever belongs to her is hers alone and that no one, neither her father nor husband, can claim it. This being so, there was no immediate danger of landed property being distributed, as a woman could retain her share without dividing the land as long as she pleased. So it is a fixed share in all properties by way of inheritance, movable and non-movable, landed or non-landed.

Friedl argues that Greek women in Vasilka owe much of their domestic power to the land they bring to their husband's households as dowry. 'The

10 See Tucker (1993,) *Arab Women*, Indiana University Press.

economic power of women lies in their ability to bring land into the household as part of their dowry and to maintain control of that land, which cannot be alienated by their husbands without the consent of their father's brothers or guardians. The trousseau and the household goods a woman brings with her add to the prestige of the new household but only indirectly to its ability to produce income' (Friedl 1967). Therefore men sought wives who would bring land to their family as well as domestic goods, but if they obtained such wives they also had to accept that as husbands they would not necessarily obtain total and unmediated control over this land (Friedl 1967, p.105).

The property which a village woman brings to her marriage as dowry is not usually 'income-generating' property in the sense that land is, and it is not necessarily the case that she will enjoy personal control over it. Even her husband's control over it is likely to be subordinate to that of his parents so long as the latter are alive. A new bride's very subordinate position in the household, and the submissive attitude which she must adopt, make it out of the question for her to assert control at the very point in time at which she would have to intervene if she wished ever to maintain her right to dispose of dowry as she properly wished. In Shayfoun, dowry property can only enhance a woman's position in the household insofar as it engenders respect for her parents and her family (Sharma 1980). It does not provide her with any more tangible source of power in her husband's household. So while land is registered in the name of the male head of the household, he is regarded as holding other forms of property on behalf of the other members, male and female. In this broad sense it is as much theirs as his, but of course he has immediate control over it and it cannot be alienated or divided unless he agrees. In this respect, women are only in the same position as junior men who have not yet attained the position of head of a household. But a woman knows that she will never be in such a position; her control over property held on her behalf will always be indirect.

What is the exception to this general expectation is the case of the widow. The right to inherit land as a widow has not always been easy for a woman to assert in practice. A widowed woman cannot alienate the land – in effect she merely acts as custodian of it until her sons grow up. A widow who has no children is unlikely to be able to claim the property in practice, exercising only the right to maintenance for herself from her husband's family which custom has always permitted (Abu Saud 1984). If she has small children it may still be difficult for her to assert her right to take over the land on their behalf unless her own kinsmen are prepared to help her put up a fight. Otherwise her husband's kinsmen are likely to put up every obstacle in the way of her registering the land in her own name. Investigating the court records of Shayfoun, an interesting case has to be mentioned to support the situation of widows and the difficulties and complexities they face. The piece of land that a widow inherited after the death of her husband in 1985 had to be divided between herself and the three nephews of her brother-in-law. The dispute between the three nephews was that their aunt had no children and she had no right to register or inherit land in her name since there could be no question of her acting as custodian for non-existent heirs. On the other hand, they thought that their aunt was unlikely to sell the land and the land would come to them eventually in any case, so why begrudge their aunt control over it during her lifetime? The court's decision was in favour of the aunt keeping half of the land and the three nephews supervising the remaining partition of the land.[11]

This was a case of a widow with no children, but what about the case of a widow with children? One of my respondents drew this case to my attention. A Shayfoun widow had one daughter and decided to manage the land on her own. Various problems faced her. First the problem of honour (*sharaf*) came seriously to the fore. The widow who had inherited the land depended heavily on others for help in crucial matters such as selling the produce in the market, and therefore could not be said to enjoy the same degree of control over her property as a man. Secondly, with a girl daughter there was the danger and real possibility that land might eventually pass to the control of outsiders when the girl married. This could not have happened when the widow had merely enjoyed the right to maintenance from her husband's estate because, although she might have enjoyed a good deal of control over how the land was managed and the produce disposed of, she would not have been able to alienate it or to will it to anyone else.

The only other possibility for female inheritance of land is the case of a woman who has no brothers. In the absence of sons, land could go to daughters rather than to male collaterals, although this principle has not always prevented male collaterals from staking their claims. So whether the land of a man who died without sons is actually registered in the name of his daughter or in that of her husband, the practice is essentially similar to the practice of allowing the widow the control of her husband's estate during the minority of her sons, that is, it is a custodial form of inheritance. The custodial inheritance of land represents an interruption of the ideal pattern of inheritance of land by males from males. Such interruptions are unavoidable given that men cannot choose when they die any more than they can choose the sex of their children, but as soon as possible the ideal of men inheriting from men is asserted again. There is certainly no question of females inheriting land from females in the normal way of things, although I suppose it could happen in the event of an only daughter bearing female children only and being widowed while these children were still young.

In the area of Shayfoun that I studied a woman who inherits land generally has a choice between two alternatives. She might give the land as a free gesture of goodwill to a brother. Goodwill between brothers and sisters is an important principle and a cousin will count as a brother in a situation like this. This principle of solidarity between brothers and sisters is often given as a

11 Shayfoun's Court Registers 1980–89, Vol. 3, pp.662–669.

reason why daughters seldom claim their share of land even though the law entitles them to do so (Sharma 1980). Another alternative would be for her to rent it to tenants and enjoy the income from the land. This would be worthwhile if the amount was fairly substantial, but the problems of recovering rents from small and distant landholdings are often so great as to cancel out the benefit. In my field work, out of the 46 household respondents only seven rent their land for cultivation.

The moral of this question of land is that if we want to understand how property rights actually work we have to look at customary patterns of practice and the values they presuppose, as well as what is on the court's books. What actually takes place is the product of the interaction between all these different sets of rules. But what is remarkable in Shayfoun is that, even in communities where women's right to inherit property is acknowledged by ancient custom or religious laws, there are still countervailing pressures which prevent women from actually claiming this right. Judith Tucker notes that among Muslim women, women waive their claim to the stake in their father's property to which they are entitled by Islamic law. It is more important to these women to consider their brother's needs than their own, since it is the brother who will send gifts to a woman in her husband's home, and who receives her back if she is divorced (Tucker 1993). The priority given to women's ties of dependence on both brothers and husbands prevents them from becoming or even wanting to become independent property-holders, even where there is no institutional or legal obstacle to their doing so.

Women continue to stand in quite a different relationship to landed property from men. It is not a relationship of total exclusion, since there are circumstances in which a woman may hold land, and it is likely that these circumstances will become more common. But frequently a woman's holding is either nominal, that is, land is registered in her name but it is managed by her husband or some other male relative, or conditional, where she holds it until a male heir is produced or reaches maturity. As I shall show later in my book, many women in fact exercise considerable control over land which is formally registered in the name of a male, especially where the migration of males means women have to take over the day-to-day management of land. Table 4.3 shows the type of agricultural spending in which women are involved in Shayfoun.

Even if she can modify that dependence to some extent, so long as land remains the main type of wealth-generating property she is still dependent in that she can gain access to it only via her relationship with men.

As I mentioned in my introduction to this book, the best place to begin a discussion of the contribution made to the understanding of gender divisions and women's subordination is Engels's *The Origin of the Family, Private Property and the State*. Engels located the emergence of women's subordination in the transition from non-class to class societies and specifically in the emergence of private property (Engels 1972).

Table 4.3 Spending of women on agriculture

Type of Investment	Number %
Agricultural investment	50
For animals	36
For machines	8
For land	6

Source: Village Survey, 1993.

Note: Multiple responses are possible. The data were compiled during field research work.

Central to this analysis is the view that the relationship of the direct producers to the means of production creates systems of exploitation and oppression within societies. This notion is developed by Sacks, who argues that women's relationship to the means of production is crucial in determining their position in society. She argues that this relationship is mediated through the way in which societies organise marriage (Sacks 1979). She compares two types of society, one characterised by what she terms a communal mode of production and the other by a kin corporate mode of production. In the communal mode of production there is no private property. The land is a common resource. In the kin corporate mode of production, however, property is owned by the kin corporate group, and access to land and the means of production is dependent on membership of this group. In the communal mode of production, women's status in terms of their access to the means of production is not affected by marriage, but in the kin corporate mode of production it is. This, I argue, is the same syndrome as I have described for Shayfoun, because ownership rights are invested in the kin corporate group which collectively owns lands on which it grows food and rears domestic animals. As I have discussed, women have ownership rights in the group they are born into but they do not enjoy the same rights in the kin corporate group they marry into. Their status as wives, therefore, differs from their status as sisters; their relation to the means of production is determined by kinship relations. Thus, in the kin corporate groups that they are born into, women maintain rights to the means of production and to products by means of their status as sisters, and they have rights to the labour of wives of that group, but their position as wives in the kin corporate group which they marry into is mediated through their husbands.

Women's relationship to the means of production affects their status (into which I will go in more detail in the coming chapters). In Shayfoun, the more women are defined as wives rather than sisters and the less direct access they have to the means of production, the lower is their status. The correlation between the decline in women's status and the emergence of class societies was prefigured by emerging inequalities in the kin corporate mode of production. Without access to the means of production women's status in other areas of their lives is likely to be reduced also.

4.3 Conclusion

In this chapter I have dealt with women's position in the family and community in terms which have been largely negative, namely, their exclusion from public space and from the control of property. Women's position in Shayfoun community are severely limited by general standards of female behaviour in public which stress women's invisibility and passivity and which circumscribe their movements, especially their contacts with men. Their political effectiveness, whatever their role in production, depends on their domestic power and their contacts with other women; the direct routes to political influence are blocked and for the most part they have to exploit the opportunities offered by their situation within the household. The main kind of property which it is relevant to consider in this book about rural women in Shayfoun is land, or rights in land. These rights are transmitted through a thoroughly male inheritance system. Familial values are not merely congruent with this male property system, they are actually geared to maintaining its maleness. Sons must be produced at all costs. As is well known, sons are given a religious and cultural value that is not given to daughters; the birth of a son is marked with much more elaborate ceremony than that of a daughter, and women who cannot produce sons are regarded with pity. In short, while female children remain legally the residual heirs of male property, as far as it is within their power, people see to it that there are male heirs to inherit.

One beneficial point which I made clear is the dowry practised in Shayfoun as a form of inheritance. Dower money belongs to the wife alone. Neither her father nor her husband can claim it. She can spend it the way she likes. As I mentioned, as a wife she adds to whatever she received by way of inheritance as a daughter and, moreover, without any obligation either to maintain herself or her children.

Although the positive role of women in production and in the control of family resources will be dealt with subsequently, it is important to delineate these negative principles at the outset, since they provide the boundaries within which women are obliged to operate and which define in advance the economic and political opportunities which are open to them, and also indicate the ways in which these boundaries and possibilities are different from those experienced by men. This will lead me to find out what characterises women's position in the process of production in the coming chapter. The situation of women in four types of farmers' families will elaborate on the status of women from rich households to poorer ones.

5 Economic development and change in Shayfoun

Much has been written on the process of development in underdeveloped countries and the increasing economic differentiation despite the egalitarian policies so ardently pursued by the governments concerned. But very few empirical studies can evince such detailed evidence as will be found here, of the degree to which the wealthier sections managed to become richer while the poor became poorer, not only relatively but also in absolute terms. It is this aspect of my research, to be analysed in this chapter, which I regard as the most interesting, and it is in this respect that this book advances at least a little of our understanding of the process of economic development in Jordan as well as in other underdeveloped areas. In my own interdisciplinary approach to the study of development at micro-level, I have tried to examine the interaction between economic and other variables within the social system of the village.

The aim of this chapter is to elaborate thoroughly on the subject of this book, which is the inequality found in Shayfoun village and the position of women in the process of increasing economic differentiation which has taken place during the last fifteen years. The chapter will conclude that farmers should be induced to adopt modern technology to improve their economic and social status.

In this chapter I seek to elaborate on such themes as the habitat of Shayfoun, ownership of land and its use, the crop pattern in the agriculture of the village, the non-agricultural economy and standards of living – all of which will be analysed thoroughly.

The chapter will conclude with four case studies ranging from rich farmers to poorer farmers. There is a realistic assumption that families will continue to grow faster than the increase in village food production. The decreasing supply of farm output per family in Shayfoun will put increasing pressure on a growing number of households to seek income from other sources. This is likely to lead to greater economic diversification among villagers.

5.1 The habitat of Shayfoun

Shayfoun is a cluster of houses surrounded by the green or golden brown of the agricultural fields. Approaching it from some distance, the impression of a dusty, grey-brown homogeneity prevails. However, inside the village a handful of households have a small kitchen garden, planted with an orange or palm tree, grapes and peppermint.

Cars have a hard time finding their way through the generally narrow, unpaved streets, but up to now hardly any household owns a car. It is therefore mainly itinerant merchants and rich farmers who on their occasional visits to the village try to find their way by car through the narrow alleys. The newly erected buildings give proof of the villagers' defiance of the government's regulations which strictly prohibit the building of new houses on agricultural land, given the extreme scarcity of fertile agricultural soil.

The great majority of Shayfoun houses (83.4 per cent) I counted are built of the material which for centuries has been used for this purpose – sun-dried mud bricks. These bricks are usually produced by the villagers themselves – chopped straw, mud and ashes from the oven are mixed and shaped into bricks, then dried in the sun.

The social life of the people living in these houses also conforms to a rural characteristic to some extent, as some 30 per cent live in extended and joint families, in which married sons live together with their wives and children and their own parents. They jointly organise the work and share in consumption of the output.

Most households have been equipped with electricity since it came to the village in 1977. Electricity has illuminated the farmers' homes in a twofold way. First, all the houses equipped with it have installed light bulbs, and secondly, it has brought the TV set and radio to the home. The availability of water pumps to nearly every household has had a beneficial effect for women. In Shayfoun, they no longer wash clothes and dishes outside and they no longer have to carry water over long distances. However, poorer farmers, needless to say, do not have the rich families' power and influence. Their access to space and their freedom to create and occupy space consequently are much more restricted, as I mentioned in Chapter 4. The most obvious instance is of course their lack of agricultural soil. They do not have land, or if so, only tiny plots.

Land has remained the pivot around which almost all village economic activities revolve. This holds true even for Shayfoun. Shayfoun lands are still only bypassed by the River Ouja without deriving any water from it. In 1975, the residents had practically exhausted the extent of cultivable land within the boundaries of their own village. The population increase since then in a period when rainfall has been abnormally low has made matters worse. To increase agricultural output, farmers have had to acquire more land outside the village boundaries and/or increase the productivity of their village acreages. They have in fact tried both these possibilities.

Table 5.1 Amount of acreage bought outside Shayfoun

Types of farmer	1975	1992
Rich farmers	40 acres	130 acres
Middle farmers	75 acres	118 acres
Poor farmers	60 acres	112 acres

Source: Shayfoun municipal records, 1993.

Note: The data compiled for 1975 figures were collected from Shayfoun Municipal Records, V. III 1978, for a comparison with 1992 figures compiled during field research work.

First, they purchased about a hundred more acres in neighbouring villages, of which approximately 20 per cent is dry land. Second, they attempted irrigating their dry land with the aid of pumps. Mohammed (H13), one of the most enterprising village farmers, was the first who, in 1985, decided to buy a diesel pump set to help him irrigate his six dry acres. He paid 1 500 JD for it out of his savings; he explained that it would have been much too cumbersome a procedure to try and get a loan from the credit organisation: 'First you have to get the village accountant's certificate to show how much land you own, then you have to complete innumerable forms; in my own case it was just not worth all the effort,' he said.

Mohammed claimed that irrigation enabled him to double-crop his acres, producing an annual yield per acre of about ten tons of wheat altogether, which just about trebled the productivity of his land. In spite of this obvious gain in yields, Mohammed used his diesel pump for only three years and then sold it in a nearby village for no more than half what he had initially paid for it. He complained that it had been much too costly to irrigate land with the aid of the diesel pump. In the mean time two other Shayfoun farmers had followed Mohammed's example and each bought such a diesel pump set. They too found operating costs prohibitive. Accordingly, they decided to rent their sets out to other farmers in Shayfoun and nearby villages at the rate of 5 JD per day. This at least offered some compensation for the high cost of using the pumps on their own lands. While Mohammed was telling me about his problems a crowd of farmers gathered. Many of them claimed that the

British pump sets from the Mandate period, which at present are the only ones available to them, are too big and clumsy for their purposes; some said they had heard of Japanese or German pumps which are much smaller and more efficient. They requested my help in securing the necessary import licences, which unfortunately I was unable to do. It is interesting to note here that Shayfoun farmers were aware of different makes of foreign-produced pumps.

The high running cost of diesel pumps (5 JD per day) is not the only obstacle Shayfoun farmers encounter in their attempts to bring water to their lands. Assad, one of the *Shaykh's* younger brothers, who is also a keen entrepreneur, had bought six dry acres in a neighbouring village. The land bordered the river. He arranged to have a well dug at a distance of about a hundred feet from the river – at least so he claims. To avoid the problem his fellow farmers had encountered with their diesel pumps he bought an electric pump set which altogether cost him 2 500 JD to install. Assad bitterly complained that as soon as he was ready to start using his new pumping system, an irrigation officer came along and told him not to proceed because the well was too near the river and therefore illegally diverting river water. He was still negotiating with the authorities while I was there; he asked my intervention on his behalf, which I had to refuse. The case had not been finally settled by the time I left Shayfoun: since he is a brother of the *Shaykh*, who has many contacts with the influential officials in Amman, the capital, Assad may yet be allowed to use his well to irrigate his land. In the mean time he feels bitter that his venture is being frustrated.

Mohammed and Assad's experiments with pump irrigation reveal the serious difficulties dry land farmers face in their attempts to keep pace with developments in an irrigated region. Purchases of land in neighbouring villages have helped somewhat in this respect. The additional land Shayfoun farmers have managed to acquire since the 1967 war has in terms of area not fully compensated for the population growth in the intervening years. Consequently, the average landholding per indigenous Shayfoun household has declined from 4.9 acres to 3.7 acres.

The 32 per cent of produce which is bartered within the village of Shayfoun reveals that the village is not self-sufficient in providing necessary items, for only 28 per cent of the produce is sold outside Shayfoun and the cash received will not cover the expenses of the households, leaving women and children worse off.

However, the proportion of wetland has gone up; it was less than 20 per cent and is now approximately 25 per cent. Since the yield of wet land is considerably higher than that of dry land, not only in monetary but also in real terms, the appropriate weighting shows that the average landholding per Shayfoun household did not decline very much over the last fifteen years.

However, economic differentiation has considerably increased during this period, as no more than seven of the richest Shayfoun farmers purchased about sixty of the additional hundred or so acres acquired by villagers.

Table 5.2 Amount of average yield per acre of dry land

Types of farmer	1975	1992
Rich farmers	4.9 tons	3.7 tons
Middle farmers	3.5 tons	2.5 tons
Poor farmers	2.3 tons	1.8 tons

Source: Ministry of Agriculture, 1993.

Note: The data compiled for 1975 figures were collected from Ministry of Agriculture Records, V. II 1978, for a comparison with 1992 figures compiled during field research work.

Table 5.3 Amount of average yield per acre of wet land

Types of farmer	1975	1992
Rich farmers	5 tons	7.5 tons
Middle farmers	3 tons	4.2 tons
Poor farmers	2 tons	3.5 tons

Source: Ministry of Agriculture, 1993.

Note: The data compiled for 1975 figures were collected from Ministry of Agriculture Records, V. II 1978, for a comparison with 1992 figures compiled during field research work.

Shayfoun's dry land economy has continued to force farmers to participate in the regional expansion. Previously this pressure was felt most by the village entrepreneurs on the one hand, and the poorest on the other; the former did not want to be left behind by their counterparts in neighbouring irrigated villages, whereas the latter, having lost the protection of traditional hereditary labour relations with farmland owners in the village, were forced to supplement their meagre subsistence income by wages earned outside (Madi 1984). During my earlier stay, Shayfoun farmers cultivated altogether 549 dry acres, which yielded about 116 500 bags of flour for the total population of 2 650. One bag of flour weighs slightly more than 2 lb and contains about 3 000 calories. Accordingly, the per capita subsistence supply of wheat amounted to approximately 88 lb per year or 0.24 lb per day, which provided 360 calories per day per head of Shayfoun's population. By contrast daily per capita calories available in the form of home-grown wheat have now fallen to 475. Two major factors are responsible for this drastic drop in dry land output per head: firstly, population has increased and secondly, unfavourable weather conditions during the last few years, especially abnormally low rainfall, played havoc with Shayfoun dry land farming. Many acres partially or even completely failed to produce crops for several successive seasons. This made Shayfoun farmers wary of investing labour and money in preparing their dry fields without much hope of getting due returns. Thus they reduced their wheat cultivation from 549 acres to 460 acres – which, due to lower yields, provided no more than 68 250 bags. Employing the same conversion rates as above, this total wheat output provides only 475 calories a head daily, which is less than half the 1 035 calories each refugee is given daily in the form of 300 grams of rice just to keep them alive. Shayfoun's aggregate supply of home-grown basic food therefore falls a lot short of villagers' total demand. This, probably more than anything else these days, accounts for the increasing number of Shayfoun villagers attempting to buy land outside and to earn profits or wages in the wider economy. It is their fundamental need to supplement their own wheat output with basic food either grown on wet land or purchased with cash. The only alternative is to migrate, which villagers are reluctant to do as long as they own even small plots of land (Badran 1989).

Shayfoun residents encounter great difficulties in their attempts to buy more wet land outside the village. Very little such land comes on the market and there is a big demand for it. Therefore land prices are booming. However, it is not merely a matter of raising the money, in itself quite a considerable problem; more important is the need for prospective Shayfoun land buyers to have a network of links in neighbouring villages. Without this they would not find out about land until too late. Only those Shayfoun farmers who carefully cultivate their kinship and friendship ties outside their own village are successful in getting to know in good time about the rare occasions when wet land is offered for sale. Moreover, they have the necessary local contacts to help them approach the seller and can count on indigenous support in their quest to conclude the transaction. Thus Shayfoun farmers have to spend much time visiting neighbouring villages, not just for social purposes but to remind their kin and friends of their keen interest in acquiring more land (Badran 1989).

5.2 Crop pattern

The most important food crops still grown in the Ajlun region are wheat and maize. Olives have remained the major cash crop. As already mentioned, the dry yields have declined drastically in the Ajlun region during the last few years due to abnormally low rainfalls. The major Shayfoun farmers therefore concentrated on producing as much as possible of their staple dietary crops instead of trying to diversify their output (in my field work 29 farmers from the sample of 46 concentrated on farming staple crops).

Their attempts to make themselves self-sufficient in basic foods is shown

Table 5.4 The productive season of various crops

Type of crop	Season
Maize	Summer
Wheat	Summer
Tomato	Summer/Winter
Olives	Summer

Source: Field Survey, 1993

Table 5.5 Percentage of production of wet land

Types of farmer	1975	1992
Rich farmers	40%	80%
Middle farmers	50%	70%
Poor farmers	20%	60%

Source: Ministry of Agriculture, 1993.

by the fact that they grow maize on about 80 per cent of the wet lands in spite of their full awareness that olives are a far more remunerative crop. The various reasons why Shayfoun farmers preferred to grow maize included their small and dispersed wet plots, the lower cash requirements for maize cultivation and so on. These factors still operate. To them must be added another important one, namely the rapid rise in maize prices over the years; while the retail price of maize has almost trebled since 1982 the olive price has only doubled. Shayfoun's concern with food self-sufficiency reflects a rational attitude in a period of rapidly rising food prices. Informants did tell me, though, that like so many others in the area, some Shayfoun farmers had planted more olive trees (which take five years to yield olives) while prices were booming. As soon as these prices dropped again, they returned to growing maize on the majority of their wet acres.

It is often asserted by economists that farm output in underdeveloped countries responds very little to movements in prices and costs. This lack of responsiveness is attributed to production being oriented primarily towards subsistence and the bulk of the inputs being available within the producing units.

Shayfoun farmers are no doubt still basically subsistence farmers. They supplement rather than substitute their own food production with cash crops.

Table 5.6 A sketch of agricultural produce and marketing in Shayfoun

Kind of produce	Produce %	Market %
Maize	100	100
Wheat	100	90
Olives	100	90
Tomatoes	100	100

Table 5.7 Distribution of maize yields per acre in Shayfoun sample households

	Number		%	
Tons	**1977**	**1992**	**1977**	**1992**
0<20	0	1	0	4
20<40	4	5	20	18
40<60	16	18	80	64
60<80	0	3	0	10
80<100	0	1	0	4
Total	20	28	100	100

Average yield per acre (tons): 43.3 (1977); 45.2 (1992).

Source: Ministry of Agriculture, 1993; Village Survey, 1993.

Note: The data compiled for 1977 figures were collected from the Ministry of Agriculture Records, V. XI 1979, for a comparison with 1992 figures compiled during field research work.

I suggest that in their case their self-sufficiency enables them to be sensitive to price fluctuations for the cash crops they can grow on their surplus wet land; for example, Ahmed sold 10 tons of wheat for 1 000 JD and 5 tons of maize for 1 500 JD. Farmers with not enough or just sufficient land to meet their own basic food needs are not as flexible in their crop pattern as those who have surplus land. The different attitudes displayed to rocketing price movements reveal the importance of subsistence farming in price responsiveness. Shayfoun farmers had to make the choice whether to grow more olives for sale or to plant wheat for their own subsistence needs on their

Table 5.8 Cost, output and income per acre of maize cultivated by Shayfoun farmers (estimated average)

Cost	1977		1992	
	JD	**%**	**JD**	**%**
a) Subsistence labour	256	17	103	3
b) Hired labour	325	22	450	13
c) Subsistence seeds and fertilisers	196	13	415	12
d) Cash	480	33	976	29
e) Hired equipment	82	6	73	2
f) Subsistence overhead expenses	73	5	982	29
g) Cash	48	3	367	11
h) Tax	14	1	27	1
i) Total cost	1474	100	3393	100
j) Subsistence cost a + c + f	525	35	1500	44
k) Cash cost b + d + e + h	901	62	1526	45
l) Output cost	1701	100	4090	100
m) Cash cost b + d + e + g + h	949	65	1893	46
n) Income: farm wages and profits l − k	800	38	2564	55

Source: Village Survey, 1993.

Note: The data compiled for the 1977 figures are an estimated average of prices available at that particular time.

limited wet land in neighbouring villages; most of them decided in favour of wheat. Moshin (H11), one of the rich farmers, insisted on growing 5 acres of olives in 1991 instead of growing wheat like the other farmers.

The further extension of irrigation over Shayfoun land has enabled farmers to cultivate maize: of the 28 sample households cultivating maize in 1992, no more than 20 had done so in 1977. The average yield per acre of maize has increased somewhat from 43.3 tons to 45.2 tons. The range of yields per acre produced by the sample's maize farmers has widened from between 24 and 56 tons in 1977 to between 19 and 80 tons in 1992.

Table 5.9 Cost, output and income per acre of wheat cultivated by Shayfoun farmers (estimated average)

Cost	1977		1992	
	JD	%	JD	%
a) Subsistence labour	145	37	81	8
b) Hired labour	64	16	182	18
c) Subsistence seeds and fertilisers	61	16	112	11
d) Cash	40	10	193	19
e) Hired equipment	10	3	6	1
f) Subsistence overhead expenses	32	8	198	20
g) Cash	22	6	214	21
h) Tax	14	4	19	2
i) Total cost	388	100	1005	100
j) Subsistence cost a + c + f	238	61	391	39
k) Cash cost b + d + e + h	128	33	400	40
l) Output cost	382	100	1260	100
m) Cash cost b + d + e + g + h	150	39	614	61
n) Income: farm wages and profits l − k	254	67	860	60

Source: Village Survey, 1993.

Note: The data compiled for the 1977 figures are an estimated average of prices available at that particular time.

There is a high positive correlation between years of experience in maize farming on the one hand and yield per acre on the other. The six sample farmers who in 1992 produced less than 40 tons per acre have had only two or three maize crops whereas the others have planted maize for many years.

Farmers rarely try to evaluate their subsistence inputs. To them the difference between gross yields and cash expenditure represents the most important aspect of return. The proportion of cash inputs per average maize acre cultivated in Shayfoun have declined from 56 per cent to 46 per cent. There is a shift from cash to subsistence input.

More farmers use their own cattle for ploughing these days. Consequently, farmers now try to provide their animals with home-produced fodder rather than purchase it. These changes in farm management are reflected in the considerable increase in subsistence overheads: cattle maintenance constitutes the bulk of this cost item. The greater farm self-sufficiency in animal power resulted in less cattle being hired. In 1990 all the charges for hired equipment involved the rent of ox teams for ploughing and other operations. The comparatively small average charge for hiring equipment per acre of maize in Shayfoun indicates that mechanisation of agriculture is still in its infancy. Only three of the 28 sample maize farmers used any large mechanical equipment.

Average labour input per acre has fallen from 328 days to 290 days. This reduction in labour requirements is only partly due to increased mechanisation; more important is the fact that experienced maize farmers have learned to rationalise their maize cultivation. In Shayfoun there has been a considerable substitution of hired for subsistence labour. In 1989, only 56 per cent of average labour input per acre of maize was hired. In 1994 this percentage had increased to 82 per cent. Shayfoun farmers find it more efficient to act in a supervisory capacity and engage more casual labour from their own household members, rather than walking miles to their fields in neighbouring villages and then performing labouring jobs themselves. This accounts for the 10 per cent reduction in average labour day inputs Shayfoun farmers have achieved over the years. Moreover, they now employ more female workers than they used to do, to reduce labour costs. Females are paid only half the rate of males per day.

Table 5.10 Shayfoun crop labour requirements: estimated average labour days per tomato acre

1985					1992				
Male		Female		Total	Male		Female		Total
No.	%	No.	%		No.	%	No.	%	
178	86	30	14	100	159	84	31	16	100

Source: Village Survey, 1993

5.3 The non-agricultural economy

The increased wealth in the Ajlun region which resulted from river irrigation is now reflected in a growing number of business ventures in the rural area. A period of rapid agricultural growth in small developing economies is usually followed by the establishment of processing and service facilities.

Olive oil refineries and small-scale tomato juice factories were established soon after 1987. It is in these factories that women in Shayfoun do most of their wage labour work. In 1992, 26 women worked in the olive refinery and 14 women in the tomato juice factory, earning 50 per cent less than the men. The average salary per month was 20 JD in 1992.

In 1976 there was only a single small café, nowadays there are five cafés. One of my informants told me that he got the idea of opening a café in Shayfoun from a relative in a nearby village. He thought of it as a profitable proposition. Utilising the links he had with his relative he managed to rent an old house from a farmer who built a new one. He pays 15 JD per month and lives there with his wife and six children. He uses one room as a kitchen and another one and the verandah to accommodate his clients. His total investment was no more than 20 JD for cups and plates and 10 JD for benches and one table. His average daily turnover is about 25 JD, made up from sales of 150 cups of tea and coffee at 0.10 JD each and light refreshments; the raw ingredients required for preparing all this cost 10 JD and fuel, electricity and rent amount to another 2 JD per day. His business profit and his wife's wages per day amount to approximately 8 JD, which is more than double what the two of them could earn in a day working as agricultural labourers.

Village cafés are places where men meet fellow villagers as well as outsiders, and where news is passed on and gossip exchanged. It is generally regarded as wrong for village women to sit down in a café and take drink and/or food there; by doing so they would imply that they were too lazy to prepare this for themselves. I never saw a single village woman in any of the many cafés I visited during my stay. None of the cafés sell on credit; payment is always cash down. This is essential in business where a high proportion of the clientele is from outside. My informant estimates that less than 50 per cent of his income is derived from intra-village customers; the rest are men who pass through Shayfoun on the way to or from their work.

Shayfoun men have established a reputation in the region for being expert livestock traders. Frequently farmers from neighbouring irrigated villages go there to buy or sell cattle. One day when I sat talking to some of my informants, a party of four farmers arrived, wanting to purchase ten sheep. One Shayfoun farmer immediately invited the visitors to come to one of the local cafés, where he treated all of us to coffee and where the negotiations were conducted in an informal atmosphere. The farmers spent almost four hours during which they were shown the sheep and treated to three coffees each. They carefully examined the sheep and then argued over the price of the pairs they were interested in acquiring. The seller asked 120 JD and the buyer offered 100. The deal was finally clinched at 110 JD. The vendor had bought the sheep two weeks previously at a nearby village for 80 JD. He thus made a profit of 30 JD on the transaction, having had to keep the sheep for no more than two weeks. This is a handsome amount. However, the seller was lucky on this occasion in finding a buyer so quickly. On other occasions he had to wait many months before managing to find a buyer. If and when they do, their profit is not always as high as it was in the case I myself witnessed, and they have the expense of feeding the livestock in the mean time.

The customary type of middlemen in crop and in cattle trading (*dalal*) seem to have a strong presence in Shayfoun. According to tradition each village in the area had its few men who were known to act as intermediaries in cattle transactions. Many of these *dalals* had come to their office by hereditary succession. Their function was to bring buyers and sellers together and to narrow the gap between the price asked by the latter and that offered by the former. A *dalal's* fee was very small, no more than 5 JD irrespective of the value of the transaction he mediated. The sale and purchase of cattle represents a very important economic transaction and has therefore always been the subject of keen haggling even among fellow villagers. *Dalals* act as intermediaries in all sales between inhabitants of the same village; these mediating activities enable the two parties to a sale from the same village to continue social relations after they have faced each other as bitter opponents in the process of bargaining. *Dalals* act in the role of the stranger and are essential in avoiding the disruptions in personal relations likely to result from the opposition between a buyer and a seller. In Shayfoun, where intra-village relations have continued to be strong, *dalals* still operate in the customary way, whereas in nearby villages, where the increasing range of social relations has reduced the intensity of intra-village links, *dalals* have become cattle traders in the modern context of impersonal cash transactions.

5.4 Village tradespeople

Shayfoun's population still includes a number of resident tradespeople, some of whom are migrants living temporarily in the village. Only three of the seven professional households in Shayfoun still pursue their traditional occupation: one washerman, one barber and one blacksmith. The others work as factory or agricultural labourers.

The more flourishing rural economy sustains a great number of men who still follow their traditional crafts. Some of them continue to have hereditary relationships with indigenous farmers and receive fixed annual rewards in kind disregarding the quantity and quality of work they perform. However, there are 12 households who earn their income from non-agricultural household resources – these comprise a variety of occupations, such as carpet-weavers and washerwomen.

One household of washerwomen washes for the village farmers. The tools and instruments of labour are rudimentary. The business is self-activated and the washerwoman keeps her earnings for herself. The washerman family is still washing the farmers' dirty clothes, for which they get the customary rewards. The blacksmith, who by 1985 had already taken over the hereditary role of Shayfoun's indigenous blacksmith, continues to repair farmers' wooden ploughs and other traditional equipment and gets paid in kind. The blacksmith who was thus replaced still makes and repairs iron ploughs and other tools on a purely cash basis. He kindly allowed me to copy the book in which he records in detail his income and expenditure. From this it emerges that his gross income for six months from January to June 1993 was 1 073 JD, giving him an approximate average monthly net income of about 130 JD just from his craft activities. Besides this he cultivates two acres of dry land. In terms of income he now ranks among the centre stratum of Shayfoun middle farmers. He managed to raise his economic status simply on the basis of his own initiative. None of the other indigenous professional households displayed anything like the drive shown by this one blacksmith.

The potters and goldsmiths have more or less surrendered their craft occupations because of serious competition from outside. The potters have completely given up making clay pots. Village households now prefer to use brass, aluminium or stainless steel. Village pottery craft is therefore dying out. Two of the potters in Shayfoun village opened a small shop and a café to increase their monthly incomes. Hassan, one of the potters, is making an increase of 10 per cent on his monthly income. Yet some of the young gold-smiths in Shayfoun are still highly skilled in their craft, having served their apprenticeships with their own fathers. One of them made for me by hand a silver pendant which is superbly finished. However, the decline in village crafts leaves no alternative for the villagers but to give up their traditional craft occupations and turn to other income-earning activities. Those who are fortunate enough to own at least some land tend to remain in their villages and try to supplement their farm income by working as casual labourers for larger landowners. The landless usually seem to have no other option but to join the mass of migrants in search of work.

5.5 Wage labour

The economic expansion of the Ajlun region has brought in its wake an increased demand for urban as well as for rural labour. This in turn has attracted a growing influx of migrants from other villages. The streets of Shayfoun throng with men and women, many of whom walk around in search of work. Frequently farmers from the rural areas use the facilities of urban cafés to engage some of these migrants to come to their villages to perform certain tasks on their lands. Although demand for various types of labour has increased, supply still outstrips it.

Urban growth has provided an increasing number of more regular indus-trial employment opportunities. It appears that the regionally dominant farmers exert prior claims to these new jobs. A large number of these more permanent workers are farmers who live in surrounding villages. Their estates are too small to keep them fully occupied or provided with at least a minimum of subsistence. They therefore seek to supplement their meagre farm income by earning an urban wage. Shayfoun offers a good example to illustrate this point.

Shayfoun land is still dry; irrigation and the resulting indigenous economic growth has passed the village by. Many Shayfoun farmers acquired wet land in neighbouring villages. Their need to have local workers on the fields there and the limited labour demand for dry cultivation led soon after the arrival of the canals to the disappearance of the traditional hereditary labour relationships which had previously existed between farmers and indigenous households.

I estimated that in 1986, 32 men working 300 days in the year should have been able to cope with all the work necessary to cultivate Shayfoun dry lands. However, as agricultural labour requirements are highly seasonal, particularly in dry areas, and men have other jobs to do besides cultivating their fields, I made a 100 per cent allowance for these factors. Even then 64 of the 199 men of working age could easily perform all the jobs within the village. Accordingly, Shayfoun's male labour force could then have been deemed more than 65 per cent underemployed within the boundaries of its home economy. As already mentioned, some Shayfoun farmers now try to irrigate their dry land with the aid of pumps. Altogether about fifty acres of olives are cultivated in this way. This wet olive culture requires more than double the male labour input needed for dry olives. Moreover, the increased population and the abnormally low rainfall during the past few years appears to be responsible for a greater number of male labour days worked even on dry crops. Although the Shayfoun dry acreage cultivated in 1989 was about 10 per cent less than in 1985, the total number of male days spent on cultivation have increased by about 50 per cent from 99.4 to 146.46 days.

The size of the male working population has also increased by about 50 per cent to 300 men in this period. Household members perform about 75 per cent of the male cultivating tasks. It is therefore possible that the increase in village underemployment may have induced farmers to spend more days cultivating their dry land by working less hard or fewer hours per day. The total male labour input of 146.46 days may therefore represent an exaggeration of labour day requirements. However, even if we assume that this is the case, about fifty men each working 300 days per year would suffice. Then, if we double this number to allow for various contingencies, as for the earlier estimate, the total number of men required to meet all the intra-village labour requirements is no more than one hundred. This means that Shayfoun's whole labour force is underemployed to the extent of 66 per cent of its capacity within the village. This fact, together with the low productivity of dry land, which cannot provide any more than even the bare minimum of staple crops for the growing population, has made outside work a dire necessity for many Shayfoun residents.

The number of Shayfoun men in regular employment outside has increased from 26 to 41: 33 of these workers are farmers who own some land; for them wages represent a necessary supplement to their small subsistence output. In spite of the fact that some of these farmer–wage earners have by now been in regular employment outside the village for about twenty years – a few of them have even lived in towns for as long as ten years – they still regard themselves as villagers and look upon urban employment as only a temporary phase in their lives.

Shayfoun municipality has appointed special staff for the implementation of minimum wages in agriculture, but unfortunately this was not enforced by the landowners. Consequently, while consumer prices have almost trebled, the daily rural cash wage for Shayfoun men has increased by only 33 per cent, from 1.2 JD in 1975 to 2 JD in 1992. In the same period the monthly wage of an unskilled worker in the Shayfoun olive oil pressing plant has risen by as much as 152 per cent, from 0.46 JD to 1.16 JD.

Table 5.11 Cash wages

Wages	1975	1992	1992 Index
	JD	JD	(1975=100)
Agricultural daily male	1.25	2.00	160
Agricultural daily female	0.50	1.00	200
Shayfoun daily male	1.50	2.00	133
Non-agricultural daily female	0.62	1.00	161
Shayfoun monthly unskilled	0.46	1.16	252

Source: Department of Statistics, 1993.

The disparity between agricultural and non-agricultural average income is obviously tied to the urban–rural differential as cause and as consequence, and both are linked intimately with regional inequalities (Myrdal 1968, p.579).

5.6 Standards of living

At the root of the prevailing inequalities in income is the inequitable distribution of the means of production. A major means of production in the Jordanian economy is land, but there is not enough of it to redistribute so that everyone may employ himself on his land and earn a minimum desirable living. The process of development during the past decade has affected different sections of the rural population differently. It has benefited the upper-middle and the richest sections more than the middle, the lower-middle and the poorer sections. Consequently there has been a growing inequality in rural

Jordan. Yet the Planning Commission does not appear to have concerned itself with inequality trends in the last decade and assumes that the pattern of inequality in consumption as observed in 1987–88 will remain unaltered until at least 1997–98. The World Bank Report on poverty in Jordan takes the Planning Commission, as well as the National Sample Survey, to task for the unrealistic appraisal of inequalities existing in Jordan. The report concentrates on examining the level of per capita personal consumption of the different strata of Jordanian society as it emerges from published statistics (World Bank Report 1993). The National Sample Survey estimate of per capita consumption in 1987–88 is more than 10 per cent below the official estimate. This carries weight, and the conclusion is inescapable that the National Sample Survey estimate of per capita consumption in 1987–88 is an underestimate and that it underestimates the consumption of the upper-middle and the richer sections much more than that of the middle, lower-middle and the poorer sections. What part of the consumption of all sections has been underestimated is a matter of judgement, and a certain subjective element is unavoidable.

Such subjective judgement certainly plays an important role in revising consumption estimates which have been found inadequate, but it has hardly any part in the material I collected in Shayfoun. My village data not only show the trend of consumption for the different strata in Jordan's rural societies but also indicate changes in income pattern. The most affected in the income pattern are women, who find themselves with virtually no institutional provision as potential workers. Women from the poorer families have difficulty in getting effective access to credit, suitable and safe facilities for saving and investment, accessible information about services, raw materials and markets, or adequate and equitable access to training and skills acquisition. The full extent of inequalities cannot be grasped just by examining different levels of personal consumption – though this is an important aspect of it – nor can future trends be predicted, without an understanding of income distribution. The differences in per capita personal consumption between the richest on the one hand and the poorest on the other are unlikely to reflect fully the extremes of economic differentiation in existence if the richest have a low range of variation in money expended on current consumption, which is what I found in rural Jordan. Differences in per capita incomes indicate much more clearly the level of inequalities. Moreover, a comparison of income distributions over time illustrates the process of the growing concentration of Jordan's means of production, in particular land, in the hands of a small rich élite in spite of various measures taken to prevent this.

For reasons mentioned at the outset, I have chosen to examine with the aid of case studies the changes in economic differentiation that have taken place in Shayfoun during the last fifteen years. The case study method has become a valuable tool in the study of economic development. The study of particular cases represents a much more modest approach than working with averages for large groups of people or whole populations. At the same time, if the cases examined can be shown to be typical of a larger section of the population, they can throw light on aspects of development which are hidden by statistical treatment of the data. Moreover, case studies which record individual choices help to bring development problems to life. Individuals are now seen as actors in a series of different circumstances who make greater or less use of an element of choice. This makes for a much livelier appreciation of development problems than mere quantitative analysis where individuals become engulfed in averages. I realise of course that the detailed collection of reliable socioeconomic data relating to individual cases is a painstaking process, but I hope that what follows will show that the effort is worthwhile and may encourage other researchers in this field to advance the techniques and approaches of the case study method.

The various cases I discuss represent the four main economic strata in the village of Shayfoun. In addition to other information on these cases, I collected a monthly household budget for April 1993 – except for the poorest migrants, who are a new element in Shayfoun society. I contrasted the 1993 figures with data similarly collected for the same households during my earlier stay in the village. In order to eliminate the impact of the different sizes and age compositions of households I utilised the concept of the consumption unit. As previously described, I accepted Lusk's coefficient.

Table 5.12 Lusk's coefficient

Age	Consumption unit
Men above 14 years	1.00
Women above 14 years	0.83
Either, above 10 years but below 14 years	0.83
Either, above 6 years but below 10 years	0.70
Either, above 1 year but below 6 years	0.50
Either, below 1 year	Nil

Source: Ministry of Labour, 1951, p.51.

I evaluated 1992 Shayfoun expenditure and income in real terms at 1975 prices, and 1992 Shayfoun cash income I deflated by an index of 285 to make allowances for price rises that have taken place in the intervening years. 1975 prices had risen by about 5 per cent a year later when I collected Shayfoun budgets; therefore I employed an index of 280 to deflate the 1975 Shayfoun household income data. A rural consumer price index of 285 for 1990 with 1975 as the base year may appear to reflect an unduly high rate of inflation as compared with official statistics. For instance, the Jordanian consumer price index for agricultural labourers with a 1975–76 base shows, for 1989, 232 for food and only 211 for general items. There are, however, no details stated as to the weighting given to the various items which make up household consumption. Moreover, it is difficult to harmonise the consumer price index for agricultural labourers with that of wholesale prices. The Jordanian cereal prices with 1989–90 as the base year have risen from an index of 280.6 in 1987–88 to one of 309.4 within only one year (Ministry of Agriculture 1993). The consumer food price index for agricultural labourers, on the other hand, shows a rise in the index number from 230 to 231 for the very same year (Ministry of Agriculture 1993). Official statistics indicate that wholesale prices of all agricultural commodities taken together have risen faster in Jordan. 'This index tends to understate price increases in so far as the prices are controlled rather than "true market" level . . . The index of consumer prices has followed a similar pattern' (Badran 1989). In view of the difficulties involved in unravelling official statistics on consumer price movements and Badran's note of warning about the unrealistic picture they may present, I decided to rely on my own data and compile a consumer price index specifically for Shayfoun.

I had carefully enquired into details of the prices charged at the bazaar for various commodities villagers bought, at the onset of my pilot survey. I repeated this exercise in my second visit, during my final survey. On both occasions the various prices were first collected from different suppliers and in some instances even involved buying the commodities. Subsequently I compared the prices I had managed to get with those that village friends had paid for the various articles they purchased. In this way I managed to reach a consensus on the various prices (see Table 5.13), which I feel confident represent the real market values. I then weighted the different items according to the proportion each constituted of middle farmers' total cash expenditure. This resulted in a price index of 285 for Shayfoun budgets.

I outline and analyse altogether six cases to represent the four economic strata in Shayfoun:

Rich farmers: Massoud can be regarded as typical of the other three richest farmers in the village; the four of them still constitute the avant-garde in village entrepreneurship. Similarly, Assad is a good example of the way the four richest men in a dry village operate in order to try to keep up with their counterparts in irrigated villages.

Middle farmers: Mohamed is representative of the middle stratum in Shayfoun society. As with so many others of his kind, the increase in the size of his family has depressed his standard of living. Likewise the study of Ahmed indicates the sort of options a small dry land farmer has within an irrigated region and how he is likely to respond to the various opportunities offered.

Table 5.13 Comparative prices of essential household commodities at Shayfoun Bazaar

Commodity	Unit	June 1975 JD	April 1993 JD	1993 index 1975 base = 100
Staple food				
Rice	bag	0.41	1.10	290
Lentils	bag	0.22	0.65	285
Vegetables				
Potatoes	kilo	0.50	2.00	400
Tomatoes	kilo	0.22	1.00	455
Spices				
Garlic	small bag	0.50	1.00	200
Pepper	pound	3.00	10.00	333
Salt	pound	0.10	0.17	170
Misc. foods				
Oil	bottle	0.28	1.00	357
Sugar	bag	0.25	0.75	300
Clothes				
Blouse	each	1.75	4.50	257
Shirt	each	3.50	10.00	285
Trousers	each	10.00	30.00	300
Shoes	each	1.50	4.00	265
Sundries				
Cigarettes	packet	0.12	0.25	208
Matches	packet	0.05	0.08	160
Kerosene	bottle	0.27	0.60	230

Source: Village Survey, 1993.

Note: The data collected for the 1975 figures were compiled from respondents in the field research work to reach a consensus on various estimated prices in real market values.

Poor farmers: The case of Mahmoud illustrates the extreme difficulties under which village farmers are labouring to try to make a living. Their experiences and the way their lives have been affected by changes during the past fifteen years clearly expose the fact that, far from having been able to improve their position, they have not only lost out in comparison to other village households, but even their standard of living has suffered in real terms.

Poorest farmer: Ali, the Shayfoun labourer, like most other migrants in search of work, is landless. Landless labourers reflect the increased demand for labour but also indicate the greater number of people now looking for work after the Gulf War of 1991.

Rich farmers

Massoud is now a dignified elder in his early sixties. He speaks softly but his words always command respect. In 1975 he lived with his wife and four children: two sons and two daughters. In the intervening years his family has extended to three generations. The first-born son married and his wife and three small children have joined the household; the second is an undergraduate. Both daughters are married; one has brought her small baby and rejoined her father's household. Massoud's family unit increased from six to ten; in terms of consumption units it grew from 4.86 to 7.19.

In spite of his age, Massoud is a dominating personality and controls all the family ventures. Though fragile-looking he is still very active. To talk to him I had to pursue him to his land where he was supervising a team of migrant labourers in the cultivation of his crops. He told me there and then that 'to get your work done according to your requirements you just have to be on the spot and supervise your labourers'.

In 1975, Massoud owned six acres wet and one acre dry land and lived with his family in one of the typical small farmhouses in the interior of the village. In the mean time he has purchased another 13 wet acres, on ten of which he is cultivating wheat. The sale of wheat provides his household with a monthly net income at 1992 prices of about 350 JD per consumption unit; sales of his surplus add another 75 JD to this figure, amounting to a monthly net income from cash crops at 1992 prices of 425 JD per consumption unit. By using a deflation index of 285 so as to reduce this income to 1975 levels we arrive at 149 JD.

Altogether Massoud's monthly deflated income per consumption unit has almost trebled since 1975. Like many other Shayfoun farmers he has increased his subsistence output by diversifying it. This household's food consumption nowadays consists almost wholly of home-produced items. His current expenditure pattern indicates a low rate of variation in money required. The value of his household's monthly food intake per consumption

Table 5.14 Shayfoun rich farmer: Massoud's monthly budget per consumption unit at 1975 prices

Income

	1975 May		1992 June	
	JD	%	JD	%
Subsistence	18	25	22	10
Barter	1	1	2	1
Profits	11	15	23	11
Rent and interest	10	14	6	2
Crop sales	30	41	149	76
Animal products	3	4	1	–
Total	73	100	203	100

Source: Village Survey, 1993.

Note: The 1975 figures are estimates of averages at that period of time, compiled from the respondent during the field research work.

Expenditure

	1975 May		1992 June	
	JD	%	JD	%
Food	22	30	22	11
Clothes	8	11	10	5
Sundries	3	4	2	1
Miscellaneous	0	0	12	6
Household overheads	4	5	4	2
Gifts	2	3	4	2
Rent and interest	0	0	0	0
Family expenses	0	0	4	2
Savings	34	47	143	71
Total	73	100	201	100

Source: Village Survey, 1993.

Note: 1975 – 4.86 CU, 1992 – 7.19 CU. Deflation index 285.
The 1975 figures are estimates of averages at that period of time, compiled from the respondent during the field research work.

unit has remained unchanged: in 1975 his household used up monthly about 50 lb of rice and 10 lb wheat per consumption unit (in 1970 they had completely avoided eating rice and monthly cooked about 65 lb lentils per consumption unit). This substitution of the dearer rice for the cheaper lentils increased Massoud's expenses on staple diet items by about 20 per cent at 1975 prices; the daily calorific intake of basic foods per consumption unit increased from about 2 700 to 2 980. Massoud's household possesses a vacuum cleaner, a radio and television. In my field work, out of 46 respondents in the sample survey, 22 households owned televisions and all 46 owned radios. Products imported into the villages are due to the inter-regional and intra-regional trade, as well as to international trade between Jordan and other parts of the world.

The only noticeable increase in Massoud's regular household expenditure is the money he spends on the education of his son, which appears under the miscellaneous items. While there have been marked improvements in the absolute educational levels of both sons and daughters, the data presented in Table 5.15 cannot be used to infer changes in the relative educational positions of the two sexes because they are affected by differences in sibling statuses. Among parents in Shayfoun, a major strategy for raising the educational level of their sons is to educate their daughters a little.

Table 5.15 Years of total education obtained by sons and daughters in different socioeconomic groups

Socioeconomic group	1975		1992	
	Sons' years of schooling	Daughters' years of schooling	Sons' years of schooling	Daughters' years of schooling
Rich farmers	6.8	4.5	7.6	6.0
Middle farmers	10.4	6.9	10.3	9.0
Poor farmers	7.9	6.9	9.9	9.2
Shopkeepers	13.1	10.1	12.0	13.3
All groups	9.6	6.9	9.6	10.1

Source: Village Survey, 1993.

If this strategy has worked, we should find a direct relationship between the number of sisters a boy has and the amount of schooling he obtains.

Otherwise Massoud's expenditure pattern has remained unchanged. Consequently his household savings have increased considerably. In 1975, he saved 47 per cent of his monthly income; by 1992 this proportion had increased to 71 per cent. Massoud has not allowed his savings to remain idle, he has invested his money in several different ways. His first priority was to acquire more land. Secondly, he established an olive crusher. Thirdly, he invested in religious capital. He built a small mosque near his home and spent on pilgrimage expenses for his fellow villagers. Lastly, he invested in non-productive property, acquiring a prestigious plot by the side of the main road to build a two-storey house. This new house combines the amenities of traditional quarters with modern building innovation.

Villagers still talk of the big weddings Massoud arranged for his daughters. He spent lavishly on big feasts for hundreds of guests and bought costly clothes and jewellery for the brides and their grooms. He is still preoccupied with intra-village affairs. In this he differs greatly from his counterpart, Assad.

Assad is a tall and well-built man with an imposing personality. He is in his early fifties and is still most actively involved in making money. His household, like Massoud's, has also increased in size and now represents a three-generation-depth joint family. Most families are of the extended type and in addition mostly range in size from six to ten members. The fact that most families are extended must be related to two points which affect women's position in the area: firstly, that due to the serious housing crisis and, more generally, the economic crisis, it is rather difficult for couples to set up an independent nuclear family household; and secondly, that the family remains the main focus of support for women. Widowed, divorced or single women will almost invariably reside with their original families.

Table 5.16 Size of the family household

Size of household	Number of households
Less than 3	3
3–5	26
6–10	9
Over 10	8
Total	46

Source: Village Survey, 1993.

In 1975 Assad already occupied a spacious farmhouse supplied with electricity. His family was then composed of himself, his wife and three young sons, as well as one of his young unmarried brothers. Now his eldest son is married and has one child. Already his family has increased in numbers from six to nine and in terms of consumption units from 4.86 to 7.99. He had proved himself an outstanding entrepreneur, active in different spheres of activities. He was at that time one of the small number of village magnates all of whom were known to have made their fortunes on the black market during the last war. He established a flour mill at a bus junction not far from his village. There 'black' grains could be milled away from the watchful eyes of town administrative officials. To cater for the needs of lorry drivers, who often waited in a queue to have their loads processed, he opened a small retail store. At the time of my earlier stay in the village Assad was thus already a well-established entrepreneur. Moreover, he owned five acres in neighbouring villages. He was at that time one of the most advanced cultivators.

The increased wet acreage and his progressive cultivation have enabled Assad to extend his cash cropping. Assad's monthly net income per consumption unit at 1975 prices has almost doubled by 1992 (see Table 5.17). Yet, like Massoud, his expenditure pattern also displays a low variation rate in the amount of money required.

Like many other rich farmers in the area, Assad has tended to substitute the more costly rice for the cheaper lentils in his household consumption – in 1975 they prepared monthly 38 lb rice and 48 lb lentils per consumption unit; the respective figures for 1992 are 52 lb rice and only 36 lb lentils. This resulted in a 15 per cent increase in the value of basic foods consumed per month per consumption unit and left the daily calorie intake practically unchanged at about 4 000 in the form of rice and lentils. The overall food intake per consumption unit in Assad's household has increased only slightly, and by diversifying his dry land cultivation almost all the food eaten in his household is nowadays home-produced. The greater monetary value of food intake per consumption unit in Assad's household, as compared with Massoud's, represents a diet modified by urban influences, including more meat. Assad keeps goats, sheep and chickens which he periodically slaughters for his home consumption. By contrast, Massoud keeps a vegetarian home (at least he claims to do so), and therefore little, if any, meat is consumed.

The increase in Assad's income accompanied by an almost stable consumption pattern has resulted in considerable household savings. He has invested his savings in different spheres of activities. Firstly, he purchased more wet land. He would have liked to buy further wet acreages but, as I have described, wet land is hard to come by for dry land villagers. Secondly, he has established a wheat mill at a strategic spot along the major highway near his home village. The increased manpower that his sons provide enable Assad to cope with his various business ventures as well as looking after his wet and dry lands. His eldest son, Mohamed, is in charge of the wheat mill. His two younger sons are responsible for the shop and lands. Assad's productive investment outside agriculture amounts to approximately 15 000 JD yet his net gains from running different ventures constitute less than one-third of his net income from cash cropping, whereas his total agricultural capital of about 10 000 JD provides almost all the rest. Here, however, it must be remembered that I have not included any interest charges in my calculations of returns from land. This helps to explain why even alert and outward-looking men of

Table 5.17 Assad's monthly budget per consumption unit at 1975 prices

Income

	1975 May		1992 June	
	JD	%	JD	%
Subsistence	24	21	34	17
Barter	6	5	6	3
Profits	30	27	63	30
Rent and interest	17	15	7	4
Crop sales	36	32	96	46
Total	113	100	206	100

Source: Village Survey, 1993.

Note: The 1975 figures are estimates of averages at that period of time, compiled from the respondent during the field research work.

Expenditure

	1975 May		1992 June	
	JD	%	JD	%
Food	32	29	34	17
Clothes	9	8	9	4
Sundries	8	7	9	4
Miscellaneous	1	1	1	–
Household overheads	5	4	8	4
Gifts	2	2	7	3
Rent and interest	15	13	0	0
Family expenses	8	7	10	5
Savings	33	29	128	63
Total	113	100	206	100

Source: Village Survey, 1993.

Note: 1975 – 4.86 CU, 1992 – 7.19 CU. Deflation index 285.
The 1975 figures are estimates of averages at that period of time, compiled from the respondent during the field research work.

Assad's type are so eager to extend their wet land holding so as to be able to grow more cash crops. Wheat-growing still yields a greater return on capital than does operating a rice mill or olive crusher.

Unlike Massoud, who had invested in religious capital, Assad is concerned mainly with the wider economy and polity. Consequently, he had spent a lot of money on financing his son's election campaign when the latter was a parliamentary candidate in the 1989 election. It is generally recognised that the young man's success in getting himself elected was due largely to his father's generous support. Assad knows very well that his continued economic advance depends on his contacts with administrative officials in influential positions as well as with farmers in neighbouring irrigated villages. He was therefore prepared to spend money helping his son to achieve a formal position in the political structure.

These two brief case studies reveal several features of the way the richest farmers of the village organise their lives. First of all, wet land farming is by far their most remunerative activity. It is only the limited availability of such land which leads them to invest outside agriculture in processing plants, shops and other rural services. Secondly, Massoud, who lives in an irrigated area and has all his wet lands within its border, spent a lot of his savings on elaborate weddings and financing religious pilgrimage activities, thereby reinforcing his intra-village social status. By contrast, Assad looks outside his own village for opportunities to participate in the regional expansion. Consequently, he is no longer so concerned with intra-village prestige and instead prefers to spend his money on launching his son on a political career. He wants to establish a niche for his family in the wider economy and polity. Lastly, but possibly most important, is the fact that, in the richest farm households, per capita expenditure on daily consumer necessities appears to have reached saturation point; they tend to spend at least part of their savings on improved housing facilities, wells, lavish weddings, and so on, which can be labelled consumer luxuries, but their consumption pattern in real terms changes only a little as their income increases.

Middle farmers

Shayfoun's Mohamed is an unassuming and retiring man in his early fifties. He does not show any signs of ambition and never complains about his lot, but seems to accept as his well-deserved fate what God has awarded him. He and his family still live in the same traditional-type home in the centre of the village which they already occupied during my earlier stay there. The appearance of their home has hardly changed over the years. In 1975, the household was composed of Mohamed, his wife and four young sons; now his two eldest sons are married and each of them has two small children. The family is now composed of 12 individuals and 9.55 consumption units whereas in 1975 there were only six individuals and 4.23 consumption units.

Table 5.18 Mohamed's monthly budget per consumption unit at 1975 prices

Income

	1975 May		1992 June	
	JD	%	JD	%
Subsistence	13	38	12	46
Barter	2	6	2	8
Rent and interest	2	6	0.3	1
Crop sales	17	50	11.7	45
Total	34	100	26	100

Source: Village Survey, 1993.

Note: The 1975 figures are estimates of averages at that period of time, compiled from the respondent during the field research work.

Expenditure

	1975 May		1992 June	
	JD	%	JD	%
Food	14	40	12	46
Clothes	8	24	4	14
Sundries	2	6	3	12
Miscellaneous	0	0	1	4
Household overheads	3	9	2	8
Gifts	0	0	0	0
Rent and interest	1	3	2	8
Family expenses	0	0	1	4
Savings	6	18	1	4
Total	34	100	26	100

Source: Village Survey, 1993.

Note: 1975 – 4.23 CU, 1992 – 9.55 CU. Deflation index 285.
The 1975 figures are estimates of averages at that period of time, compiled from the respondent during the field research work.

Mohamed then had 3.75 wet acres and half a dry acre. He cultivated two acres of wheat and 1.75 acres of maize as well as dry tomatoes. When his first son married, he got himself so much into debt that he had to sell 0.75 wet acre to appease his creditors. Like many other farmers of his kind Mohamed is just about managing to make ends meet. To do this he has had to adjust his household consumption: he has substituted cheaper lentils for more expensive rice. In 1975 his wife cooked monthly about 43 lb rice and 10 lb lentils per consumption unit; in 1992 she prepared approximately 32 lb rice and 20 lb lentils. This reduced the monthly value of basic foods per consumption unit by about 10 per cent at 1975 prices and reduced the daily calorie intake per consumption unit from 2 430 to 2 240 in the form of rice and lentils. The value of these basic items used to make up about 65 per cent of total food consumption in Mohamed's household; now it composes as much as 75 per cent. This means that greater emphasis is now placed on the staple items just to fill their stomachs, while their ability to vary their diet has somewhat declined.

Mohamed's total monthly expenditure per consumption unit decreased by about 10 per cent since 1975. When his family was smaller he managed to save 18 per cent of his monthly income. Now he just about breaks even.

The increased size of his household, which necessitates greater overall expenditure on food, clothing and other essentials, is responsible for the difficulties Mohamed is now encountering, yet as long as he can produce sufficient food crops to meet his household needs and also grow some cash crops to be able to make the essential cash purchases, he is likely to keep his head above water. However, his joint estate will probably be partitioned in the near future; his two married sons are not happy about living in a joint household and want to break up the unit. Mohamed tries to persuade them that each family unit will be worse off independently than they now are sharing. In spite of his arguments the sons are adamant and Mohamed seems too weak a person to withstand them much longer.

Shayfoun's Ahmed is quite a different man from Mohamed: he is a lively, extroverted man in his early forties. Already in 1975 he was eager to become an urban worker. He then persistently kept asking for assistance in his quest. He could get factory employment in cement manufacturing in the capital, Amman. As in Mohamed's case, Ahmed's housing has also remained unchanged; only the size of his family has increased. In 1975 he lived with his mother, wife, and a little boy. Since then his wife has borne him two daughters. His household has thus increased from four to six in numbers and from 3.16 to 4.69 in terms of consumption units. His landholding has remained the same. He still has only one and a half wet acres and two dry acres. He keeps to the same pattern of cropping, growing half an acre of wheat and one acre of potatoes on the wet land he owns in a neighbouring village. This accounts for the drop in the subsistence output per consumption unit and his attempt to make up for it by bartering (in June 1990, he exchanged one sheep for 210 lb flour so as to meet his household's food needs). Ahmed's

Table 5.19 Ahmed's monthly budget per consumption unit at 1975 prices

Income

	1975 May		1992 June	
	JD	%	JD	%
Subsistence	13	43	8	29
Barter	0	0	5	19
Crop sales	8	26	6	22
Wages: Agriculture	6	18	1	4
Other	0	0	7	26
Miscellaneous	4	13	0	0
Total	31	100	27	100

Source: Village Survey, 1993.

Note: The 1975 figures are estimates of averages at that period of time, compiled from the respondent during the field research work.

Expenditure

	1975 May		1992 June	
	JD	%	JD	%
Food	15	48	13	47
Clothes	5	17	5	19
Sundries	4	13	4	15
Household overheads	3	10	1	4
Gifts	1	3	0	0
Rent and interest	2	6	4	15
Savings	1	3	0	0
Total	31	100	27	100

Source: Village Survey, 1993.

Note: The 1975 figures are estimates of averages at that period of time, compiled from the respondent during the field research work.

wife still prepares about the same quantity of staple diet items per consumption unit, namely about 21 lb rice and 30 lb lentils per month, which together yield about 2 300 calories per day per consumption unit. In 1975 the cost of rice and lentils accounted for about half of the household's food consumption. Nowadays it composes 60 per cent. As in Mohamed's case, here too there has been a shift back to relying on basic starchy foods and a decline in the variety of other items consumed.

Ahmed has cut down his overall expenditure per consumption unit by 10 per cent; only in this way does he manage to break even these days. His household budget for June 1992 clearly indicates that without his factory wages he would have great difficulty in making ends meet.

In May 1975, he worked six days as an agricultural labourer and his wife and mother each worked eight days as such. In June 1992 his wife worked three days for one of the wealthier farmers in the village and he himself earned 100 JD in the factory. He explained that now that his son is a young farmer in his own right he expects him to take full responsibility for cultivating the family lands. The son, however, is not very happy about this arrangement and would prefer to work in the town. This creates tension and difficulties between father and son and frequently necessitates Ahmed absenting himself from his factory employment to ensure that his land is cultivated properly. During the previous twelve months he had to absent himself from his job for 40 days for this reason.

Mohamed and Ahmed provide good examples of the middle range of middle farmers in their respective villages. Mohamed's economic status has declined because of the considerable increase in the size of his family, yet he still belongs to the 70 per cent of households who have sufficient land to satisfy their requirements. In Shayfoun, there are a number of farmers falling into the category of middle farmers who are considerably better off than Mohamed. In most of these cases this is because their families have not increased by nearly as much as Mohamed's. Therefore demographic accident plays an important role in the economic placing of Shayfoun's farmers, in particular middle farmers. If, as is highly likely, Mohamed's estate will be partitioned shortly, the emerging households will increase the number of farmers without sufficient land to meet their basic requirements. Without his factory wages, Ahmed would have great difficulty in meeting his household needs. He, like so many others of his fellow villagers, is dependent on income derived from outside Shayfoun to keep his family going: irrigated lands and employment outside Shayfoun provide the major sources of such exogenous income for Shayfoun middle farmers.

Mohamed's case study also illustrates the way middle-range farmers are affected by the increasing size of their family. This brings me to illustrate and examine the category of the poor farmers in Shayfoun.

Mahmoud is an alert and lively young man in his early thirties. In 1975, he was still unmarried and lived together with his widowed mother and two younger siblings. In the mean time, both Mahmoud and his brother got married and they partitioned their one acre so that Mahmoud has now only half a dry acre. Mahmoud now lives with his mother, wife and two young children. In terms of members, his family has increased from four to five, but in terms of consumption units it has remained at 3.66.

Mahmoud's household was severely affected by the decline in the number of days his family worked per month, coupled with the fall in the purchasing power of daily wages. His household's income from wages had fallen by approximately 70 per cent at 1975 prices. This drastic decline in real wage income is reflected in his considerably lower standard of living. He still lives in the same small house but which now looks even more dilapidated than it did previously; he and his family walk around in clothes which are almost in shreds. In May 1975, Mahmoud's mother cooked about 20 lb rice and 29 lb lentils per consumption unit, which yielded 2 140 calories per day. In June 1992 Mahmoud's wife cooked 6.5 lb rice and 40 lb lentils per consumption unit, yielding 1 960 calories per day. The staple diet of rice and lentils constituted 55 per cent of Mahmoud's household's food consumption by cost during the earlier period; in 1992 the proportion had increased to almost 70 per cent. In relative terms food now occupies 53 per cent of Mahmoud's household consumption by cost at 1975 prices as compared with only 42 per cent during the earlier period; in absolute terms he has reduced the value of his food consumption by about 25 per cent, from 13 JD to 10 JD per consumption unit, while reducing the calorie content of basic food per consumption unit by no more than 8 per cent. The total reduction in the calorie content is probably considerably greater than that as he had to substitute rice and lentils. I am afraid I am unable to give a more precise account of his dietary changes.

Mahmoud has to reduce his expenditure per consumption unit on clothes, sundries such as cigarettes, and household overheads, just to try to make ends meet. The greater emphasis placed on food in his household expenditure illustrates the well-known fact that people living at the lowest levels of income have to give first priority to food to ensure their survival. In spite of Mahmoud's attempt to cut down his overall household expenses he still cannot pay everything out of his income and is getting more and more in debt to his wife's family.

Mahmoud feels very bitter about the fact that he is in debt. Now he has to turn to professional moneylenders in Shayfoun or nearby villages, as he cannot meet even his household running expenses. He has difficulty in paying interest, let alone repaying his debts. When I questioned him on how he manages to get moneylenders to continue advancing loans to him when he seems unable to repay them, he explained that last year he had sent his eldest

Table 5.20 Mahmoud's monthly budget per consumption unit at 1975 prices

Income

	1975 May		1992 June	
	JD	%	JD	%
Subsistence	5	35	2	22
Barter	4	30	3	32
Gift	2	14	1	10
Sales: Animal products	1	7	0	0
Wages: Agriculture	1	7	0.33	3
Other	0		1.33	14
Net borrowing	1	7	1.84	19
Total	14	100	9.5	100

Source: Village Survey, 1993.

Note: The 1975 figures are estimates of averages at that period of time, compiled from the respondent during the field research work.

Expenditure

	1975 May		1992 June	
	JD	%	JD	%
Food	8	58	5.5	59
Clothes	1	7	0.5	5
Sundries	1	7	1	10
Household overheads	2	14	1	10
Gifts	1	7	0	0
Rent and interest	1	7	1.5	16
Total	14	100	9.5	100

Source: Village Survey, 1993.

Note: 1975 – 4.19 CU, 1992 – 4.69 CU. Deflation index 280.
The 1975 figures are estimates of averages at that period of time, compiled from the respondent during the field research work.

son to work in the house of a moneylender. His wages of 12 JD per month went to pay off his father's debt and interest. Mahmoud thought this was a satisfactory arrangement. It enables him to borrow the necessary money just to keep his family. It provides periodic regular employment for at least one member of his family and makes sure of a free meal whenever he visits the moneylender when his son is there.

The creditor–debtor relationship in Shayfoun goes with the system in which agricultural labourers are advanced petty sums of money in their time of need. They are bound so that they are not able to repay the debt out of their meagre wages, because under the terms of the bond they get food, clothes and a small salary only. The result is that they are not only unable to repay the loan but also have to add to it. Even their children are obliged to take upon themselves the repayment and become involved in it. Mahmoud regards himself as fortunate; at least he has a permanent home and owns one acre of dry land.

Poorest farmer

Ali's case is typical not only of Shayfoun's poorest households, but of the thousands and thousands of farmers in nearby villages who are landless. The family consists of six members: Ali and his two younger brothers, one of whom is already married and has his wife with him, as well as Ali's own wife and little boy. These six individuals constitute 4.99 consumption units. They use their small hut as a base from which to explore employment opportunities.

The two women in Ali's household formed part of a team of ten women who performed agricultural tasks as a group in June 1992. This team was engaged for ten days, yielding a cash wage of 20 JD for Ali's household. The head of the family and his younger brothers worked altogether seven and a half days during the month, for which they received 15 JD. This meagre wage income deflated to 1975 prices yields no more than 2.40 JD per consumption unit per month, which covers only half the necessary expenditure on food. Ali and his wife claimed that they receive the remainder of their necessary food in the form of gifts from rich farmers. Ali's wife cooks monthly about 10 lb of rice and 160 lb lentils for her household, which together yield a daily calorie intake of no more than 1 500 per consumption unit.

Ali's expenditure on rice and lentils composes about 80 per cent of the total daily food consumption. Therefore the calorie content of his household is likely to be no more than 1 800 per consumption unit, which is well below the minimum requirements of 2 500 calories. The lack of sufficient nourishment is obvious when one looks at these farmers, in particular their children. No one is prepared to risk lending them money because, as they have no permanent abode, they can pack up their few belongings and leave at very short notice. They are regarded in the area as the scum of society and have no choice but to accept the lowliest social position; their very survival is at stake.

Table 5.21 Ali's monthly budget per consumption unit at 1975 prices

Income

	1975 May		1992 May	
	JD	%	JD	%
Wages	2.4	38	2.4	38
Barter	1.5	24	2.4	38
Gift	2.4	38	1.5	24
Total	6.3	100	6.3	100

Source: Compiled from personal interview.

Expenditure

	1975 May		1992 May	
	JD	%	JD	%
Food	5	79	5	79
Clothes	0.40	6	0.40	6
Sundries	0.54	9	0.54	9
Household	0.36	6	0.36	6
Total	6.30	100	6.30	100

Source: Compiled from personal interview.

Note: 1975 –4.99 CU. Deflation factor 285.

5.7 Conclusion

The case studies presented here clearly indicate the process of increasing economic differentiation which has taken place in Shayfoun during the last 15 years. The wealthiest farmers have become considerably richer. The maize boom provided the possibility of a windfall profit to all farmers who owned more than two or three wet acres: the greater the maize acreage the greater the benefit a farmer derives from soaring prices. This encouraged the wealthier and more enterprising farmers to invest in more and more wet land. In a period of rapidly rising prices, investment in land and processing capital enabled the wealthiest farmers who still produced their own subsistence needs to ride on the tide of inflation.

Middle farmers managed on the whole to hold their own during this period of inflationary pressures, as long as they either had at least three wet acres to enable them to grow most of their own food as well as some cash crops, in order to make their essential purchases of clothing and so on, or if, as shown in the case of Ahmed, they managed to get regular employment to supplement their farming income. The fate of these middle farmers is largely determined by the rate of increase in the size of their families: the more rapid the increase, the quicker the decline in their economic status.

The case studies of the poor households show that the greater a household's dependence on rural cash wages for meeting necessary expenditure, the greater has been the deterioration in the standard of living.

In developing economies wages often lag behind price rises, and rural wages are notoriously slow in adjusting to rises in the cost of living. In periods when rural wages lag considerably behind price rises, agricultural labourers are bound to suffer, while landowners and entrepreneurs operate with an obvious advantage.

The difficulties the Shayfoun farmers experienced are by no means peculiar to this specific village. A study set up by the Ministry of Agriculture in June 1982 deliberated on the question of what should be regarded as the desirable national minimum level of consumer expenditure. The study recommended that a per capita monthly consumer expenditure of 30 JD (at 1970–71 prices) should be deemed the national minimum (Ministry of Agriculture Report 1985). According to the second Agricultural Report, about 85 per cent of people belonging to agricultural labour households were below the minimum.

The study of the farmers' situations therefore provides a reasonably accurate forecast of their future development and the changes that can be expected in their lives. It is likely that in the throes of change the poorest will suffer greater hardships than before. There just does not seem to be any one panacea for the vast socioeconomic problems; the most to be hoped for is to be able to suggest means to ameliorate major areas of difficulty. This will be the discussion carried forward in the next chapter concerning the position of women in the household economy.

6 Women and the household economy

6.1 The composition of the household as an economic unit

In order to analyse the specific factors that characterise women's subordinate position in the process of production, one has to understand, among other structures, their position in the household. This is because the household constitutes one of the basic units that comprise the economy. If households ever were discrete and self-sufficient units in the area I studied, this is certainly not the case now. It would be impossible to study the household in isolation since it is a unit where a number of processes take place, including the earning of income from a variety of different activities. We need to examine the household because it is still largely through their domestic roles that women are allocated work or leisure. Through their position in the household the pattern of their work is organised and their control over its products defined. So I shall discuss the household as a unit of both production and consumption, examining the structure of economic relations among its members.

In order to do this, I shall have to clarify some problems of definitions. There are a number of concepts of meanings attached to the term 'household', and are the groups which I have termed households genuinely comparable? There has been a tendency in studies of the family and household in the Arab world (Hijab 1988; Mernissi 1975; Morsy 1990) to look at the household mainly in terms of its composition. The key problems have been 'What categories of relatives normally live together?' and 'How are we to describe households which contain members of more than one nuclear family?' Less attention has been paid to problems such as 'What kind of things do members of one household do together?' or 'What is the structure of cooperation among its members?' Badran points out that while modern sociologists are aware that the family and the household are not the same thing, 'a considerable confusion, however, still persists because of the tendency to use the words "family" and "household" as synonyms' (Badran 1989). This conflation of the genealogical model and the residential group has led to a tendency to treat the household as first and foremost a kin group, albeit 'influenced by economic factors' (Mandelbaum 1972), when it should be treated as both a kin group and an economic group. An inordinate amount of energy seems to have been devoted to deciding what precise term should be applied to a nuclear family household augmented by the presence of, say, the husband's widowed sister, instead of looking at the structure of cooperation and exchange within this group.

In this chapter I seek to elaborate on the complex pattern of collaboration between men and women in the household and on the inequalities of the status of women in rural employment. The conclusion of the chapter will be that women continue to depend upon men to handle most of the important issues involving their income and the budgeting of their monthly expenses.

The household is indisputably a kin group in the obvious sense that it is constituted by relations of blood and marriage. In only a very few households in the village that I studied were there non-kin living as members of the same domestic group. Invariably these non-kin were living on small farms. On the other hand the household is more than just a kin group 'influenced by economic factors'. It is a unit of consumption: its members budget together for their needs and to a large extent share common rations and lodging. A household possessing land is also usually a unit of production – its members constitute a work team in cultivating and managing the land and preparing its products for sale or consumption. And in the case of households where the household itself is not a unit of production, as in labouring or tenant families, members may still cooperate in production activities or work alongside each other.

But if the household is not just a kin group, what are the economic dimensions which we should regard as defining it? This is the real problem, because in the north of Jordan the group of people who hold co-parcenary rights in a piece of land or other property may not all live together. Brothers frequently farm the patrimonial land jointly while living separately, as in the case of (H7), whose land is not partitioned from that of his elder brother. Or the land may be partitioned from that of the elder brother, or partitioned and registered in the brothers' several names but in reality farmed as one unit, with only one of the brothers staying in the village to manage it. This was the case in Mohamed's (H4) household; his two brothers worked in a nearby city while Mohamed devoted himself to full-time farm management. In some cases the brothers who are employed outside the village leave their wives and children behind, sending remittances to them or to their parents. This is more common among the lower-income households (H9) (H11) (H13). Or they may take their wives and children to live near their place of work, sending money to their parents or brothers from time to time. In such cases, a group of people related through kinship live separately for most of the year but share a high degree of financial responsibility for each other and budget together for major items of expenditure (a tractor, or a daughter's wedding).

That there are several dimensions of household cooperation and joint living which do not necessarily coincide has been recognised by most authors. Gore distinguishes residence, property holding and use of a common hearth, evidently giving primacy to co-residence, as have most other writers (Gore 1968, p.6). This, however, leaves out the question of joint budgeting and sharing of general financial responsibility insofar as this relates to matters other than land. Friedman tried to overcome the complexity of defining the household by adopting a dual classification of households according to 'jointness'; one classification refers to jointness in terms of common responsibility and cooperation. According to this schema, two brothers who lived separately would not be 'joint' at all in the first sense. But if there were a high degree of mutual financial responsibility or other kinds of regular cooperation between their families, then they could be considered to show jointness according to the second sense of the term (Friedman 1993, p.34). Friedman's contribution is helpful in that he recognises that if we treat residential units as discrete groups then we risk ignoring the very important relations of economic cooperation which exist among close kin who do not necessarily live together. This results in the arbitrary isolation of a unit which may or may not be isolable if we are primarily concerned with the economic dimension of family life. So any strict definition of the household will be arbitrary to some extent; relations of economic cooperation and financial obligation overflow the physical boundaries of the family home, and it is difficult to isolate the core of kin who have primary economic responsibility for each other from the vaguer set of relatives who have less definite rights and duties towards each other. In the case of Fatima (H8), for instance, her son Ali lived at some distance from the village where the family owns land, and was employed as a factory employee. Most of the time his wife and children do not live with their grandmother but with Ali. Should Fatima and Ali be considered as one household or as two? They budget separately for their everyday needs, to be sure. On the other hand, Fatima cannot manage the land on her own. She relies on Ali and on his younger brother Abdullah to visit her regularly to supervise the farm, and in most months one or the other of them manages to come for a few days. The land is managed on a joint basis, though in fact it is registered in the separate names of Fatima and her four children in order to avoid the effects of land ceiling laws. Fatima and her sons are mutually reliant so far as farm management is concerned and for all major expenses. Therefore, on the grounds that most of their budgeting is collective, I have treated them as constituting one household. For the purpose of this study I have conceptualised the household as comprised of a group of people where there is substantial economic co-operation, common property and mutual financial responsibility. Most of the time most of its members will live together (a definition of the household which made no reference to common residence would be stretching the meaning of the term well beyond its conventional meaning), but at any one time some members may live away from the common home. This may seem an arbitrary definition, but as I have suggested, some arbitrariness is inevitable and I am not making any claims for this usage other than its appropriateness for the purposes of this study.[12] However, I have tried not to be arbitrary in my application of this definition and there is consistency in the procedures by which individuals have been included or excluded from the sample.

One final point needs to be made. Any household is always in the process of development (Sharma 1980). It continually loses members, gains members, divides, and becomes more or less complex in its composition. The households in the sample are seen as though 'frozen' at the point of time when I studied them. In case the processual character of the household is lost from view in the subsequent discussion, let me point out that after I left the village Ali left his employment in the factory to come back to the village and live with his mother. Fatima, his sister, will probably leave to get married. If I were to revisit the village now, after six months of field work, probably almost every household would require some amendment.

6.2 The household as a unit of diversified economic activity

In Shayfoun the household is not an economically self-sufficient unit (in the sense that its production covers its consumption costs), yet self-sufficiency is celebrated as a value. While the household maintains its own internal system of social relations and legitimating ideology, it also contains mechanisms for linkage with the outside ecological and political economic systems. Minor alterations in productive strategies and patterns of distribution and consumption take place during changes in the agricultural cycle (Chayanov 1966; Deere and Janur 1979) or at times of recession and high unemployment (Jelin 1982). Major transitions such as those accompanying a modification in the dominant mode of production necessitate more radical changes on the part of households (Sacks 1979; Tilly and Scott 1978; Young 1978). The change may cause a transformation in the internal relationships of the household.

In the area farmers yearn nostalgically for a bygone age, almost certainly mythical, when each household produced all that it needed to feed and clothe its members. Food which one has not produced oneself is often considered to be less nutritious than home-grown food. One woman told me that she felt

---

12 Note that all definitions to some extent are selective in this respect: 'The value of a definition lies not in its supposed descriptive accuracy but in the analytical question it allows us to ask' (Nazir 1991, p.29).

111

depressed when her sheep went dry: quite apart from the expense of buying milk each day, milk which you have bought from someone else does not taste so sweet. It is true that in the past many households produced items which they now buy from the *suq*, but the modern rural household is far from being the autonomous, self-sufficient unit which remains a strong ideal, even in the case of those families who own large amounts of land. Very few informants of any social class felt that they could manage entirely on the proceeds of the land they owned. In Shayfoun, this was mainly due to pressure on cultivable land because of the increase in population; holdings have been partitioned to the point where individual units are no longer economical. In Jordan as a whole, this is true of the smaller farmers. This category of farmers own between 2–5 acres. In general the character of these small farmers is that production is family-based, relatively independent of capital, and they adapt to the constraints imposed by access to only a small quantity of land and other resources. But there has also been a general rise in the standard of living and of people's expectations. New needs have been created for consumer goods and other items which the household cannot produce itself and must obtain with cash. A regular cash income over and above the proceeds of agriculture was felt to be needed in all but one or two capitalist farmer's households. That is, one or more members of the household must find regular paid employment. However, the types of households in Shayfoun are threefold:

a) those which can fully meet their consumption and also have a surplus;
b) those that can only partially meet their needs;
c) those that have to rely completely on outside employment for income.

In Jordan, when I speak of households 'needing' cash income in addition to the produce of their own land, I am referring to practical needs and not to any absolute standard of need. Of course, a household such as Mohsen's (H12) could not survive without some source of income other than the grain they produce from their own land, or they would starve. But many of the larger landowners equally felt that they could not manage without some other source of income. Fatima (H1) did not feel that her household could manage on the proceeds of their farm at the moment, even though the combined land holdings of the family amounted to over eight acres. That is, they could not maintain the standard of living which they considered appropriate with any security unless at least one of the sons had a paid job. Partly, this is an effect of the process of transition to capitalist methods of farming. This family had only begun to farm their land themselves about five years ago on the death of Fatima's husband. They still had substantial repayments to make on loans taken out for the purchase of a tractor. Other households who had made the transition to this kind of farming earlier (H3 and H4) could maintain a high standard of living on their farm income alone.

The combination of agriculture with wage labour in the farming household is, of course, very widespread in Third World countries. The particular division of labour which we find in Jordan and among the poorer Jordanian families, where men enter paid employment and women farm, is common where an agriculturally undeveloped region lies within reach of an industrially advanced area (as in many parts of southern Africa). Where the returns of agricultural production are low and industrial wages are also low in relation to the urban cost of living, then this pattern of interdependence is necessary for the survival of the poorer families. Note that only five households in my sample relied on a single type of income. Two of these were wealthy capitalist farmers, emancipated from the need to sell their labour (H3 and H4). Another two were families that were becoming more orientated towards professional work and the fifth was an impoverished family which existed entirely and precariously on the produce of their land.

This dependence on multiple sources of income has various consequences in Jordan. It is noticeable that occupational diversity favours the persistence of joint families; there are economic advantages in members of complex households staying together when some members can specialise in urban employment and others in agriculture.

Secondly, it has consequences for class formation. The class position of individuals can be defined, but households are harder to characterise, since their members may participate in more than one economic activity either simultaneously or serially. Aisha (H5), for instance, is a farmer–proprietor farming her own land, while her eldest son keeps a small shop and her other sons work as labourers in a city. Mohsen (H12) owns a little land, rents land from time to time, and works as a farm servant. For Fatima (H1) class exists in an objective sense, but class consciousness does not develop easily where the individual identifies with a household whose members' economic positions are so diverse (this is especially true in the middle ranges of the rural hierarchy). The *hamula* is a more accessible focus for self-identification than class. The classifications which I have used to characterise households (teacher, farmer, labourer, and so on) must of necessity be very crude and are only a rough guide to such things as income and standard of living, level of education, or self-identification.

The third consequence of which we need to take account here is that women are doubly dependent. As I demonstrated earlier, they seldom possess land in their own names; now they also largely depend on men to bring cash into the household since, for reasons which I shall describe, women play little part in wage employment. There is an intimate relationship between women's work in the household and family and their acceptance. As specific kinds of wage- and income-generating workers, women turn their domestic skills into market skills as do men, but to a lesser degree – they value their domestic work as a commodity. As Nelson put it, 'The boundary between women's unpaid domestic labour and the paid work they perform in the formal or informal sector is often a tenuous one' (Nelson 1979, p.299). As a result women become involved in child care, washing, cleaning and making clothes or carpets for the market.

6.3 Rural women and employment

It is usually the men of the household who are the chief wage-earners. There are two reasons for this; firstly, women are less educated relative to men and therefore are less qualified for some kinds of employment, and secondly, the restrictions on women's mobility and public visibility described previously in my book severely limit their opportunities for employment. In Jordan, rural women of low socioeconomic class in the *hamula* can obtain seasonal agricultural labouring work, and in any case most women are too fully occupied working their own holdings or those which they rent in the absence of their menfolk to have time to work for other people. In my field work, the figures show that 26 men are chief wage-earners whereas 20 women work as teachers and carpet-weavers.

In my field work the picture looked a little bit different in the matter of seasonal employment. However, the data on seasonality shown in Table 6.1 suggest that the female sector as a whole is still dependent on the viability of the male occupations. The seasonal trend in women's incomes and expenses reflects the cycle in the male agricultural economy; women's incomes are higher in November, when men have cash from olive sales, than they are in July. Women's cash receipts are 75 per cent higher in November than in July;

Table 6.1 Women's average cash income

	JD		%	
	July	Nov	July	Nov
Sales of tomato	12.80	21.67	39	37
Resale	2.38	8.25	7	14
Olive work	–	6.11	–	11
Subtotal	15.18	36.03	46	62
Transfers				
Husband	10.32	15.33	32	27
Other men	3.79	2.37	12	4
Women	3.45	3.94	10	7
Subtotal	17.56	21.64	54	38
Total	32.74	57.67	100	100

Source: Village Survey, 1993.

this is accounted for, not by gifts and transfers from men to women, but by additional money earned by the women themselves through market activities.

In the entire sample there were only 20 women, representing eight households, who worked for wages at any time during the field work. These included three teachers, seven agricultural labourers and ten carpet-weavers. Only the teachers worked on a permanent basis. All the others simply worked when the opportunity arose.

6.3.1 Women outside their own village

In the confines of the village the prejudice against women moving about freely in public militates against their seeking work outside their own villages, even when they are qualified and when work might be available in some other district. In one household, the daughter had passed her teaching examination with excellent marks but was currently unemployed as there was no post vacant in the local schools and her parents were unwilling that she should go to live elsewhere away from their home. Married women are somewhat less restricted, especially in the nearby villages of the district. It is not unusual for a woman teacher to take up work away from home, living separately from her husband for the duration of her service.

6.3.2 Women in professional employment

In the past there was little scope for rural women to find professional employment because they had not been educated to the same level as men. Amongst the generation of women born after the Mandate period it would be unusual to find one able to say of herself, as many of my older informants could say, that she 'never went near a school in her life', but girls are still educated to a lower level than their brothers. This persistent inequality is found in the Indian culture too (Sharma 1980). Or perhaps a more accurate way of putting it would be to say that there are various educational strategies for girls, but few of them lead to the girls being able to obtain the kind of qualifications which will help them to get work. Nowadays the logic is not that they will get too independent but that it is just not worth it, since they are not going to be seeking employment after all (a self-fulfilling assumption). The exceptions are the high-status *hamulas*, where education enhances a girl's position in the marriage market, and where the aim is to use the education to get a good husband. The husband's family might then decide for her to work or not.

6.3.3 Women in rich families

In Shayfoun, girls of the very highest status *hamulas* are automatically educated to a high school and university level, but with even less expectation that they will use their qualifications. The impression remains, however, that many of the women who become teachers are drawn from the upper *hamulas* nonetheless. Status is still a vital consideration in determining what kind of work a woman may do, but education is regarded as more than simply an ornament.

Girls of all socioeconomic groups seem to enjoy their education and take it seriously even if, as in many poor families, they cannot manage very regular attendance. It is one sphere in which they can achieve and be appreciated for their personal performance yet in a suitably enclosed and feminine environment (most secondary schools are single-sex schools and even in co-educational schools there is considerable segregation of the sexes (Sharma 1980)).

Another factor which militates against girls from poorer families gaining useful qualifications is the domestic and farm work which they are often expected to do. Mohsen's daughter (H31) had worked her way rather painfully to the sixth grade, but had difficulty in keeping up with the work since as soon as she reached home each afternoon she was expected to do a number of routine tasks, such as washing clothes and cleaning the house. Boys are also expected to help at home and run errands, of course, but to a lesser extent than girls.

Where girls of poor families are concerned there is yet another factor which deters them from seeking paid work, namely that the wages for female labourers are much lower than those of male labourers and the work available for women labourers is seasonal and sporadic. There is little incentive for poor women to regard such work as a source of regular income. Rich farmers in Shayfoun seldom employ more than one or two permanent labourers, invariably men. Women are employed for seasonal work, such as weeding wheat or planting vegetables. Women such as Meriam (H11) and Muna (H19) are therefore liable to regard money earned in this way as a bonus to be used for meeting occasional expenses, such as clothing, or to put by for weddings and the like. I remember Muna being very elated with the 10 JD she had just earned for a couple of weeks' work in the fields and which she was about to spend on cloth for a new outfit for herself.

I should perhaps make it clear that if there is limited scope for employment open to rural women, this does not mean that finding work is easy for all rural men. There is a great deal of unemployment among the men, some of it 'hidden'. A farmer's son may spend his time working on the family land, all the while making unsuccessful attempts to find work elsewhere. But there are still important differences between the employment chances of boys and girls. For one thing, as I have already made clear, a man has the advantage of being more mobile. He can, without prejudice to his reputation, move about alone in search of work and travel long distances if necessary. A young man of poor family who cannot find work in his own locality will often go to stay with a relative in some more promising area in the hope of finding work there. Secondly, while personal contacts are always important in finding employment, they are particularly important for women. A young girl may have professional qualifications, but her parents will be unwilling to allow her to work in a situation where the family have no prior contacts or where there is no trusted person who can 'keep an eye on her' and vouch for her safety and welfare. So far as labouring women are concerned, large farmers tend to advertise their needs for casual labour through their own personal contacts in the local villages (Mernissi 1975).

The desire to take employment, therefore, is not disapproved of in a woman of high- or middle-status family, provided that there is work available which her family regards as suitable and provided money is available for her training, but it is not expected of her as it would be of a boy. Girls of poor families, on the other hand, are definitely expected to help contribute to the family income if they possibly can, either directly by taking seasonal labouring work or indirectly by giving extra help in the home so that some other female member of the household can take on such work outside the home when available. This point has been discussed by researchers (Morsy 1990).

How do women themselves regard paid work outside the home? Studies indicate that apart from the financial rewards, many women derive social satisfaction from paid employment since it enables them to avoid the isolated tedium of housework. However dull the work, some companionship and social importance derive from it. In my field work, the rural Jordanian women whom I studied regarded work outside the home in quite a different way, since they did not usually experience the home as somewhere they needed to get away from. The ideology of honour teaches a woman to regard the home as the one place where she feels particularly secure and important. And, as the home is the focus for interaction among kin and neighbours, even women who observe fairly strict seclusion do not experience it as a place of isolation. So they derive satisfaction from paid work in proportion as they find the work intrinsically interesting or agreeable. This issue I referred to in discussing the issue of territory (see Chapter 4).

However, although women are not obliged to seek paid employment in the sense that many men are, and although the decision to do so is not one which a woman can make alone, once the decision has been made she will not regard work as in any way marginal to her role as a woman. What the female role demands is the subordination of the individual woman's personal inclinations to the needs of the whole group, whether those needs be primarily for prestige or for cash. If suitable work is available, there is no reason why she should not fulfil her role as dutiful wife or daughter by going out to work – this is likely to be rather different from that of many European women who see their work role as something either conflicting with or subordinate to their role in the family.

The role of a Jordanian village woman as paid worker is only 'marginal' in the family in the sense that she is likely to be paid less than the men of her household. Her pay is certainly not regarded as 'pin money'. Even the richer families have not reached that standard of living where extra income brings much scope for choice in expenditure. Most households will have a list of priorities which are dealt with as income rises, no matter who is responsible for actually earning the money. Women's earnings are not really different from those of men in this respect. So, while in the community women are devalued, to the extent that they are offered less money than men for the same or similar work, within the family a female earner is valued in the same way as a male earner in the sense that her contribution is taken seriously.

Having said this, however, I must stress again the point that cannot be re-iterated too often, namely that women seldom command the kind of income that would allow them to be independent of their husbands or fathers. Further-more, the senior members of the household have ultimate control over the labour power of the female members of the group and to some extent that of the junior males also, even where women obtain and spend their own quite substantial incomes. A woman can only get access to training if her parents are willing and if her father or some other relative is prepared to pay the fees, and having obtained it will not be able to work outside the home without her parents' consent. In practice, unmarried girls often need the help of male relatives in getting work in the first place, as they will not have the contacts which are needed to locate and obtain work in rural areas (Tucker 1993).

In a sense, no member of the household is regarded as having the right to sell his or her labour or to enjoy the income thus earned without reference to the other members of the group, and their needs and wishes. But because of their particular moral role as repositories of family honour and their particu-lar economic position as financial dependents, women are less likely to be able to resist this control and to participate in the labour market on the same terms as men. Only in very exceptional cases will a woman's role as earner mitigate her role as dependent.

6.4 The organisation of work in the household and the sexual division of labour

Most writers who have addressed the question of the organisation of labour within the household have looked at it primarily in terms of the way in which tasks are allocated among men and women and the degree of overlap, if any, between male and female tasks. Certainly this is important, but we also need to know how routine tasks are organised, that is, not just who does what but who decides what, and who is responsible for seeing that specific tasks are done. This involves looking at the whole structure of household work: how work teams are constituted, what kind of cooperation takes place between men and women in the household, and what other criteria besides that of sex are important in the domestic division of labour. The table summarises the way in which routine agricultural and domestic tasks are allocated between the sexes and among the age groups for, as we shall see, age is also an import-ant principle in the organisation of household work. This table does not reflect

Table 6.2 Allocation of tasks in the household

	Tasks usually done by females	No.	Tasks done by males or females	No.	Tasks usually done by males	No.
Children	Occasional help with cooking and washing utensils	2	Fetching water	3	Helping on the farm	2
	Tending smaller children	1	Purchasing from shops	4		
			Taking cattle to pasture or water			
Adults	Cooking	16	Shopping	19	Operating farm machinery	16
	Washing clothes	18	Operating well for irrigating	11	Digging irrigation channels	12
	Sewing, knitting Raising vegetables near the house	12 8				
Elderly	Minding small children	4	Light agricultural work	2		

Source: Village Survey, 1993.

the actual division of labour which operates in any particular household; in some households women do virtually no agricultural work, not all households include elderly people, and many possess no heavy machinery. It only represents the range of tasks performed by men and women in the community in general.

From this summary, we see that the tasks which are almost exclusively performed by women are those relating to the supervision and care of young children and to the personal care and nourishment of family members. Women may perform many additional tasks of an agricultural nature but these 'nurturant' tasks are the preserve of women. There are fewer tasks which are exclusively male. Among these are ploughing and all agricultural operations which involve driven machinery. There is a very strong feeling in the village that women should not plough. One woman tried to explain this feeling with reference to the idea that for a woman to plough would be bad for her honour. However, the fact that women do not operate machinery or drive tractors does not seem to have any such normative origins.

Women explained this simply by stating that they did not know how to do these tasks; if they had ever been taught to do them, no doubt they would. One can, however, speculate about some of the reasons why women have not been taught these skills. Firstly, the advisory government personnel and development officers who are responsible for disseminating information about modern farming technology are exclusively male and tend to communicate with males. The rich farmers who can afford to purchase machinery are almost all male. So too, as I have already noted, are the permanent labourers employed by these farmers to work the land, while the nature of labour – ploughing, operating Persian wells and digging irrigation channels – is also male-orientated. This channelling of knowledge about modern farming technology through exclusively male networks is common in developing countries, as Boserup and other writers have noticed. A second 'hidden' reason is that whoever drives a tractor or operates a tube-well must collect the necessary fuel from the filling station in the *suq* or along the main road, venues which are rather too public for women to visit frequently.

On the whole, the division of labour in the household is flexible within limits; whatever pattern the particular household adopts there will usually be a range of tasks which can be performed by men and women alike. It is possible to identify three main patterns in Shayfoun, which can be summarised as follows in an order of degree of rigidity:

1   Rich farmers in Shayfoun: women of the household do no agricultural work at all, unless of a supervisory nature. Men do agricultural tasks which do not involve strenuous manual labour or actual contact with the soil, for example, (H17, H18, H21).
2   Middle farmers: men do the majority of agricultural tasks and women do domestic tasks along with a little light agricultural work and tending cattle (H27, H28).
3   Poor farmers: in most households in the village area, women participate in practically all agricultural work and also bear the prime responsibility for domestic work (H13–17)(H22–H29).

But age is as important a principle as sex. In all but a few rich landlords' households, children are expected to do a fair amount of domestic and agricultural work. A work team engaged in operations such as sowing or threshing will typically include a man and his wife with one or more of their children. Elderly people withdraw from heavy work of any kind but will continue to do whatever light or sedentary tasks are within their capacity, such as cleaning grain.

The sexual division of labour is not very pronounced in early childhood; little boys and little girls are asked to do much the same kind of work until they are about nine or ten, although girls are more frequently left in charge of younger siblings than are boys. But children have to learn the skills appropriate to their sex from the parent of the same sex, and the sexual division of labour becomes more apparent as they approach adolescence and are drawn into the adult work pattern.

In some households the difference between tasks allocated to girls and to grown women reflects an actual change in the aspirations of the family. For instance, Aisha (H39), Mohsen's elder sister, did not do any work in the fields, although her mother did a fair amount of agricultural work. This girl was studying to become a teacher, the first of her family to pursue a course of higher education, and it was felt that it was not proper for her to do manual work out of doors. In some households the reverse is true, that is, the young daughters do tasks which their mothers cannot do for reasons of status. Fatima (H14), for instance, scarcely ever left her own house except for social visits, but she would send her eight-year-old daughter to the shops on minor errands as it was not considered improper for the children to go to the *suq*.

But we cannot understand the significance of the sexual division of labour unless we also know about the division of responsibility. That is, we need to know not only who normally does a particular task, but who gets blamed if it is not done. We may obtain a very false picture of the relations between men and women in the household if we do not look at the distribution of responsibility (Oakley and Marsden 1984, p.159). We have seen that in households of all social classes it is women who perform such tasks as cooking, cleaning the house, washing clothes and caring for small children. We can add that these tasks are also the responsibility of women. Let us examine what this means in respect of one particular task – cooking. In Shayfoun, most men know how to cook and some can cook very well indeed. Most men have lived away from their womenfolk at some time in their lives and have learnt how to do most routine domestic chores for themselves. The same is true of many Shayfoun men of lower socioeconomic status, especially those who have served in the army. But village men will hardly ever be seen doing this kind of work in their own homes. If the wife is sick then some female neighbour or relative will take her place at the hearth. This is partly because it is shaming for a man to do a woman's work if there is a woman who could do it instead. But it is also because cooking is the responsibility of women. If the woman who normally cooks is unable to do so, then it is up to her to arrange for someone to act as her understudy, and she will not appeal to the men of the household unless she has really exhausted all possibilities of a female substitute from her own household work team or from a neighbour's. An interesting situation arose on one occasion, when a man's wife had not accompanied him to the village. Fatima, his younger brother's widow, felt concerned that he did not have anyone to cook for him. She felt that, as a closely related woman, it was her responsibility to see that he had proper meals. Yet she also felt anxious that if she invited him to share her own meals this might be construed as taking an improper interest in him. She resolved the situation by sending him hot food, carried to his home on a tray by a neighbour's son.

The care of children is less exclusively the woman's responsibility, but it is still the mother who will be criticised if her children are unruly. For instance, the children of Munira (H29) were reputed to be somewhat wild, and when the eldest girl (who was about nine) insisted on climbing on farm machinery when she had been bidden not to, a neighbour remarked, 'Munira's daughters are totally without fear and it is a pity that she does not discipline them better.' That is, it was assumed that it was the more immediate responsibility of Munira to punish the daughters for climbing on farm machinery.

If there are several grown women in one household they will form a work team for the performance of domestic tasks under the leadership of the senior active woman. The leader need not necessarily be the oldest woman; an elderly woman who has retired from active work has probably also relinquished her role as work organiser even if the fiction is maintained that she still has this authority. The women will usually work out a regular division of labour for themselves. For instance, in Muna's household (H31), Muna herself did most of the cooking and she also milked the cattle. Her elder unmarried daughter generally washed the clothes and occasionally cooked. The younger daughter and the son, who were still at school, took it in turns to fetch water. The senior active woman will usually take the initiative in allocating tasks, but daily reminders that this or that must be done are seldom necessary except in the case of young children, for whom, understandably, the idea of another ten minutes in bed or another half-hour's play may be more attractive than that of fetching pots of water or of sweeping the yard.

In households where the women do little or no agricultural work, the men of the family form an independent work team, similarly organised under the leadership of the senior active male. Hassan (H26), for instance, did little strenuous work on his farm after a severe illness, but he would usually accompany his two sons to their fields and would give instructions as to which fields should be ploughed or irrigated, how many labourers should be hired for a certain task, and so forth. That is not to say that the sons took no initiative, but they would not undertake any major task without reference to their father. In this kind of work team the role of the senior male is more obvious, though not necessarily more important, than that of the woman who leads the domestic work team, largely because domestic work is more repetitive at a day-to-day level than agricultural work. Its cycle of tasks is shorter and more regular and the need to make major decisions is less frequent.

What about those households in which agricultural work is done by both men and women? In such cases, the men and women of the household will form one work team so far as cultivation is concerned. The prime mover may be the senior active male or the senior active woman – or it may be impossible to decide who actually takes the main initiative. Where the men are employed outside the village or where there are no adult male members the senior woman must organise the day-to-day routine work. The husband of Aisha Ali (H16) had his own taxi business and also did agricultural work, but it was Aisha Ali who played the more active role in actually organising the work. She did not do much work in the fields herself, but she would go daily to the shed in the fields where her husband and the farm workers gathered to eat their lunch. Her pretext was that she took them their food to eat there, but in actual fact she would use the visits to supervise what was going on, to allocate tasks, and to survey the progress of the work already started. On her way home she would collect money from the households where she sold milk. In Muhsin Ali's (H26) household, however, it was very much Muhsin Ali's father who directed the farm work, even though he was absent from the farm for most of the day.

To summarise, we might say that while it is more usual for a senior man to lead the agricultural work team of a household than for a woman, there is a good deal of variation according to the circumstances of particular households. It is only in the more highly segregated households of the rich farmers that the leader will invariably be a man. Although there is a good deal of social segregation of the sexes in Shayfoun, there is no real feeling that men and women ought not to work together in the fields. If a mixed group is engaged in a common task, either as members of the same household or as hired labourers on another person's land, there is a tendency for the women to congregate and to work at a little distance from the men, but if a man and his wife are working alone or just with their children they will not space themselves in this way. The rules of etiquette which separate the sexes in most situations do not seriously inhibit communication among men and women cooperating in the same work team, and young wives learn to reap and weed deftly with their faces modestly veiled from their fathers-in-law.

There is a third area of responsibility which I have not referred to explicitly in this chapter so far, namely the responsibility for the household's dealings with other groups and agencies – what might be called extra-household business and liaison work. I am dealing with it now to defend my thesis on the roles of women in production and the inequalities they encounter. As far as day-to-day shopping is concerned it is more often the responsibility of the women to see that the household is stocked with provisions and everyday necessities. It is not necessarily the women who actually do the shopping, but it is their business to see that it gets done and to commission some other member of the household to go to the *suq* and fetch any item that is needed. On the other hand, most other kinds of dealings with official or commercial agencies are a male responsibility, in accordance with the idea that the public sphere is primarily a male sphere, which I dealt with earlier. Dealing with matters of taxation, registration of land, government agents, or registering children in school – these are all tasks which are primarily, though not exclusively, the business of men.

We therefore have two basic patterns of organising work performed in the household. In one type, there will be two distinct work teams – a female work team performing domestic work, and a male work team doing agricultural work and extra domestic tasks – or there may be two overlapping work teams – a female work team doing the domestic work, and a mixed work team doing agricultural work and extra-domestic work. There are two minor variants of the latter pattern. In the first, women are rather marginal in the agricultural work team and are only drawn in to perform certain specified tasks or only at certain very busy seasons of the year. In the second variant, which is more common in Shayfoun, it is the men who are marginal to agricultural work, for the reason that they are absent from the village for much of the time and the main burden of organising and performing farm work falls on the women.

In the latter case, the women have a very heavy load of work and responsibility. One Shayfoun villager remarked to me, 'Our women are slaves; they are never free from work. Men can sit in the *suq* and smoke or drink tea, but the women always have something to do.' In fact few men spent much time in total idleness, nor did the women think of themselves as slaves, but they did think of themselves as tied to a never-ending cycle of work and activity. Domestic work alone is seen as being of itself without beginning or end. 'Housework is never finished' makes just this point and can be compared to the English saying, 'A woman's work is never done.' When the responsibility for farm work is added to this, the women understandably see themselves as doubly burdened.

6.5 The life cycle and the domestic cycle: meeting labour demand

It will be evident from what I have said about the organisation of labour within the household that an individual of either sex passes through a characteristic ordered cycle of work and responsibilities. In farming households, a girl spends her childhood learning domestic tasks and agricultural work under the supervision of her mother. When she marries she may spend further years working and gaining more farming experience with her mother-in-law, or perhaps with her husband's elder brother's wife. As daughter-in-law she will initially have more work than responsibility, but she will assume further responsibility for the performance of tasks in the household either when her husband sets up an independent household separate from that of his parents or brothers, or more gradually when her mother-in-law begins to retire from active management of household work. As she grows older herself, and as her daughters grow up and her sons' wives join the household, she is in turn in a position to withdraw from the more strenuous routine work, eventually taking a place on the sidelines so far as day-to-day work is concerned. This is a typical sequence, but there is no way of predicting at what age a particular woman will experience these stages, only the order in which they are likely to occur. At precisely which point, for instance, she will be able to shuffle off some responsibility onto the younger generation will depend on the cycle of household organisation which a domestic unit undergoes as its members marry, bear children, separate their property and die. Decisions about whether

124

to get a son married early or late, whether to divide property, or whether a particular son should leave the village to work elsewhere are not made without reference to the labour requirements of the household at the time.

The case of Ali's household illustrates these points. Ali's parents-in-law (H21) had been anxious to arrange their son Abdulla's marriage as soon as possible because another female hand was badly needed at home. All their sons were now working outside the village, and all but one of those who had already married had taken their wives with them to the various places where they worked. The elderly couple were left to work the family land with the help of only one daughter-in-law. This daughter-in-law had several tiny children and therefore could not be expected to do so much of the outdoor work. In Shayfoun it is usual for a girl to spend a good deal of the first year of her marriage at her parents' home, visiting her in-laws' home regularly and gradually extending the length of her visits there. In Ali's wife's case, however, her incorporation into her husband's household was hurried along for the simple reason that her labour was badly needed. Her parents were not very happy about this, partly because they themselves were facing a similar labour crisis.

It happens, therefore, that a household is liable to experience occasions when its labour requirements cannot be met or can be met only with difficulty. This can happen for a number of reasons. It may occur for demographic reasons, for instance, if the first two or three children of a marriage are daughters and have to be married off before their brothers are ready to marry and bring home wives who will replace the daughters. However, in the rich farmers' households in Shayfoun the crises which occur are liable to be of a different nature. The household will be in a position to hire extra domestic or agricultural help when it is needed, and heavy manual work is not done by household members anyway. Crises in this kind of household will relate to the need for there to be at least one active male member of the household at home to take charge of the day-to-day management of the farm, since women cannot stand in for men as they can in households of lower-status groups.

When labour crises occur in farmers' or labourers' households it is generally the women who bear the brunt of the work burden. It is a male responsibility to earn cash; women, as we have seen, cannot be expected to contribute so much here. The women are liable to be left to deal with shortages of household labour as best they can. Frequently these crises are of long duration, especially when they are due to the absence of males in wage employment at a distance from the village.[13] Couples are generally pleased to have a large family as it is hoped that the sons will all find employment and will be able to support their parents in comfort when they are older. But if the husband

13 The absence of migrant males tends to favour the persistence of joint family living since this allows some rationalisation of tasks among the women, although there are other considerations involved besides the question of labour (Sharma 1978, pp.297–8).

himself is absent for much of the time the double burden of agricultural and domestic work is liable to fall on his wife at precisely the period when she is also bearing children, and in such cases her load is a triple burden. Meeting one need (the need for cash) can create another (the need for labour).

The one area in which women can translate their income into decision-making power is in buying food for the household. In order for this to occur, it seems necessary that women have more than a negligible income as well as the ability to control this income. In half of the cases in which men do the food shopping themselves, they spend the minimum amount necessary for survival: 30 JD per month or less on food. Whether or not women also shop for food is, therefore, crucial to the family's nutritional status. The data show that in practically every case in which men do the shopping, women also report shopping for food, alone or with their children, spending most of their income on food. In fact, in 39 per cent of all households in the 52 per cent of households in which the wife earns more than 100 JD per year, the wife shares the breadwinner's responsibility with the husband.

Husbands are the sole breadwinners only when the wife does not earn an income or her income is minimal. It is therefore clear that women's contribution, whether implicit or explicit, is crucial.

Table 6.3 Who pays for food expenditure?

Wife's income per year JD	Husband		Husband + wife + children	
	Number	%	Number	%
Less than 100	15	100	4	27
100–200	11	73	7	78
201–300	2	22	5	50
301–400	5	50	4	50
401–500	4	50	8	73
501–1000	3	37	1	100
Total	40	55	29	39

Source: Village Survey, 1993.

6.6 Decision-making in agricultural production

However, the wife of a migrant labourer will have not only more work than a wife whose husband is at home, but also more responsibility. She will have to be prepared to make decisions regarding the management of the land and to carry the can if things go wrong. Most migrant workers do their best to be at home during critical periods of the agricultural year, especially the wheat harvest and the olive collection, but this is not always possible – for instance if the husband is in the army and is posted to a distant part of Shayfoun.

I had the impression that the nature of agricultural decision-making differed considerably according to the kind of farming unit concerned. While I was doing my field work, I made efforts to identify the processes of agricultural decision-making. Who, for instance, decides when to plant the wheat or the olives, and on the basis of what kind of information? How do people make judgements about what kind of crops to sow? I found that as far as many farmers in Shayfoun were concerned, these were the wrong kind of questions. Firstly, they did not see themselves as having much scope for choice as to what crops could be grown or where they could be marketed. In any agricultural/social/economic zone, there is a relatively limited inventory of crops that can be grown or have been grown – the permutation and combination of these crops depends on a number of factors, including the risk-bearing capacity of the cultivators. There were thus very limited possibilities open to them, due to the lack of agricultural development in this area and the lack of capital for investment; if there is no possibility of irrigation then you have little choice but to cultivate one of the few local varieties of drought-resistant wheat. Secondly, many farmers in Shayfoun seemed to perceive agricultural decision-making as more of a collective than a household matter. That is, if a farmer gets up in the morning and begins to plough a particular field, in reality it can only be because either he or someone else in the household has considered that this would be a good thing to do. But also farmers see themselves as being very much guided by a kind of local collective conscience. For instance, when I asked farmers how they judged whether it would be better to wait a little at the start of the season, I would receive replies such as, 'I started to sow because everybody else was sowing; it was the right time for sowing.'[14] This does not mean that the farmers did not make decisions on an individual or a household basis, only that they were not conscious of the decisions as individual ones. They tended to see themselves as managing their land according to a set traditional pattern, which left less scope for conscious choice and deliberation (Badran 1988).

This contrasts strongly with the rich farmers and slightly less strongly with the smaller cultivators, who saw their own practice in a very different light. Here there was a tendency to see decision-making as very much a household matter. Farmers would certainly discuss agricultural matters with each other; evenings in winter would often be spent sitting round a stove, talking over the progress of the wheat crop or the certain demand for types of vegetables. Conversation would usually revolve around farm management and there

14 The decision to sow at the beginning of the season is the most critical decision of the agricultural year. If the farmer sows and it turns out the seed germinates but soon shrivels from lack of water, or, on the other hand, if he delays too much, valuable growing time is lost.

would be a good deal of exchange of personal experience and opinions. But farmers saw their judgements as being based on information gathered from a variety of sources. These sources would include the views of one's neighbours, but also of commercial firms and their representatives, government agencies, radio or television programmes, and so on. It would be up to the individual farmer to collate this information, discuss it with the men and women of his family and come to a decision that would be right for his circumstances and for the type of farm he had.

The particular tasks done on farms by men and women have certain common patterns. In general, men undertake the heavy physical labour of land preparation and jobs which are specific to distant locations, such as livestock herding. From my field work, it was deduced that 26 per cent of the farmers' households did 100 per cent of the preparation of the soil. Women carry out the repetitious time-consuming tasks like weeding and those which are located close to home, such as care of the kitchen garden. The sample from Shayfoun showed that out of 46 households, 39 household kitchen gardens were taken care of by women. Marketing is often seen as a female task: 29 per cent of the females in Shayfoun were involved in selling eggs and milk to neighbouring houses.

We may note that this discussion does not necessarily exclude female members of the household, even when the women are minimally involved with the material aspects of agricultural production. The long deliberations which Abdullah (H17) engaged in with his family involved his wife, Aisha. She played an active part in discussions, as I can attest from personal observation. It is difficult to decide how much weight women's opinions carry in such consultations, but obviously we cannot assume that, because women are not seen in the fields, they have no control over what goes on in them.

The point which I am trying to make is not that rich farmers make decisions in a calculated and rational way while small farmers blindly follow tradition. It is rather that there are differences in the way in which they perceive their decision-making, and these differences are ones which are important for the purposes of this study. For if decision-making is not seen as resulting from interaction among individuals with different interests, opinions and information, but as a matter of intuitive sensitivity to prevailing conditions of climatic, sociological and ecological nature, then it is going to be all the harder to identify the specific role which women play in agricultural management. This point will be important in the next chapter, when I discuss changes in the part which women play in farm work and management.

Summarising the foregoing sections, we can say that it is not possible to predict precisely what degree of control over the organisation of work in the household any particular woman can hope to enjoy, but that there are certain factors which are very important. We can ask about a woman's position in the household. Are there other women to help her? Is she the senior woman? What is the composition of the household? What is the proportion of men to women, and are the men employed away from the village? What type of farming is practised? I now turn to the question of the extent to which women participate in control over household resources.

6.7 The disposal of agricultural produce and the control of income

Besides the wages of its members the other source of cash for rural households is the sale of agricultural produce. In Shayfoun, only the farmers with the largest holdings, that is, ten acres and above (and such holdings are very few), can ever hope to have a surplus worth marketing.

In Amman district, on the other hand, with more productive land and larger holdings, the capitalist landowner can expect to obtain a good part of his annual income from the sale of grain or other produce. Wheat and maize are sold either to government agents or to private dealers at, at least in theory, government-approved prices. Vegetables grown in the Ajlun area may be sold to dealers in the wholesale market in Ajlun itself, but some farmers prefer to take their vegetables to Amman city and trade with larger dealers (Badran 1989). In either case a good deal of the produce ends up in the central wholesale market in Amman. In Ajlun there is no such local wholesale outlet. A vicious circle operates, as there is little incentive for dealers to visit rural areas to buy up goods when the surplus product is so scanty and uncertain. But, there being no regular market for any small surplus they might have, farmers have no incentive to switch to the cash crops which could be grown in the area and tend to stick to staple grains for their domestic consumption. If they have a little extra wheat or maize such farmers usually sell it privately to neighbours or other local people. Small quantities of grain can also be sold direct to local shopkeepers. Much the same practice is found among some small farmers in Ajlun district. Where large amounts of produce are to be sold and a visit to the wholesale market is necessary, then the marketing of the produce is invariably in the hands of the men of the household. It would be considered inappropriate and unseemly for a woman to go on business to the vegetable market at Shayfoun, where she would be gazed upon by the male public in general (Badran 1989).

This does not mean that women do not have any control over the agricultural produce of the household at all. In the household the grain kept for domestic use is stored in large bins or baskets to which all members of the family have access. There is nothing to prevent any member of the household from removing grain, selling it or giving it in exchange for other goods,[15] though it is generally considered the senior woman's responsibility to monitor the domestic grain supply to judge how long it will last, and to control consumption if a shortage is likely. If the household produces eggs or milk in

15 Small shopkeepers will often accept grain in lieu of cash for goods sold, and sales between neighbours are also often made in this way.

excess of its needs then the sale of these will usually be managed by the senior woman of the household, and the cash earned will be kept by her. Such sales are usually made to close neighbours. So in my analysis of the Shayfoun rural women I can conclude that women have the initiative and power to display their work in the small market at the village and take the decision to sell the produce.

There was no household in the sample which did not have one or more sheep or goats. For some of the poorer households in the study area of Shayfoun, the sale of a young sheep or goat was an important means of raising money to meet some important but non-recurring need. In my field work examination of the livestock of Shayfoun village the following table illustrates the ownership of sheep and goats of the household.

Table 6.4 Average number of livestock in Shayfoun household

Size of household	No. of households	Owning sheep	Owning goats	Income per month	Expenditure per month
Large households	12	12	10	20	14
Middle households	18	15	8	15	11
Small households	10	10	6	11	9
Poor households	6	5	3	9	4

Source: Village Survey, 1993.

For instance, Hamida (H15) sold two sheep and three goats to pay for the installation of a hand pump in her courtyard. She hoped to raise the money for the marriage of her daughter by selling the cattle which she was rearing. Hamida's husband had been chronically ill and was likely to remain bedridden, so the family had little hope of being in a position to save cash to meet such demands. The sale of the young cattle was all that had stood between this family and the moneylender. Cattle may be sold at fairs held periodically in many country districts or by private treaty. In either case a good deal of travelling outside the village is needed and the transactions will therefore generally be dealt with by the men. It is women who actually tend the cattle and it is often a woman who has located a prospective purchaser for a goat or a sheep through her network of kin and contacts in other villages; but the cash accruing from the sale of the cattle is controlled by men.

6.8 The control of cash and household budgeting

From the foregoing it will be clear that while some women have a cash income of their own, the major portion of the household's cash income,

130

whether earned through the sale of produce or through employment, will be received in the first place by its male members. But who controls the spending of this income? What role do women play in the disposal of cash? Patterns of gender-specific expenditures are similar among the households in the survey, suggesting that the wealthier, more educated families do not exhibit consumption behaviour more consistent with the New Household Economic Model (Rosenzweig 1986). Table 6.5 illustrates that among rich households, as well as among middle and poor families, more than 80 per cent of the husbands were primarily responsible for expenditure on furniture.

Table 6.5 Husband's proportional contribution to furniture expenditure

Types of families	Number of households	%
Rich families	9	10.7
Middle families	70	83.3
Poor families	5	6.0

Source: Village Survey, 1993.

On the other hand, wives paid for their own and their children's personal items, such as clothing. Only 37 per cent reported that their husbands paid for more than half of their expenditures on children's clothing. An even smaller amount, 17 per cent, stated that their husbands paid for more than half of their expenditures on personal clothing. But 85 per cent of the women did report that their husband's clothing expenditures were primarily his own financial responsibility.

Table 6.6 Average family expenditure

Expenditure item	Number of households	%
Rent	5	2.1
Husband's clothing	32	13.3
Furniture	22	9.2
School fees	34	14.2
Children's clothing	46	62.0

Source: Village Survey, 1993.

Arrangements in this respect are very various. In households where the husband is in employment outside the village, he will usually send regular remittances to his wife to meet the household's day-to-day expenses. If his parents are alive and are living with the couple or nearby, he may send the money to his mother or his father instead of his wife. Where a wage-earning husband is living at home, there is more scope for him to maintain a close control over the budget himself. Ahmed, the policeman in Shayfoun (not included in the sample), gave his wife very little cash each month (not more than 15 JD) but did almost all the shopping, but Mahmoud (H12) would ask his wife what should be bought and she would give him the amount they estimated was necessary for these purchases. He made over his entire wage to his wife when he received it and asked her for cash if he wished to make personal purchases.

The following table summarises some of the common arrangements among the families in the sample. It is only a very crude summary since some of the categories could be broken down further. We cannot predict much about the relative financial power of women in category C, for instance, since much depends on whether the wife receives a large and regular income for her labour or a small sporadic one. The men of category B may be ceding a lot of financial control or a little to their wives, according to how great their incomes are in the first place.

Also, I cannot be sure that all that my informants told me about their household budgeting was true, this being a rather sensitive area of enquiry.

Table 6.7 Control of household budgets: summary of households in the sample

	Types of control	Numbers of households
A	Man gives fixed allowance to wife for household expenditure only	15
B	Man gives all monthly cash earnings to wife for most kinds of expenditure	4
C	Man and wife each keep respective earnings and share responsibility for budgeting	8
D	Man keeps all the cash and does all kinds of budgeting himself	0
E	There is no male member of household; the woman receives all cash and budgets for herself	1

Source: Village Survey, 1993.

However, taking this distribution as a crude guide, we can see that the most usual arrangement is that which is also most usual in Western industrial countries, that is, the man gives a more or less regular allowance to his wife for her to use for housekeeping expenses, keeping the rest back for his personal expenses and for saving.

However, traditional economic theory has suggested that a rational pooling of household resources leads to economies of scale and thereby to increased family consumption (see Lewis 1977; Oppong 1981). Economic autonomy permits a wife to invest in extended family relationships and social networks, thereby improving her bargaining position in her ongoing marital relationship. Such social relationships provide a measure of insurance in case of marital disruption. Economic independence also lessens the risk of asset loss under traditional inheritances, as I have mentioned and analysed earlier.

But where a woman has control over cash there are a number of factors which may inhibit her from exercising that control in a free and independent way. A number of the women from farming households feel embarrassed that exposing their illiteracy in public places such as banks is a detriment to their status. The sense of having trespassed on 'male' territory was quite real enough to deter them from visiting places such as the bank independently. The same feeling deters some women from independent shopping expeditions. The wives of big landowners in Shayfoun do not visit the *suq* at all; if they go shopping it will be to make some personal purchase in a large urban shopping centre such as Amman where they are not known to the shopkeepers. The everyday requirements of the household will be brought in by a servant or by male members of the household, albeit under instructions from the woman herself. So far as women of other social groups are concerned, much depends on the individual preference. Munira (H11) felt self-conscious about visiting the *suq*; she claimed that she seldom went shopping as she had never been to school and was afraid of being cheated or made to look foolish. The fear was probably unfounded – many non-educated village women are quite capable of making rapid and accurate calculations in spite of having had no formal education – but the feeling was real enough to her. In other families, the women would go to the *suq* to make purchases but would go about their business briskly, not making it the occasion for casual gossip as men might do. Muna (H4) said that she never visited the *suq* if she could help it as she did not think it was proper for women to be seen there. Her husband would fetch the important items and a child could be sent for minor errands. She was prepared, though, to visit her husband's shop and that of her husband's brother; they were, in a sense, family territory and, to her, less public than the other shops. Similarly Sara (H25) had no compunction about going to the *suq* to sit in her son's shop from time to time, but she would not be seen hanging about chatting in any other part of the market. Social norms do not explicitly forbid any but a few high-status women in Shayfoun from visiting shops to spend money as they think fit, but they do ensure that a shopping expedition will be experienced as a venture into territory which a woman does not feel to be her own.[16] Village women usually feel more confident about making shopping expeditions in the company of other members of the family or with other women whom they know. Alone, they often feel uncomfortable about moving freely from shop to shop in search of just the goods they want at precisely the price they wish to pay.

A third factor is one which has been identified in studies of women in Western societies, the sense that money given as a regular allowance by the husband from his wages is not truly 'one's own' to spend with complete freedom. The woman not only feels that she has been entrusted with responsibility for seeing that housekeeping needs are met, but also feels positively guilty at the idea of spending any small surplus left over after meeting these requirements on herself, unless such expense is approved by other members of the household (Sen 1990). This leads to an asymmetrical situation: while a man does not question his right to spend what he chooses on personal items, such as cigarettes or tea, a woman will feel such expenditure on herself to be an indulgence. Village women in Shayfoun are less likely to be ignorant of what their husbands earn than working-class women in the West; a man's salary is one of the more public aspects of his status and a rise in wages is an occasion for family celebrations. But however large a share of it she receives in the form of a monthly allowance, she will feel responsible to the rest of the household for the way in which she decides to spend it, in a manner that is different from the responsibility felt by men for that part of their wages which they withhold.[17]

6.9 Women's control over their own earnings

Lower-socioeconomic-class *hamula* women who earn money by doing agricultural labour, odd domestic jobs for other households, or by carpet-weaving, do not usually surrender their earnings to any other member of the household, but spend or save their cash as they think best. When I called to collect a small carpet I had commissioned to be made up by Halima (H24), her mother told me to give the money to Halima herself and did not seem curious about how much her daughter had charged me. Halima planned her spending without reference to any other member of the family as far as I could see, but her purchases were usually of a fairly essential nature and were as often made for another member of the household as for herself. She would, for instance, commission me to buy wool for her when I went to Amman so that she could knit sweaters for her brothers. She also bought her own clothes

---

16 It does not provide her with her main chance to meet and gossip with her neighbours as is the case in many Western communities, where a trip to shops, even if there is no item which is urgently needed, represents relief from the isolation of the home.

17 Hunt cites that however a couple may handle their money, it is usually more difficult for the woman to earmark part of their money for her own use. This is due to ideological and practical reasons (Hunt 1980, p.47).

out of her earnings. Her mother used most of the money which she earned as a labourer on general household expenses such as groceries and fuel. Certainly neither woman spent her money on personal indulgences. Women who earn money in this way often save privately, hiding the money against a 'rainy day' by storing it under the bedding. As one informant told me, 'Every woman likes to give her husband and her children a surprise when the family runs short of money. They will be impressed that she has been saving money all the while and they will praise her.'

A professional woman will retain control of her earnings herself if she is the one who has prime responsibility for household buying and domestic budgeting. The teacher at Shayfoun whose husband was employed elsewhere kept her salary to pay for the household expenses which she and her children incurred while they were staying at Shayfoun. Her salary was more than adequate to cover these expenses, so that her husband did not have to contribute anything to their day-to-day expenditure. The schoolteacher Meriam (H37) had always had full control of her own salary, as she had saved it for future expenses. But Hania (H29) gave a substantial part of her earnings to her mother, who used it to help with general household expenses.

The number of professional women which a study of small rural localities is likely to include will be too small to reveal any general patterns in the way in which such women dispose of their earnings, but it is likely that much will depend on the woman's position in the household. A junior woman may be expected to hand over a large part of her wages to her parents or parents-in-law. The literature on urban women, at least, suggests that this often happens.[18] The fact that a woman can command a responsible job where independent decision-making is required of her does not mean that her family regard her labour as other than a household resource whose fruits should be put at the disposal of the whole family. But a woman who is effectively head of the household, or at least its senior woman, is less likely to be expected to hand over her earnings to anyone.

If this is so, it is in contrast to the pattern in labouring families, where junior women are more likely to spend their money individually with minimum reference to other members of the household and without regular pooling of resources. The expenditures are summarised in Table 6.8. The women's budgets are clearly dominated by supplements to the family food supply in the form of meat, salt and oil, and household needs such as kerosene and soap. These account for 74 per cent of cash expenses.

But perhaps it is a mistake to look at household budgeting from the point of view of the relative independence which women enjoy *vis-à-vis* their husbands or other male members of the household. It might be more useful to

18 There are several cases in which professional women were expected to hand over their earnings to their parents-in-law or husbands, this often leading to great friction and dissatisfaction on the part of the wife.

Table 6.8 Women's average monthly cash expenses

Expenses	Amount (JD)	%
Food and minor household	33.41	74
Personal	7.18	16
Clothes (own and children)	4.33	10
Total	44.92	100

Source: Village Survey, 1993.

look at family styles of budgeting as they affect both men and women. For instance, it seemed to me that among the lower socioeconomic *hamulas* of labouring families I knew in Shayfoun, the individual earners, whether male or female, junior or senior, had greater autonomy in spending. Some money would certainly be reserved for collective expenditure and would be pooled, but individuals were less likely to have to consult others about minor purchases. But this is less a case of greater personal freedom than of there being less scope for any kind of decision-making by anyone, owing to the poverty of the families.

A second common pattern is found in many more prosperous farming households in Shayfoun, where the chief source of cash income is the wages of the senior man, especially where this chief wage-earner is a migrant labourer. In these households it makes more sense to ask questions about discretion and choice, since there will be more cash to spend or goods to dispose of. Here we find a style of budgeting where there is a far sharper definition of the financial responsibilities of men and women, and responsibility is less diffuse than in the poorer labouring families. Typically, the wife or senior woman will receive a monthly remittance from her husband or son. She will have almost complete control over this allowance, using it for all short-term domestic expenditure or non-recurrent items, for example, house construction and repairs.

A third pattern is found in the households of rich commercial farmers. Here also there is a demarcation of financial responsibility between men and women. The wife or senior woman is given a monthly allowance for house-keeping and the husband sees to saving and major expenses, as in poorer farmers' families. But here the area of control is much narrower. Firstly, the sum given to the wife will represent a smaller proportion of the entire income of the household. Secondly, her responsibility may be more restricted, limited to a rather specific set of expenses, mostly relating to fuel and food. A house-wife in this kind of household may well receive far more money than the wife of a migrant labourer or rural employee, but her sphere of discretion is far narrower when seen in relation to that of her husband.

These types are not exhaustive. For example, I have not dealt with budgeting in households where the control of finances is entirely or almost entirely in the hands of a senior woman. But it should be clear that if we want to assess women's part in the control of household resources this control has at least two separate dimensions: firstly, the absolute size of the household's income – does the family have enough money for the question of choice and decision-making to be important? And secondly, the demarcation of responsibilities for expenditure of different kinds – what is the range of a woman's responsibility relative to that of her husband or other members of the household?

6.10 Conclusion

The structure of the household economy is more elaborate than would appear at first glance. There is a complex pattern of collaboration between men and women in the household; all members of the group who are not infants are expected to contribute to the group in ways appropriate to their sex and age and capabilities. The contribution of women to this work is central; even in households where the women do no outdoor agricultural work, their domestic labour is essential. Men need women for the work they do in the household. I came to know of no household in either area where all the resident members were men, though there were a few all-female households.

Why, then, do we speak of women being dependent upon men, rather than of men being dependent on women? Firstly, however large a role individual women play in decisions about the household resources, land is still held by men for the most part, and men, therefore, have a source of power in the household to which few women can ever aspire. If men share control of land and household income with women – and, as we have seen, most of them do to some extent – this sharing takes place because the men have permitted it. Secondly, women continue to depend upon men to conduct transactions concerning the household in its relation to outside agencies, most importantly transactions which concern the household resources – marketing goods and registering land. Women are implicitly debarred from this kind of function by norms which restrict their mobility in public places and their contacts with unrelated men, and frequently by their lack of education relative to men. Furthermore, there is one agricultural operation which women are explicitly barred from performing – namely ploughing – and this renders every woman farmer dependent on her menfolk for carrying out this essential piece of work twice a year.

Men, of course, depend heavily on women to cater for their domestic needs – to cook, clean, wash clothes and care for their small children. These are tasks which few men would care to perform for themselves at home. But if a man's wife is sick or absent from home he is likely to be able to find a female 'substitute' to do the essential domestic work in her place from among female relations or neighbours. A woman whose husband is away will find it harder to manage without her man, though many are obliged to do so. Moreover, the decline in self-sufficiency of the household unit has actually increased the dependence of women upon their husbands and sons.

In this chapter I have analysed a number of factors: the position of women in the household economy and their roles in diversified economic activity; the inequalities of the status of women in rural employment; the sexual division of labour and how work teams are constituted; what kind of cooperation takes place between men and women in the household; and, finally, the life cycle and domestic cycle in which women can translate their income into decision-making and control of their income.

I will continue my analysis of the rural women of Shayfoun by elaborating on women's perceptions of agricultural and domestic work, in the following chapter.

7 Women's work: agricultural and domestic

7.1 Women in agricultural production: changes over time

To further my discussion on the thesis of the inequality of rural women and their role in production, in this chapter the analysis will be of women in agricultural production. Women's roles and status will be elaborated. The conclusion will be that the economic development in Shayfoun during the last fifteen years has worsened the relative position of women and led to more poverty and social problems.

The diverging experience of urban women in the early twentieth century had a parallel in the experiences of rural women. In the latter case, however, the differences were not class-based, but rather were dependent on the degree to which commercialisation of agriculture took place. Sources on the productive activities of rural women are even sketchier than for lower-class urban women. Even noted female observers like Gertrude Bell in the later nineteenth century, someone who lived in the Middle East for many years and spoke the language, left the impression that the countryside was curiously devoid of women. However, from a knowledge of the general patterns of change, it is possible at least to suggest some hypotheses about what happened to rural women during this period.

Rural areas of northern Jordan were basically similar to peasant societies in other parts of the Middle East and other parts of the world. The basic social unit was the peasant household, which was a unit both of production and of consumption, but this unit was still a part of a larger economic system. To bear out my thesis that the role of women in production does indeed explain much else about their social roles and the inequalities they experience as partners in the development process, the exact division of labour varied from village to village and perhaps within the village according to relative economic standing.

The first fifty years of this century brought major economic changes to Jordan, as commerce and production were affected more and more directly by the pressures generated by the forces of the global economic system. However, these changes can be more accurately described as an adaptation of the traditional commerce and production to changing global conditions rather than as a full integration into the world market. Through continued access to and control of traditional markets and sources of supply, the producers of Shayfoun were able to respond to changed conditions on their own terms and to retain a certain degree of autonomy from the major upheaval in its social structure.

It is a common observation that an increase in prosperity among farmers in Shayfoun goes together with a withdrawal of their menfolk from outdoor agricultural labour. The increased profits from irrigation, better technology or opportunities to buy more land are invested in status and leisure, and labourers are hired to do work which was formerly done by the women of farming households. In the community of Shayfoun a religious principle favours the tendency of women to be kept where their honour can be preserved, in their own homes.

Since the growth of modern technology and the implementation of mechanised agriculture, however, there is a third factor to be considered. Are women really withdrawn from agricultural work, or are they squeezed out of agriculture by the expansion of a technology which is controlled by and disseminated by men? Writers including Boserup have drawn attention to the fact that, with capitalist farming, the opportunities for women to participate in agriculture and to benefit by this participation have actually diminished in some parts of the developing world (Boserup 1970).

Given the 'subsistence ethic' of farmers, families whose women derive income as wage-labourers constantly strive to gain access to land. The pattern of wage-labourer in Shayfoun belies the assumption of a land consolidation–proletarianisation dichotomy and by extension the allegation of a transition to capitalism in Jordanian agriculture. The designation 'landless peasant' is seasonally highly variable for any given peasants. But besides differences in standards of living, as I analysed in Chapter 5, there is a notable contrast at the more fundamental level of production. In other words, there is a greater differentiation in the extent of the agriculture of the peasants. This is evident in the variation of their access to productive resources and of the related differential control of surplus products and accumulation of resources – that is, differential investment capacity, the extent of employment of wage-labourers, and differences in crop mixes and agricultural mechanisation.

For a small number of farmers from landless households work in the nearby factories was second best. Their preferred choice is to own and make a living off the land. This would raise their socioeconomic status, or at least the latter would not slip downwards within the scale of the traditional social hierarchy (Nazir 1991, p.146). As it is, work in the factory is seen to have an ambiguous status both by the incumbents in the factory and by the better-off peasantry in Shayfoun.

Let us examine the factors affecting the degree to which women participate in agriculture in Shayfoun.

From data collected during field work concerning women's participation as family labourers working on their fields, we find 100.71 females per 100 males in 1952 compared with only 34.04 females per 100 males in 1992. When it comes to participation as agricultural labourers, that is, paid workers on another person's land, the difference is just as great. There are 49.88 females per 100 male labourers in 1952 and 42.3 females per 100 male workers in 1992. The contrast is striking (Al Masry 1992, pp.30–32). This low rate of participation also invites us to enquire why the women in such an agricultural area should take so little part in farming? Adnan Badran, writing in 1989, notes that, in a village in central Jordan, women:

> Probably never worked in the fields in the way in which women of some other cultivating groups do. But the trend towards women not doing any work in the fields is recent. The change has occurred only during the last 20–30 years and is related to increase in education and urban influence (Badran 1989).

Many of my informants from the ranks of rich farmers, such as (H8) and (H10), made similar observations. Ahmed's brother's wife told me,

> I do not work in the fields. I only go sometimes to take my husband his food if he cannot come back to the house. My mother did more work than I have to do. That is because in the old days there was more poverty. People nowadays can afford to hire labourers, but people like us could not afford that when my mother was young.

Statements like this from young or middle-aged women would corroborate Badran's suggestion that if there has been a shift in the number of women working, it has taken place during the period since the Mandate. Yet in the late 1930s and 1940s Talal Asad noted the tendency in the changes of *hamula* structure over time. The historical evidence is that which I analysed in Chapter 3. (Asad 1975).

We might do worse than accept the general picture given to me by many informants in Shayfoun. I was told that there were some women who have never done such work. As traders and professionals, these groups were definitely part of the rural scene, but many had urban connections and until recently they had mostly rented their land out to tenants rather than cultivate it themselves. Among the landless labourer and tenant class, the women had always worked in the fields and there was no indication that they would change this practice as long as the opportunity remained.

141

It was only among the women in the intermediate groups that things had changed much, I was told by my informants among the larger owner-cultivators, who were largely though not exclusively from rich *hamulas*. The withdrawal of women in this class from outdoor agricultural labour has taken place over time and is probably not complete even today. There is certainly no reason to suppose it has been solely a product of a non-capitalist mode of production. It is certainly a product of rising living standards in this group, a rise which has been taking place over a long period and for a variety of reasons. Members of this class have invested money earned through military service in the purchase of land, or had been rewarded for their services during the Mandate with grants of land. Nowadays these families have prospered either through the application of modern technology on their farm and the rise in the value of agricultural produce, or through well-paid urban employment in the cities.

Even this general picture does not tell us whether there has been a real decline in the proportion of Shayfoun women engaged in agricultural work, because for all we know, the withdrawal of women which takes place in substantial peasant households may have been compensated for by the re-entry into agricultural production of women from groups which have been downwardly mobile.

Yet we can know with some certainty that there is not much likelihood that women will play a greater part in the near future. The increase in mechanised farming discourages the participation of women in two ways. Firstly, farming involves direct contact with dealers, commercial firms and government agencies – the whole world of public commerce and the market from which women of 'good family are effectively barred'.[19] In fact, men as well as women in capitalist farming families withdraw from most outdoor labour in the fields, if by that we mean the actual manual work of sowing, weeding, harvesting, and so on. But they continue to perform the supervisory and managerial work which it is difficult for women to do. Secondly, at the lower end of the social hierarchy, mechanisation displaces both men and women of the labouring tenant class, though probably more women than men, since any permanent farm servants who are hired will be men, and women are retained only for poorly paid seasonal work. This shows a degree of inequality.

In the area around Shayfoun, the situation is rather less complex, although there are fewer historical accounts available to help us judge the extent of change. It is clear that in the lower foothills the vast majority of women do all kinds of outdoor agricultural work apart from ploughing, and that in all probability they always have done.

19 Women are also debarred from this world by the nature of the education they receive. Girls are not sent to college to learn agriculture or commerce, so it is difficult for them to acquire the knowledge of management and modern technology which would be necessary for them to participate in capitalist agriculture on the same terms as men.

What about the past? Is this abstention on the part of some Shayfoun women a remnant of a once more rigorous observance of honour, or is it a movement towards a withdrawal from agriculture such as we have seen among some groups in Shayfoun? Aisha's husband, Mohamed (H13), gave the following account:

> In the old days, about fifty years ago, we Bani Hani *hamula* were military people. Our work was ruling and fighting. Even now, if you ask a Bani Hani boy what he wants to do he will tell you straight away that he wants to go into the army. Bani Hani were experts in fighting, the men went into the army and the women stayed at home. They kept their honour and did not work in the fields. All the work was done by tenants. In those days tenants were glad to get work. Now they do not want to work for us any more because they can get good wages mending the roads or working in towns. And so our wives have to do a lot of hard work.

In other parts of the hills in Shayfoun district there seems to be evidence that Bani Hani did once practise a stricter form of honour principle than they do now. The rules by which they maintained their claims to status included the injunction that women should be secluded, but nowadays no one observes this rule and it certainly seems to have been the norm to do some outdoor work.

The even greater reliance of households on earnings brought in by migrant male members, and the consequent absence of many men for most of the year, means that it is less likely that women will withdraw from agriculture in the near future. It is true that in some households where migrant men are earning a good wage in secure employment the family could, if they choose, employ others without becoming insolvent. But in such families it is only the substantial cash savings derived from employment which made tolerable the social cost and inconvenience of the men's absence.

7.2 Women, work and status

Obviously, if we wish to explain why some women work in agriculture and others do not, we must look at the traditions of particular *hamulas* and the local social ethos, as well as economic factors. *Hamula* groups have their own work ethics so far as both men's and women's labour is concerned. Although not all *hamula* ethics discriminate between men and women in respect of the acceptability of outdoor labour, because women are the repositories of family honour it is likely that the more rigorous prescriptions will nevertheless apply. Not all people can afford to live to the pattern which they feel is dignified and fitting for people of their *hamula*, but these traditions do affect the ways in which people evaluate themselves and others. The practice of a particular household is the result of the interaction between the economic position of that family and pressures to conform to a self-image which they feel is appropriate (Abu Lughod 1986).

While all groups regard land-owning as prestigious, agricultural labour even on one's own land brings no positive credit. In some ways it is seen as non-work, in much the same way that housework is regarded as non-work in Western societies. I remember how one woman, when asked what her husband's occupation was, replied, 'He does not do anything, he just stays at home.' It took further questioning to reveal that she had not meant to imply that he was idle, only that he cultivated his own fields and had no outside employment. When Shayfoun women take over the share of work which their husbands formerly did so that the men can go outside the village to work, they undertake a burden which brings them absolutely no additional credit or prestige. Not being paid, the agricultural work of the family labourer is no more 'proper' work than washing the dishes.

Attitudes are slightly different among the new rich farmers in Shayfoun, although we should remember that the agricultural work they do on their own farms does not include the more arduous forms of physical labour. This is done by hired labourers, and the landowner will usually confine himself to the operation of machinery, driving tractors and supervisory work. On the other hand, most women in rich farmers' households are not in a position to do outdoor agricultural work and at most play a minor role in management and supervision. Some of the women whom I knew might even have enjoyed a greater involvement in their husband's farms. Munira (H12), for instance, told me that if only it were acceptable for a woman of her status, she would have enjoyed starting a little market gardening concern of her own in the village where her husband held land. But for most women of the peasant and labouring groups agricultural work meant back-breaking toil in the sun, and they would find it hard to share the disapproval of the honour woman's lack of opportunity for healthy outdoor exercise. Nor would they be much moved by the feminists' concern that they are being pushed out of agricultural production. Few regard agricultural work as satisfying, and most would welcome the chance to earn money in non-agricultural work.

7.3 Women's perceptions of agricultural and domestic work

I found it interesting that even women who actually spent more hours in the fields than on housework still tended to identify their duty as women in terms of domestic work. A woman's business is to cook and clean the house and to look after the little children. Women usually claimed to like domestic work more than farm work. When asked which routine tasks they found most enjoyable, and which they found least enjoyable, most women expressed a preference for cooking. I am still not sure how much these answers reflected actual pleasure felt in doing the tasks or how much they reflected the social value assigned to them. A woman enjoys preparing and serving food as an experience of her family's dependence upon her in a very direct way; she is conscious that she controls a vital resource. And then there is the positive moral evaluation given to the preparation of food and the ritual purity of the cooking (Mernissi 1975).

Women regarded housework as more satisfying and more related to their feminine roles than agricultural work, but they did not regard it as entailing any particular skill other than the skills of economy. For the poor families there were not enough opportunities to vary the way in which the work is done. Even in wealthy families the possibilities are limited, for in rural areas one has to buy what is available locally, and there may not be much variety. Wealthy women in Shayfoun can afford to visit the capital and obtain household gadgets and consumer goods – refrigerators, stainless steel dishes and cutlery, and so forth. In this class there was the incipient idea that a woman might show individual taste and skill in the way in which she arranged her home and organised its daily routine.[20]

Another task which many women found interesting and rewarding was the care of cattle. In all households save those of a few rich farmers who employed servants for the purpose, the care of cattle was the woman's task. There were only seven households out of a total of 46 in my sample in which women were not involved in the feeding and milking of cattle. Women take this work very seriously and they derive real pleasure from it. But even apart from the utilitarian aspect of this work, here was an activity which clearly gave many women a real sense of achievement. This kind of work brings economic gains for the women in Shayfoun, for the milk produced is sold to neighbours in the village and the money received will cover some of the expenses of the house and the children.

Caring for young children is regarded as part of the housework and therefore the preserve of women. The proper training of children was seen as something for which the parents were certainly responsible, but not as some kind of specific task for which time had to be allocated and hence which might interfere with other activities in a busy routine. Most women considered that children learn through doing. You do not have to spend time teaching your daughter to make bread. She just picks it up from doing it. 'First she plays with the flour beside you in the kitchen, then she just picks it up from doing it.' Most women recalled their own experience in this way. They could not remember anyone actually taking time to explain how you do a particular task, or deliberately instructing them. Agricultural skills are passed on in much the same way, although on one or two occasions I did observe a father giving a teenage son lessons in ploughing.

Among some of the wealthy Shayfoun families one finds a different attitude. Here women are beginning to see the children's education as something which requires their active supervision, and possibly participation. Munira (H24) complained to me that the local village schools were very poor:

---

20 Such women give attention to making the home more comfortable and devote more time to personal hygiene and personal adornment.

The teachers just sit around and gossip all day and then set the children homework to cover what they have not been able to make them understand. That means that if the child is ever to learn anything, then parents have to go over it with him at night. I have to spend several hours on seeing that my children do their homework every day.

This was no exaggeration. She really did spend the latter part of every afternoon supervising her children's studies, and they were not allowed to go out to play until they had completed their work. Parents in this socioeconomic group felt that a child was not educated just through the fact of attending school. The quality of the schooling counted and they were sufficiently educated themselves to be critical of what their children receive. They also realised that though some of their sons would become farmers, others would probably seek urban employment and that therefore a high standard of educational achievement was important to them. Here we see the beginning of a tendency which is very obvious in urban middle-class families in Jordan. One of the most important duties of a wife is to supervise the children's education, to see that they do their homework, and to help them with it if necessary. Cooking and cleaning can be delegated, but education cannot. In this socioeconomic group a wife's education is not just a status symbol. It is vital in ensuring that the children of the marriage receive a good enough education themselves to maintain the family's prestige and socioeconomic group position.

The redivision of labour resulting from the seasonal adult labour shortage has also meant an increased burden for children, at low pay. This is particularly evident with regard to the cultivation of thyme. Children, and to a lesser extent women, predominate in the harvesting of this aromatic plant for a fraction of the pay received for picking olives. It is indeed a wonder that child labour power is committed by parents to the harvesting of thyme at lower wages. Data collected during field work indicated that 34 children (20 boys and 14 girls) out of a total of 79 children participated in this kind of work during 1993. Children and women engage in the harvesting of thyme on the land of their parents so that the latter will guarantee regular employment for family members during the slack agricultural season in the winter months. Additionally, it helps to repay loans and other favours extended by rich farmers to these workers' kinsmen. Evidently the 'comparative advantage' of thyme cultivation and the international marketing of the partially processed aromatic plant are closely associated with the 'comparative disadvantage of farmer women and children' (Arizpe and Aranda 1981).

The presence of small children in themselves is not seen as interfering with the mother's capacity to do agricultural work unless they are many and there is no other woman in the household to help her. A mother can take her children, even small babies, to the fields with her and let them sleep in the shade of a tree. Or she may leave them at home with her mother-in-law or sister-in-law, even with an older child. Much depends on the structure of the house-hold. Even the village teacher did not see any conflict between the demands of her children and the demands of her work, or none that amounted to more than occasional inconveniences. During the children's school term she adjusted her work to fit in with school hours. During the vacations she took children to her school if she was doing paperwork. If she had to visit some other village she would leave her daughters on their own. The elder child was nine and quite sensible enough, she said, to be left in charge of her younger sister. Hiba (H16), who was a schoolteacher, took her two elder children to school with her, although they were not yet of school age. I did not find any feeling that working mothers ought not to work because of the effect on the children, only that combining work and children made for certain practical inconveniences. The prime responsibility for supervising and caring for children is still the mother's, even if she does work outside the home. However, the increased inequality between sons and daughters is due to the educational differences between them. After the Mandate period the expansion of opportunities led to a sharp rise in educational inequality, as parents deliberately took their daughters out of school early so they might earn the money that would keep their brothers in school.

In my field work the following table illustrates the situation:

Table 7.1 Years of total education obtained by sons and daughters in different socioeconomic groups 1987–92

Socioeconomic group	Sons		Daughters	
	Years of education	%	Years of education	%
Temporary workers	6.0	8	4.2	11
Regular workers	9.6	7	6.9	7
Farmers	7.5	24	6.7	30
Shopkeepers	12.9	17	10.1	8
All groups	9.0	56	6.9	56

7.4 The relationship between agricultural and domestic work

It should be clear from what I analysed in this chapter and the preceding chapter that we cannot discuss women's work in isolation from the work which men do, although my focus has been on women's contribution to the household. Some changes in women's patterns of work are a result of general changes which also affect the kind of work available to men, as when mechanisation pushes women out of paid agricultural labour faster than it displaces men. Some changes come as a direct consequence of changes in male patterns of employment, as for instance when women take on more agricultural work to compensate for their husbands' absence as migrant labourers. Or it may be the other way about, that is, a change in women's work responsibilities affects men's workload in the same household, when men are obliged to take on agricultural work which women no longer do but for which they cannot afford to hire labourers. What is common to all these possible patterns of change is that the domestic component of women's workload is never transferred to men. The modern way of life, together with the modern value system, have made the men in Shayfoun far less dependent on their wives. They eat less frequently at home, and they send much of their clothing to the launderette because they claim their wives would ruin the clothes if they washed them. Since they spend relatively little time at home or in the neighbourhood, they see little reason to spend much of their income at home. Women cannot organise community pressure to make their husbands conform and pay more money. These women are powerless, and they feel it very strongly. There is no trend towards any greater involvement of men in housework and child care, although some wealthy women in Shayfoun are able to shed some of their domestic tasks either by hiring labourers or by investing in labour-saving gadgets of one kind or another.

One of the problems which confronts us when we consider the relationship between agricultural and domestic work in rural households is that in many families these tasks are not discrete spheres of activity, but part of a continuum of tasks. Cleaning a cattle shed and milking a sheep might be regarded as agricultural work since they contribute to the production of a basic food, milk. But these activities could just as well be seen as preliminaries to a domestic activity, the preparation of a meal. For the woman who does the work, the distinction is not very relevant. The work is all part of a round of activities which are done in the house or in the family's fields, all of which she does in her capacity as wife or daughter. Table 7.2 illustrates the major kinds of work done by women and the time spent doing the work.

Workplace and home are only distinct and separate places for those women who are in paid employment, whether in agriculture or some other kind of work. The conceptual separation of 'work' as both generating income-producing goods for sale and as servicing the family's own needs is emerging in the rich farming families, and here it coincides fairly consistently with the division of labour between men and women. Other families model their pattern of household activity very much on the practice of the rich farmers and on the sexual division of labour operating in such homes, so the distinction between housework and agricultural work needs to be registered even if no such distinction can be made empirically in the majority of households.

It is a distinction which is certainly made by women themselves in both areas. Women spoke about work in the house as distinct from work in the

Table 7.2 Average time spent in minutes in a typical Shayfoun household

Type of work	Male		Female		Children	
	Mins	%	Mins	%	Mins	%
Preparing breakfast	60	1	103	44	77	7
Working on farm	135	36	60	4	80	9
Fetching water	60	27	60	1	60	9
Taking goat to graze	64	34	60	2	67	8
Preparing lunch	69	7	129	41	94	7
Tidying the house / washing	60	1	128	43	96	5
Bathing / raising children	60	1	116	29	100	3
Preparing and serving dinner	60	4	90	44	70	6
Social visits	78	38	88	39	60	5
Other	0	0	0	0	0	0

Source: Village Survey, 1993

fields, and as we have seen, they generally evaluate the former as more dignified and rewarding. But this distinction is a crude one, and there are some
tasks which may be performed in or near the home and which are regarded as
part of a woman's domestic duties, but which contribute directly to agricultural production. When Ahmed (H14) hired women to sort and clean peas
and seed potatoes for planting, it was his wife Aisha who supervised the hired
women working in the courtyard, even though she claimed that she never did
agricultural work herself. Munira (H12) shelled her maize on her sitting-room
floor, and in almost all households women tended the cattle, even if they were
not responsible for actually going out to cut fodder. The social segregation of
men and women in rural society means that in some ways it is easier for a
woman to supervise other women, and a wealthy farmer's wife may do such
work regarding it as a natural extension of her duties as housewife. We also
have to take into account the contribution which women make to agricultural
decision-making which, contrary to what one might expect, does not necessarily diminish when women abstain from outdoor labour, as I discussed
previously.

In almost any household where the men are involved in cultivation, the
women will also contribute to agricultural production in some capacity, even
if the women themselves and indeed the men look on this contribution as part
of the housework. We therefore need to be cautious in our evaluation of statements about the women's participation in agriculture, such as I discussed and

analysed at the start of this chapter. We need to ask whether the withdrawal of women from farm work which is being described is not really the withdrawal of women from the more strenuous and publicly visible forms of outdoor labour, while the women continue to contribute to production in more discreet ways. If there is also a positive moral and social value given to women not doing outdoor agricultural work, it is likely that informants and interviewees will encourage researchers to underestimate the agricultural work which women do. If, in addition to this, there is a tendency for family agricultural labour of both sexes to be regarded as 'non-work', then even more of the agricultural work performed by women will be lost from observers' accounts.

7.5 Conclusion

To conclude the section on women and their agricultural roles and domestic tasks, I come to the point that, although I elaborated on the growth of rich farmers, there has been a simultaneous displacement of women in some socioeconomic groups from agricultural production.

The argument that economic development could worsen the relative position of women, proposed among other researchers too (Young 1993), reveals that the important component in the bargaining power of women is the perception of self-worth, which differs widely between family members, particularly between men and women, and which influences perceptions of advantage. This is based in part on the contribution that the various household members make to household well-being. In Shayfoun, two factors enter here: actual ability to earn income or bring valued resources into the household, and the value given to different members' contributions. As we have seen, since men often get privileged access to income-earning opportunities, women's contributions are generally underrated. Asymmetries develop and the relation falls out of equilibrium and balance into one of inequality. Until women's contributions are recognised and made visible, until women themselves have a sense of their social worth, their bargaining power in decision-making will remain weak.

To carry my analysis one step further on the inequalities women encounter in Shayfoun, I shall proceed to elaborate on some of the ideological and legal processes in their daily lives – in marriage and kinship – that put them into this position.

8 Women's economic and political position in marriage, kinship and female roles

To continue my analysis of the inequalities women face as partners in the development process in Shayfoun village, a very crucial aspect of their inequality is their social and political position in marriage, kinship and the female roles they play in the household. The aim of this chapter is to elaborate on the dowry women receive and the arranged marriages and divorce which they encounter. I will seek to show the inequalities perpetuated by the ideological and legal processes, and the importance of these in reinforcing the inequality persistent in Shayfoun.

It is now time to turn to women's roles in the system of kinship and marriage and to see whether a fresh look at this area of social life will tell us more about women's economic and political position.

The concept of kinship has tended to be treated in two divergent ways. At one level, kinship can be treated as a cognitive system, a way of ordering the symbolic world, a structure of norms and representations which can be considered as having its own logic. Kinship in this sense is an ideological definition of the relationship between the social and biological worlds and, as such, may for some purposes be treated more or less independently of the economic and political system in which it is embedded. But kinship in everyday life is also experienced as practical activity. Kinship roles specify the form and direction of cooperation, exchange, mutual aid and ritual obligations. The most rigorous obligations and the most concentrated forms of cooperation are those within the household itself, but this cooperation overflows the limits of the actual residential unit.

Those researchers whose interest in kinship has been of the first kind have noted the refraction of female roles. Mernissi (1975) notes the contradiction

151

between women's role as sexually active beings, whose sexuality is negatively valued and seen as threatening, and as mothers, whose fertility is positively valued but can only be realised through sexual activity. These contradictory values are juxtaposed, though not finally resolved.

Turning now to kinship as a system of concrete rights and obligations, the crucial distinction to be made here is that between women as affines, primarily wives but also daughters-in-law and sisters-in-law, and women as consanguines, as sisters and daughters. This categorisation extends beyond the immediate household to the women of the entire village, according to whether they were born there or married there. Appropriate behaviour is specified for either kind of relationship. Daughters are a category; one gives first and foremost to one's own daughter at the time of marriage but one also participates in giving to the daughters of close kin. Daughters-in-law are also a category. One expects very specific services from one's own son's wife, but respectful and submissive behaviour is expected from the daughter-in-law of any kinsman. Also, one does not only receive gifts from one's own daughter-in-law's family. One has a share in the gifts brought by the daughters-in-law of close kin, especially at marriage and other religious feasts (Sharma 1980).

This categorisation at the level of active social roles reproduces the refraction of female roles in the cognitive scheme, but only in an approximate and distorted way. The distinction between women considered as inactive in this sense, such as sisters, is present, but mothers do not constitute a category of persons comparable to daughters or daughters-in-law: one's mother's sister or one's own father's brother's wife can be 'like a mother' but they are not referred to as mothers. Mothers are only treated as a category when a person refers to his or her father's polygamy. One woman told me 'I have two mothers', meaning simply that her father had two wives, both of whom participated in her upbringing. In general, the relationship with the mother is considered too intense and specific to be generalised (Sharma 1980).

From the point of view of the women themselves, this refraction of female roles is reflected in the duality of parents' home and in-laws' home. A woman sees her social world as radically divided between those to whom she is related in consanguinity as sister and daughter and those to whom she is related through her husband as wife and daughter-in-law. For the village woman in Shayfoun who has not travelled much these categories may be virtually exhaustive; all the members of her social universe are subsumed under one or the other, given that all members of her village are like her own kin, as are all members of her in-laws also. It is only those women who have lived in more impersonal communities who have experience of close relationships with people who cannot be assimilated to either category, but who must be classed simply as neighbours or friends.

The division between affines and consanguines exists for men also. A man will identify his wife's natal village and the people to whom he is related, but the opposition between one's own village and that of one's spouse is not significant in the same way for men because they are not required to move from one to the other on marriage. Men's experience differs from that of women further in that men, being more mobile and more likely to leave their own villages in search of work, are more likely to know a large number of people who are not related to them in any way and cannot be subsumed to either category (Mernissi 1975).

Sisters and wives have different kinds of claims upon the resources of a household. A sister has the right to expect a decent dowry at the time of her marriage and has a right to maintenance until that time. After marriage she has no automatic right to maintenance from parents and brothers unless she is the eldest of the father's children. Yet if her marriage is unhappy or threatens to break up she may need to return home. Not being entitled to maintenance as of right, she must rely on the goodwill and kindness of her brothers or parents. I think that it is confusing to regard dowry as a form of *ante mortem* inheritance on the part of the female heirs, but it does make sense to the extent that the giving of dowry is regarded as terminating the father's responsibility to maintain the woman, a responsibility which is transferred to the husband. Here the inequality of their shares will cause social and economic repercussions that are inevitable.

8.1 Dowry and the role of women

A consideration of dowry is necessary here, because some writers (Boserup 1970) have seen the nature and direction of marriage payments as being related to the economic contribution of women to the household.[21] Dower money is an essential part of Islamic marriage, without which *mahr a nikah* (dowry for marriage) cannot be said to have been properly solemnised. Dower money must be paid or fixed before the solemnisation of a marriage and it is the exclusive preserve of the women or the bride to determine the amount. Also, *mahr* (dowry) belongs to the wife alone. Neither her father nor husband can claim it. She can spend it the way she likes. However, the *Quran* does not use the word *mahr*, but *saduqatun* or *ujurun*. *Saduqatun* is derived from *sadaqa* which means truthfulness, sincerity and a gift given as an act of virtue. It is not something intended to show off one's social or financial status.[22]

Thus it would be seen that, according to the Islamic concept, the bridegroom must pay to the bride some amount as a token of his love, truthfulness and sincerity. No doubt its origin lay in pre-Islamic and tribal custom and it was essentially a bride-price, but Islam elevated it from being merely a bride-price to being a token of love, truthfulness and sincerity. Another word used

21 Boserup suggests that in regions where women do most of the agricultural work it is the bridegroom who must pay bride wealth, but where women are less actively engaged in agriculture, marriage payments usually come from the bride's family.

22 See Al Munjid (Beirut 1956) under '*Sadaqa*'.

for dower in the *Quran* is *nahlah*. *Nahlah*, according to Ragib, is something given without any expectation in return. Similarly, *mahr* is what is given purely for love, not for any return. Thus the concept of *mahr* was greatly refined by the *Quran*.

The *Quran* repeatedly exhorts men to give *mahr* to the women they intend to marry. It says '. . . and give women their dowries as free gift. But if they of themselves be pleased to give you a portion thereof, consume it with enjoyment and pleasure.'[23] Thus the *mahr* should be a free gift. This verse makes it quite clear that it is the wife who fully owns the amount of *mahr* and it is for her to allow her husband to enjoy part of it if she agrees to remit it. Is there any specification for *mahr*? According to the *Quran*, it is the right of the bride to demand as much as she desires. It could be nominal or it could be quite substantial, if the woman insists on it. There is no limit to it. It could be, as the *Quran* says, even a heap of gold.[24] No ceiling could be fixed for *mahr*; when the second Caliph and a close companion of the Prophet tried to fix a ceiling on *mahr*, a woman stood up and recited this verse from the *Quran* 'And if you wish to have (one) wife in the place of another and you have given one of them a heap of gold, take nothing from it. Would you take it by slandering her and doing her manifest wrong?'[25] Omar, on hearing this, had to withdraw the proposed ceiling.

The husband thus cannot take back the dowry which he has given to his wife at the time of divorce. It can be taken back only if the wife wishes to have a type of divorce called *khula'*, which I will discuss at an appropriate place. If, however, divorce takes place before the consummation of the marriage, the husband need not pay the entire amount agreed to by way of *mahr* but only half of it. This ordains that even if no dowry has been agreed upon and divorce takes place before consummation, the husband must show consideration to his divorced wife and give her some gifts (Kandiyoti 1991). It gives maximum consideration to women and tries to safeguard their rights in every possible manner. Some *ulama* (Islamic doctors of sacred law and theology) even maintain that even if marriage has not been consummated and husband and wife spend some time together, the husband will still have to pay the full dower amount.

Imam Malik holds this view. According to Iman Abu Hanifa, even a moment spent together would necessitate full payment of the dower.[26] Even if a person is impotent but spends time with his wife he has to pay the full amount of the dower. Of course his impotence will become a ground for obtaining divorce, as we will see later in this chapter. Also, if *mahr* has not been fixed in advance, it can be done so in keeping with the bride's status or

23 The *Quran* (4.4).
24 The *Quran* (4.20).
25 *Ibid.*
26 *Fiqh al quran* (V.1, p.550).

in keeping with the *mahr* given to other women in her family. It is known as *mahr-i-mithl*, meaning an equivalent amount of *mahr*. Here too the underlying idea is that the woman should not suffer and should get her due. The *Quran* is so specific about *mahr* being an integral part of a marriage that no contract will be valid without *mahr* ultimately being paid, though it may not be mentioned at the time of the contract. That is why the *ulama* evolved the concept of *mahr-i-mithl* as mentioned. If no *mahr* has been fixed or mentioned at the time of the marriage *mahr-i-mithl* will have to be paid by the husband. Also, part of the *mahr* could be paid at the time of *nikah* (marriage) – known as *mahr-i-muajjal*, that is, the immediately paid portion of *mahr* – and part of it could be paid at a later date or at the time of divorce. This deferred portion of the *mahr* is usually fixed in advance, since generally at the time of the *nikah* both portions of the *mahr* are separately specified. It also acts as a security against divorce, although that is not its original intent. However, during recent years, with the dark clouds of inflation looming over the village, coupled with the anxiety which parents patently feel about the settlement of their daughters in marriage, there seems to be a situation where a surplus of women are actively competing to attract mates from a reduced supply of eligible men. Many of my informants were under the impression that was the case, and told me that dowry marriages had been few. The proportion of women to men had increased to 960 women per 1000 males in the population at the last census. The demographic imbalance had long favoured women in the marriage market. In some social groups in Shayfoun the position of women seeking husbands may have been better in past times due to the practice of female infanticide. Also in the past, some high-status groups regularly married their daughters to even more prestigious groups outside their immediate locality, thereby removing them from competition in the local scene.

As I have shown in Chapter 6, in most families women perform agricultural or domestic work which is essential to the running of the household, but this contribution on their part does not lessen their dependence on men. They depend upon their husbands for their participation in rights to land, since in the normal run of things they are restricted in the inheritance of land. Secondly, they depend on men to earn cash, since few women are in a position to obtain well-paid work outside the home and some kind of cash income is regarded as essential to run their daily expenses. Only the wholesale entry of women into the cash economy as sellers of produce or as wage-labourers equal to men would make much difference to their situation as dependents. So we could regard dowry as a form of inducement to the husband to accept the responsibility for the wife's maintenance. To the extent that men's opportunities for earning cash are still far ahead of those enjoyed by women, we would expect dowries to increase until such time as this gap narrows. If this theory is right, women's dowry rates will have little to do with women's participation in agricultural production as long as we are talking about their work as family labourers (Kandiyoti 1991).

All the same, we must not lose sight of the function of dowry as a status symbol, which complicates any attempt to treat it as a purely economic phenomenon. The dowry consists of three elements: household goods and equipment to be used, personal ornaments and clothes. These gifts indicate the bride's family's aspirations to generosity and good form. From the point of view of the bride her family's status must be asserted for her benefit, since she expects that if her parents are generous she herself will be well-treated in her husband's home. Dowry is a means to impress one's neighbours as well as one's in-laws, and it is unlikely to diminish in importance while this is the case. All restrictions upon spending at the time of marriage are very difficult to achieve, and it is not surprising that legislation to curb this kind of spending has proved impossible to enforce. The marriage of a daughter can bring few short-term benefits of a tangible kind, at least if the ban on receiving anything from a married daughter or her new family is strictly observed.

8.2 Arranging marriages: the role of women

In this section and the following one I shall consider the role of the women in Shayfoun in an important area of household decision-making, the arrangement of marriages. How much control do women have over the making and dissolution of marriages, both their own and those of other women in the family? How much freedom does a woman have to choose sexual partners? The inequalities in making decisions will prevail in the discussion.

Since marriage is contractual in Islam either side can validly lay down certain conditions. It is technically known as *khayar al-shart* (freedom to set conditions). However, the option to annul the marriage is not mentioned as a condition *per se* in the contract. That which is mentioned as a condition in this respect is a particular quality, such as the bride's virginity or the groom's possessing a university degree, in a manner that, if the said quality is found not to exist, the other partner shall have a right to annul the contract. There is a difference of opinion about the validity of a contract if its conditions are not fulfilled. The Maliki, the Shafi', the Imamiyyah and the Hanbali schools have said that 'The conditions are valid and if they are not satisfied the spouse laying down the conditions acquires the option of either breaking or annulling the contract.' However, *muta'a* marriage is a temporary contract of marriage and is valid only among the Shi'as, where the marriage becomes automatically annulled after a period of validity.

Mawdudi comments on this type of marriage as lasting for a period of time, say, a week or more; the man fulfils his desire and then releases the woman. It is called *muta'a* since he 'benefits' or 'enjoys' (*muta'a* literally means enjoyment) (Mawdudi 1975). It has no common acceptability in the Islamic world. It is only legitimised by the Shi'as. Just as Bertrand Russell's concept of temporary marriage did not find many takers in the Western world, acceptance of the *muta'a* marriage also remained quite limited in the Eastern world.

156

The five arranged marriages in the following table took place in high-status *hamulas* where the father of the bride developed an extensive network of acquaintances through his work. I was able to make use of the registers of Shayfoun's *mahkama* (court) to study the marriages that took place in the period between 1982 and 1992.

Table 8.1 Marriages of 30 women in Shayfoun: mode of arrangement

Arranged by female relative of the bride to one of her husband's kin	13
Arranged by female relative of the bride to an unrelated neighbour or associate of her husband	6
Arranged by unrelated neighbour to one of her own kinsmen or acquaintances	4
Arranged by an unrelated male friend or neighbour to one of his kinsmen or acquaintances	2
Arranged by a male relative to one of his neighbours or associates	5
Total	**30**

It is clear that it is the structural role of women in the kinship system that makes them important as intermediaries in the arrangement of marriages (Hijab 1988). But what does an individual woman get out of such activity? The satisfactions are not immediately obvious. The role of matchmaker is a very responsible one. As a rule, a girl's parents are obliged to marry her into a family which they know only by repute. Yet concern for their daughter's happiness and for the honour of their own family ensures that they will not marry her off to just any boy. There must be an equal basis of partnership. They depend heavily on the person who makes the introduction to provide reliable information about the boy and his prospects, the habits of his family and their standing in the community. The closer the relative who makes the introduction, the less likely he or she will be to try to pass the boy off as better than he really is or to give misleading information about a girl, resulting in a disappointed groom. Some women avoid the role of matchmaker, just because of the great trust and responsibility it involves. Samira (H23) told me, 'I have never arranged any marriages myself. If the marriage works, then you do not get any credit. But if the bride and groom are not pleased with each other, then you will certainly get the blame. It is not worth the trouble!' There is real fear on the part of the parents of eligible boys or girls that they will be

157

duped into making alliances for their children which turn out to be unsuitable. Every village has its horror stories about marriages where some vital fact about the boy or girl or their families was not revealed in time. Sara told me, 'There was a girl, the daughter of a teacher. She used to be a pupil of mine. When the wedding ceremony was completed, the bride's father started to demand that the groom's family should promise a TV set in addition to the dowry he should pay. If you are asking a TV today, tomorrow it will be a motor car. If I cannot get it then I'll beat you and soon you will marry another.' Shayfoun is a little place. Such things do happen (Morsy 1990).

In cases like this, it can hardly be imagined that the social credit of the person who arranged the match will be much enhanced. On the other hand, it is clear that such women derive great satisfaction from the business of making matches. Once a marriage has been arranged and proved successful, the person who made the introduction receives no special recognition. The role is not formalised or ritualised and there are no very definite rewards to tempt women who are not disposed by temperament or inclination to this kind of social entrepreneurship. But a man or woman who does undertake it may indulge in a virtuous glow at having discharged the duty incumbent on the relatives of any eligible young persons to see that they are married to the credit of the whole family (Morsy 1990).

Probably the role of women as matchmakers will decline as families become more mobile and men travel farther in search of employment. This has already happened in the more urbanised families, where the men's business and professional networks are an important source of new agreement. But the important role which women play at present is the consequence of their structural position as the connecting links between groups of related men. It is also congruent with their roles as 'servicers' of the relationships between their families and other families with which they have ties. This role is not obvious at first sight, since it is the men who conduct all formal transactions between one family and another and act as the household's public representatives. Superficially, women appear as more or less passive symbols of their families' wealth and honour. But it is primarily the responsibility of women to visit the families of relatives or neighbours at ritual events and on all important occasions, such as deaths or marriages. At an informal level, it is women who act as ambassadors for their house in the community. Muna accounted for women's dominant role in matchmaking by saying that 'It is only the women who have the time for these things!' Clearly she is correct to the extent that women of all classes are expected to make time for the kind of social activity which links their own family informally with others in the community.

8.3 Arranging marriages: the procedures of matchmaking

Once an introduction is made and the two sets of kin have been brought together by the matchmaker, the process of arranging the wedding takes its own course. The part which the matchmaker plays in what follows depends on his or her relationship to the parties involved. The formal negotiations for the marriage will be conducted by the menfolk of the households concerned, but a wide range of kin and friends, both male and female, will be consulted, and indeed will expect to be consulted.

As in the matter of family budgeting, the specific role which any individual plays in decisions about marriages is hard to identify because the dominant ideological conception of the way in which a wedding is arranged is that it is a collective process, in which the whole family participates. This means that it is hard to specify the power of women in this department of life. Another problem is that much negotiation takes place in terms which are implicit; in a delicate area of operation, tact requires the use of delicate codes, indirect suggestions and discreet proposals. Consultation often does not take place in an explicit manner, and nor do negotiations in their early stages. The negotiating parties do not usually know each other already, and a false step or a careless comment might jeopardise the honour of either (Mernissi 1975).

At the level of the explicit, it is generally stated that the young couple themselves will not be consulted; the whole rationale of arranged marriages is that the boy and girl are too immature to make the necessary judgements themselves. The bride certainly ought, ideally, to be innocent of what is going on, in conformity with the idea that an unmarried girl has a maidenly ignorance of matrimonial affairs and too much sexual modesty to take an interest in her own marriage before the event. Yet it is quite clear from some of my informants' accounts that not all girls get married without their preferences being taken into account. Huda (H14) told me that when she first came to Shayfoun as a bride she was not too happy:

> I told my mother not to marry me to a farmer. My parents live near Shayfoun, where my father was working at that time, and I like my village life. My parents wanted the marriage to be done quickly so that my younger sisters could be married. So I agreed and it was all done in a month or two. I did not like Shayfoun much at first, but I soon got used to it, and now I am pleased that I was married here.

Clearly in this case, a compromise between the girl's preferences and the needs of the family as a whole was worked out, so she must have had the opportunity to make her wishes known at some point, however indirectly. Traditionally, while it was permissible for the girl's family to see the groom, it was bad form for the groom's family to ask to see the bride. I think that the idea behind this was that it is humiliating for a girl's family to have to display her when the ideal for unmarried girls demands that they be completely sheltered from the public gaze, and the best kind of girl is the one who has no reputation at all because she has never done anything to attract anyone's attention. But naturally, every boy's mother will be interested in the manners and appearance of her future daughter-in-law. As one informant pointed out, there are informal ways of trying to find out something about the girl, by trying to get a glimpse of her in the *suq*, by deputing a trusted friend to do the same and report back, or through other modes of matrimonial espionage.

Among the richer Shayfoun families there is greater likelihood that there will be some kind of viewing of the bride, perhaps under the guise of a family visit. This kind of arrangement would be totally acceptable in any sophisticated family. In my field work six brides admitted that they viewed their grooms. The parents of a marriageable boy or girl must learn to 'read between the lines' in such visits. The interpretation of coded information given by others is taken into account. The matter of dowry is seldom discussed explicitly, for this would smack of a commercial transaction.

Yet obviously, the matching of the groom's family's expectations with the girl's family's capacity to give is crucial. In some wealthy Shayfoun families, specific demands may be made by the groom's parents. Similar findings have been found by other researchers (Afshar 1985; Kandiyoti 1991). For instance, there may be demands that some particular item be given with the dowry, but even these are seldom put in such a way that they can be discussed explicitly, for this would be to make a bargain of what is supposed to be a gift. One anecdote was told me – it may be apocryphal, but it is significant nonetheless – about what can happen when the cues are misread. A family of radically modern outlook arranged the marriage of their son with a girl of respectable family, but told the bride's people that they did not want to cause any unnecessary expenditure and would be sending only a very small wedding party. Feasting the groom's party is a major expense and a point of honour for the bride's family, and it is usually the bride's father who suffers.

It is interesting to note that in Shayfoun women from a low socioeconomic *hamula* can marry and move up the ladder into a rich *hamula*, whereas it is rarely the case for a man from a rich *hamula* to drop down by marrying a girl from a low socioeconomic *hamula*. The inequality of social classes is getting more explicit in Shayfoun. More women are moving up by marriage.

The range of kin who are explicitly consulted about a marriage will vary according to the family's circumstances. An ideal which was influential among low-status *hamulas* and most *hamulas* in Shayfoun was that the whole *hamula* should be involved. If the family do not consult them this means that they are effectively outside their own *hamula*. I think that it is unlikely that every single member of the local *hamula* will be canvassed individually, although the proposed marriage will be mooted generally so that anyone having an objection may raise it in time. This statement refers to the idea that the marriage takes place with the blessing in the *hamula* community, in conformity with its standards and customary practices. An informant in Shayfoun suggested that the involvement of the *hamula* at the time of the marriage ensures that they recognise it as valid, and when the bride goes to her husband's house all his community attend the feast to show that they accept the bride as one of themselves.

In wealthy and professional families, the parents will tend to restrict their consultations to those members of their local *hamula* and kin who are of a similar social standing to themselves. A great deal depends on the composition of the local *hamula* community. What appears to happen in most cases is for a narrower range of kin to be drawn into the negotiations, relatives whose opinion is thought to be particularly useful. Trusted friends and neighbours may also be involved (Morsy 1990).

Although there are no clear rules as to who is entitled to share in decision-making regarding a match, it is obvious that the role of the women of the family is all-important. This is openly acknowledged to be the case on the boy's side, for it is the women of the groom's household with whom the bride will have to cooperate after marriage in the daily routine of domestic or agricultural work. Yet all the explicit negotiations are carried out by men and occasionally by senior women, and the symbolism of the wedding ritual emphasises the transfer of the bride to her husband's family as a transaction between men. At the wedding, which involves the ritual meeting of the male kinsmen of the bride and groom, it is the bride's father who embraces the groom's father, and the bride's maternal uncle or brother who escorts her out of her parents' house. One has to look behind the public symbolism to perceive the vital part played by women in the politics of matchmaking.

8.4 Divorce and breakdown of marriages

In this part of my book on the inequality of women as partners in the development process I contribute to the field of women and development by analysing the concept of divorce and its social applications.

What control does a woman have over her relationship with her husband after marriage? Does the economic and moral dependence of women on their families preclude them from governing their own matrimonial affairs as adults? In particular, can a woman choose not to live with a husband with whom she cannot agree? In a society where the bonds of cooperation and dependence that tie a woman to her husband are so tight, we should not expect a high rate of marriage breakdown, so I was surprised to find as many as 11 cases of permanent breakdown for Shayfoun in the past five years (1987–1992) in the registers of the national court (Jordan's Court, Register 2, Vol 12, 1992).

Table 8.2 summarises information on these cases. Nine of them occurred in the 28 households included in my sample of marriage and divorce in Shayfoun, or concerned the marriages of close kin members of these households. There are no statistics for Shayfoun on marriage breakdown which would help us gain an idea of the proportion of all marriages which end in permanent separation; divorce figures will only tell us about those marriages which end in the divorce courts, and these are a minority of broken marriages.

The ideology of the adaptable and submissive wife makes it difficult for

Table 8.2 Summary of information on 11 cases of broken marriage in Shayfoun

Outcome of separation	Number
Wife lives with parents	5
Wife lives with brother	4
Wife settled in her independent home	2
Total	11

villagers to countenance marriage breakdown as a social fact rather than an individual misfortune. There is a positive correlation of the dependence of women upon men, especially among high-status groups. One woman told me with great pride that she would never take money with her in her handbag when she and her husband travelled together since this would look like a lack of trust in him. Samira (H31) had actually lived independently of any man for many years after she separated from her husband, but for a long time had maintained the polite fiction that she was supported by her brothers – a tactful gesture to the ideal of the dependent woman. The fact that dependence is a moral value as well as an economic reality makes it very difficult for a woman to acknowledge that she wishes to break away from a husband with whom is deeply unhappy (Mernissi 1975).

To balance this, there is a strong awareness that marriage is a relationship in which trouble can be expected, if not from the husband then from his family. This realistic acceptance of the possibility of conflict underlies the sister's desire to remain on good terms with her brothers. If problems should arise in her marriage, to whom else can she turn for moral or economic support? The brother–sister relationship is celebrated in a number of festivals and rituals in which sisters honour their brothers and wish for their good fortune and long life. A woman hopes and expects to remain in touch with her brothers after the death of their parents (Sharma 1980). The tacit assumption is that while the formal responsibility for the woman's maintenance and welfare is transferred to her husband at marriage, a residual moral responsibility remains, or at any rate can be cultivated by the woman if she is wise. Sisters are not in a position to repay their brothers in any way if the latter respond to this dependence upon their sentimental behaviour.

How do women manage to break away from the men on whom they depend for their bread and butter? It is practically impossible for a woman to leave her husband unless she has first secured the support of her own family for her cause. The procedure for a woman who was in difficulties in her husband's household was described to me as follows:

She must let her parents or brothers know of her condition and tell them her troubles. If they say, never mind, go back and try and put up with it – well, she must do as they say. But if they say that she has just cause for discontent and has been really ill-treated then they will not send her back, even if her father-in-law or husband came to fetch her. Then her father will take the matter to court. The court decides in the first instance that she should return to her husband and she must comply, for divorce is the most disgraceful event in the life of a village woman.

Most of the cases I studied did not follow this hypothetical pattern very closely. Generally it proved difficult to get the two families together, especially where the geographical distance between them was great. The preference for marrying daughters far afield has the consequence that it is hard to find intermediaries when marital disputes arise, for there will be few people who know the two families equally well and who are acceptable to both sides. But if they do not often resolve marital disputes, the elders in the village do stimulate the parties to work out solutions for themselves. Take the case of Ahmed's sister (H12). This woman had a slight physical deformity and, although her parents-in-law had not been troubled by this when the marriage was arranged, her husband had never taken to her. He alternately neglected her and ill-treated her, and when she returned to Shayfoun for the delivery of her first child she told her parents how unhappy she was. They decided that they would not send her back to her parents-in-laws' house again. Her husband took the matter to the elders of his own village, who arranged a meeting of all the parties concerned. On hearing the complaints presented by the girl's family, the elders agreed that the husband had been unnecessarily harsh and the elders' chairman promised to see to it that the girl was well treated if she went back.

After that Ahmed said, 'It was all right, because the husband had learnt his lesson.' Here the role of the elders seems to have been to administer a short sharp shock to the husband in a marriage dispute which might otherwise have dragged on longer, with mutual recriminations and family pride making it more and more difficult for either party to modify their position, until a court case was needed to resolve the dispute.

Even if a woman manages somehow to attain some kind of economic autonomy, her moral position is very uncertain. It is socially unequal with that of her husband. The honour of the family depends on her behaviour, but if she cuts herself off from them she has no honour of her own. If it is almost impossible for a woman to 'go it alone', it is also not particularly easy for her to set in motion the machinery of negotiation, reconciliation and compromise without the practical assistance of others. The position of a young woman, whether as daughter or daughter-in-law, is a weak one. She has little economic leverage and no recognised authority in the household. If other members of the husband's household are unwilling to help smooth over domestic disputes, then she must rely on her parents or brothers for help. The interesting question then becomes not why so few women manage to achieve independent lives for themselves, but why so many families nowadays are apparently prepared to take a married daughter back again. In view of this whole ideology, the emphasis on the total transfer of responsibility for the girl to her husband's family, and the financial sacrifices which the parents have undertaken in order to marry off the girl, one would not expect parents to take back a discontented bride gladly, for economic pressures are great these days and one extra mouth in the family adds to the burden.

Yet it seems that a young woman who finds life with her husband intolerable will not find it impossible to transfer her economic dependence back to her natal family, in spite of the ceremony with which the husband has been invested with responsibility for her welfare. It can be argued, of course, that even if very few women can become financially independent, a returning daughter's labour in the home is still an economic asset, especially if there is a shortage of adult women in the household. This is an explanation which has conventionally been put forward by anthropologists to explain the higher incidence of divorce among low socioeconomic classes; where a woman makes an important economic contribution to the household, it is argued, it will be easier for her to control her own matrimonial destiny (Ahmed 1976; Mernissi 1975).

I find this explanation inadequate for two reasons. Firstly, it seems to me that it has been assumed that, in areas like villages, broken marriages really are common only among the low socioeconomic classes. High socioeconomic people certainly accept the fact of broken marriage as if this was the case, and low socioeconomic people do seem to find divorce less shocking, but the only rural group among whom permanent separation actually seems very uncommon was the wealthy landowners in Shayfoun. It is possible that this is a modern situation and that formerly it was true that only low socioeconomic classes practised divorce. In practice, returning daughters are taken back not only among impoverished farmers' families, where their labour might be of most economic value, but also among the landless labourers as well as the rich farmers, where the value of their labour is less likely to exceed the cost of their maintenance.

Secondly, this explanation does not tell us why parents are apparently more willing to take daughters back now than they were a generation ago. Larger amounts of money than ever before are invested in the marriage of daughters, and yet the same woman is taken back when the marriage proves a failure.

But perhaps it is not so much a matter of parents being willing to take their married daughters back as of husbands being unwilling to pursue a departing wife to try and persuade her to return to him. It has always been normal for recently married daughters to visit their parents for long periods, and unhappily married women may stay on in default of any attempt on the part of the husband or in-laws to fetch them back. Looking at the matter from the point of view of the husband's family, there is much less urgency for them to

164

re-establish good relations between husband and wife, since it is so much easier for a man to find another wife. A man whose first wife has left him may be regarded as a rather poor prospect if he is known to have been cruel to her. But he will not find it impossible to get a second wife if he is well placed and his family are prosperous.

It would be interesting to know something of the laws made by Islamic countries on arbitration between husband and wife before a divorce takes place. In Egypt arbitration has been provided for in the Text of Egyptian Family Law 1920–1929. Article 25 states: 'Arbitration shall be undertaken by two persons eligible to act as witnesses under the Islamic Law of evidence, one each either from the families of the spouses or amongst persons knowing their circumstances, and possessing the ability to effect a reconciliation.' The law requires that 'the arbitrators shall be bound to make all enquiries into the causes of discord and to take all possible measures to effect a reconciliation'. The arbitrators are required to report their award to the court, who shall pronounce judgment on the basis of the award.[27]

The Ottoman Law of Family Rights 1917 makes provision for arbitration in its articles 130–131. This is, it must be noted, in accordance with the Maliki school of jurisprudence. If there is a dispute between husband and wife and either of them approaches the court, an arbitrator from both sides will be appointed. Outsiders can also be appointed if suitable persons from the husband's and wife's families are not available. This is known as a 'family council': it hears the parties' grievances, closely examines them and makes all possible efforts at a reconciliation. If reconciliation is not possible and the fault lies with the husband, he will be asked to divorce his wife; where the wife is found to be at fault she will be granted *khula'* (see below) in lieu of part or all of the dower. If the arbitrators cannot agree, then either other arbitrators from the respective families shall be appointed or help sought from an impartial umpire whose decision would be binding on both the parties.[28]

In Pakistan, under the Muslim Family Laws Ordinance 1961, an arbitration council has been provided for. The arbitration council is a body consisting of the Chairman and a representative of each of the parties to a matter dealt with within.[29] This ordinance provides that where any party fails to nominate a representative within the prescribed time, the body formed without such a representative shall be the arbitration council.

In Iran major changes were introduced in 1967 in the family protection laws. Amongst other decisions it was laid down that all family disputes could be referred by the courts to arbitrators for settlement. However, after the Islamic Fundamentalist revolution all previous laws and amendments were declared null and void, and it was laid down that only the Islamic laws in

27 See Tahir Mahmood, *Family Law Reform in the Muslim World* (Delhi,1972), pp.61–62.
28 *Ibid.*, p.46.
29 Tahir Mahmood, *Personal Laws in Islamic Countries* (Delhi, 1987), p.244.

accordance with the Ja'fari school would be recognised and that those who followed other schools of Islamic law like the Hanfi, Maliki, Shafi' and Hanbali would be judged accordingly.[30]

8.5 *Khula'* (woman's right to divorce)

I should now like to throw some light on a woman's right to divorce. Islam is probably the first religion in the world to have recognised such a right. It is called *khula'*, which literally means to disown or to repudiate, for a woman can repudiate her marriage. It has been referred to in the *Quran* in the following words: 'Then if you fear that they cannot keep within the limits of Allah, there is no blame on them for what she gives up to become free thereby.'[31]

Of course, there is a difference of opinion among the Jurists as to whether *khula'* is divorce or *faskh*, that is, simply annulment of marriage. Some feel that it is divorce inasmuch as the husband has to pronounce it after the wife returns the dower and remains at her family home. There is no need, according to this view, for the husband to pronounce divorce – the marriage is repudiated without pronouncement of divorce. That it is *faskh* and not divorce is also proved by the fact that one menstrual period only should be observed, whereas in divorce a woman is required to observe three menstrual periods. It is also said that it is divorce in words, though *faskh* in reality.[32]

A wife can initiate *khula'* and win judicial dissolution of her marriage on account of any physical defect in her husband, of ill-treatment and of legal cruelty. Cases (such as (H14)) asking for the charges of legal cruelty are numerous and vary from locality to locality, although uniform guidelines are found regarding this in legal manuals.

Another interesting matter that is dealt with is that of divorce by a sick person and a woman's right to inheritance. Here also Islamic law has been quite meticulous in defining and protecting the divorcee's rights. The four schools differ, though, on the rights of a woman who is divorced irrevocably by her sick husband who dies from the same sickness. The Hanbali allow her to inherit as long as she is in the waiting period (*'iddah*), provided the husband is considered as attempting to bar her from inheritance and the divorce takes place without her consent. In the absence of any of these two conditions she will not be entitled to inherit. The Hanbalis maintain that she will inherit from her husband as long as she does not remarry, even if her *'iddah* terminates. The Malikis are of the view that she will inherit from him even after remarriage. The Shafi' have given three different opinions, one of them being that she will not inherit even if he dies while she is observing *'iddah*. This is the

30 Tahir Mahmood, *Personal Laws in Islamic Countries* (Delhi, 1987), p.246.
31 *Ibid.*, pp.215–16.
32 See *Islam and Modern Age*, Vol XX, No. 4, November 1988, p. 265.

hardest provision against women.[33] It is to be noted that except for the Imamiyyah the other schools speak of a divorce by a sick person only if it is irrevocable. But the Imamiyyah observe that if a man divorces his wife while he is sick she will inherit from him, irrespective of the divorce being irrevocable or revocable, on the realisation of the following four conditions:

1   That the husband's death occurs within a year of the date of divorce. Thus if he dies a year after the divorce, even if only by an hour, she will not inherit from him.
2   That she does not remarry before his death. If she does and he dies within a year of the divorce, she will not inherit.
3   That he does not recover from the illness during which he divorced her. Thus if he recovers and then dies within a year, she will not be entitled to inherit.
4   That the divorce does not take place at her request.[34]

However, there is also something in favour of women: the delegated right of divorce, or *talaq-i-tafwid*. It protects their rights. In this form of divorce a man at the time of marriage can delegate his right to divorce to his wife, and she can exercise it when any of the conditions of the marital contract are violated; however, this would not deprive the husband of his own right to divorce his wife under certain circumstances.

There are differing opinions about the validity of a divorce granted under a state of intoxication. The Hanafis feel that even if one is intoxicated divorce should be valid. The Malikis ay divorce pronounced in this state is invalid. The Shafi' accept divorce under intoxification as valid. The Hanbalis disapprove of divorce under the influence of liquor especially when a man is so intoxicated that he cannot distinguish between good and bad. It is called *talaq-i-mukrah*.

There is one case where women can obtain divorce on grounds such as the disappearance of the husband (*mafkudal khabar*), non-payment of maintenance, imprisonment of the husband for a long term, impotency, and so on. This right is separate from her right to *khula'*, because in *khula'* it is her dislike of the husband which makes her repudiate the marriage, for which she has to return all or part of the *mahr* or any property. But if she asks for divorce on the above grounds, it will be divorce by the husband obtained by the court and she will not be obliged to return the *mahr*.

Clearly women's interests have been taken into account as far as possible in matters of divorce, even by the classical Jurists of Islam in the formulation of *sharia* (Islamic law) injunctions.

33 *Ibid.*, pp.265–85.
34 See *Qanun al Ahwal al Shaksiyah*, Section 88, p.392 (Syria 1982).

8.6 Widowhood

When a woman's husband dies, does she gain any greater control over her own life or any independence which she did not have before? In the area I studied one influential ideal is that widowhood should not alter a woman's relationship with her husband's family, although not all widows can manage or wish to observe it. The husband's family should, ideally, enjoy the same rights to the widow's services and loyalty as they did before, and if her husband has not already separated his share of the family land or property then she has the same right of maintenance from the family's resources as she did before his death.

The chief change should be her own behaviour and outlook, since she ought now to follow a discipline of chastity and asceticism. A widow is ritually inauspicious and she should not expect to enjoy the things of the flesh, only to devote herself to the service of her parents-in-law and children. This ideal is not too onerous for women widowed in later life. Elderly women are expected to lead a simple life. It is the turn of the younger generation to enjoy whatever fine food and good clothes the household can afford.

So far as a young widow is concerned, there are at least three different patterns of behaviour which prevail. In high socioeconomic families, a widow will not remarry. As one informant put it:

> When a woman's husband dies, she has a choice. She may stay with her husband's family or she may return to her parents. If she goes back to her parents they may find another husband. If she stays in her husband's home, though, people will think better of her and will admire her more.

Lower socioeconomic informants did point out, though, that it would be difficult for a young widow with small children to find a second husband and so not many widows would in fact remarry. In my field work only three cases of lower socioeconomic status had remarried after the death of their first husband.

In families where women are responsible for much of the agricultural work, widowhood in early or middle life hits a woman hard. Aisha (H26) had been widowed when her eldest child was about ten and when her husband had already separated his land and property from that of his brothers. She was now the head of a household, but without any other adult to share the domestic and agricultural work with her. Even now that the children were growing up, she found it hard to manage:

> A woman cannot plough her own land, so I always have to get someone else to do it for me, since my son can never get enough leave from his work as a labourer. That means that my crops are always going to be behind everyone else's. Without a man to help you in this kind of work you face difficulties all the time.

168

Aisha was justly proud of the fact that she had managed to feed and educate her children, but she did not regard her independence in decision-making as any kind of privilege.

8.7 Conclusion

No member of any household is regarded as making decisions as an autonomous individual, even though it is recognised that some have greater authority in the family than others, so it is always hard to isolate the influence of any one person or category of people. But the economic and moral dependence of women upon men means that women are in a particularly weak position to exercise control over their own marital affairs. They may participate in the arrangement and undoing of the marriages of others in the family once they are of adult status, but they can seldom act unilaterally on their own behalf. It is not surprising, then, that they tend to regard themselves as very much passive victims of fate. It is according to one's *kismet* (destiny) that one gets a good and considerate husband or a callous and greedy one, and according to God's will that one's husband lives to a ripe old age or is cut off in his youth. Fate provides a harsh, tyrannical mother-in-law or a kind and understanding one. Young girls tend to think of themselves as burdens on their parents even when they patently contribute a good deal to the household in terms of earnings and work, since their marriages usually exhaust their household's entire savings. This means that they are diffident about asserting their own wishes in any matter on which they are not directly consulted.

I have argued that the dowry tends to reinforce all those tendencies in the economic and normative structure of the household which underlie women's dependence on others. If there is any expansion in women's higher education and technical training in rural areas, whatever economic independence this may bring will be swallowed up by the moral dependence consequent upon the expansion of the dowry system.

Notwithstanding, the women in the villages I studied often showed great courage and determination in standing up for themselves in difficult circumstances. One has to respect the women for their resourcefulness and refusal to be defeated by hard work, public disapproval and moral isolation. They have found ways of balancing their own needs with those of others in the family in a moral environment which does not acknowledge either the need or the capacity for women to act independently.

This leads me to analyse and discuss the relationships of women with other women, their neighbours and kin. The position of a woman within the community of neighbours has important consequences for all the members of her household.

9 Women's relations with other women: neighbours and kin

This chapter seeks to elaborate on the subject matter of this book: women as unequal partners in the development process. The aim of the chapter is to analyse on the one hand the role of women in the socialisation of their society, and on the other hand their perception of their lives as being unsatisfying and full of daily tensions. I am going to elaborate on their relationships, both inside and outside the home. The chapter will conclude that through the dominant use of kinship, women's relationships are defined as belonging to the private sphere and to familial life.

The modern feminist movement has stimulated an interest in the relationships that women have with each other, both in Western societies and in others (Afshar 1985; Moser 1987a). If women have been regarded as characteristically lacking solidarity with members of their own sex, is this because of the influence of an essentially male view of women: women as male property, women as adjuncts to men, and women as repositories of male honour? Or does their subordinate position really leave no room for the flowering of sincere and satisfying relationships among women themselves? This follows my previous discussion on their role in economic life and carries it further into the sphere of their social life.

Women can hardly be more isolated from each other than are housewives in capitalist societies, it would appear (see Oakley 1974, p.8). However, in many non-capitalist or transitional societies, female roles and activities are highly segregated from those of men, and women cooperate with each other in various day-to-day or long-term activities. This does not necessarily lead to any kind of political solidarity among women in their separate female world. Yet Maher (1976) has frequently revealed that informal and hence usually unrecognised networks and relationships among women may have political and economic significance. So far as the Jordanian rural women are concerned, there are two quite conflicting views of women's subjective experience of their social roles and of their relations with each other. According to writers like Al Torki, a woman's role subjects her to many trying and painful situations – separation from her own parents at marriage, or conflict with the mother-in-law or other members of her husband's household. Yet Jordanian women do not experience doubt in themselves as women and few would 'trade places with anyone else', largely because they have been firmly socialised into these roles and learn to find satisfaction in them which increases with age and authority in the household (Al Torki 1986). Lila Abu Lughod, on the other hand, paints a picture of Arab women who find their roles unsatisfying and full of tensions. Women united in the same household cooperate under conditions which make it difficult for them to obtain genuine love and support from each other; even less likely are they to find warmth or understanding from their menfolk (Abu Lughod 1986).

As observers, it is when we try to make judgements about the quality of women's lives and relationships that we are most likely to be influenced by subjective factors. We will be affected by attitudes gained from our roles as women in our own society which we have taken with us to the field. We may also be influenced by the attitudes of the women with whom we form the closest relationships in the field. But this is an important area of research; the scope for satisfying relationships which female roles offer to women is one of the things which will decide their investment in these roles and determine whether they are likely to wish to defend or change these roles in the future. So I tackle this issue of the quality of women's lives, bearing in mind that the women I studied were as much divided among themselves by class as they ever were united by their sex.

9.1 Relationships among women

Relationships among women themselves are given little specific recognition in the Jordanian culture, and when they are, they are usually seen in terms of stereotyped cultural expectations. A girl's relationship with her mother is seen as one of intimacy and affection whose interruption at the time of marriage will be a source of grief for both. The relationship with the mother-in-law is seen as one of probable conflict. Shayfoun women often say that your own mother is your mother 'in righteousness', which is an idea contained in the very term 'mother-in-law'. What they are saying is something like what the anthropologist would express by saying that one's own mother is given by nature but one's relationship with one's mother-in-law is constructed by culture (see Tucker 1986 for a fuller discussion of kinship as a dialectic between the rules deriving from nature and the rules derived from culture). One must attempt to regard one's husband's mother in the same way as one regards one's own mother, but it is recognised that this is not always easy as it does not come naturally. Other relations between women are also stereotyped in terms of the contrast between the warmth and intimacy enjoyed with women of one's own class and the antagonism likely to develop among women from different classes. This shows in the inequality of relationships. An enumeration of the cultural expectations and roles prescribed for women's relationships with the various members of the household does not provide a full or reliable map of women's social experience. What such an account does provide is a guide to the structural strains in the household and local community which are the potential source of fission and conflict. They may or may not develop into actual quarrelling, and there may be other unrecognised sources of tension to which such accounts do not alert us. If we take the case of the relationship between a wife and her husband's sister, we see that the expectations of conflict and sour relations refers to a lack of community or interest between the two women. The wife expects her husband's economic and moral support, but the sister also cultivates her brother's continued interest and affection after marriage. Yet this potential conflict does not generally ripen into actual quarrelling. The husband's sister is destined to be married elsewhere and is not likely to spend many years under the same roof as her brother's wife. Provided that she is happily settled in her new home, her demands on her brother are not likely to be excessive. Most of the women I knew had cordial though not particularly intimate relationships with their husbands' sisters, and if there were serious tensions these lasted for only a short period.

After marriage, a woman's most significant relationships are with her mother-in-law and her husband's brothers' wives – a group of women who, if they do not actually share a house, will usually live close to each other and must co-operate in family activities. In terms of kinship vocabulary women married to a group of brothers are identified with each other. They may address each other as 'sisters', and they will call each other's relatives by terms appropriate to such relationships.

The complexity of relationships among sisters-in-law can be taken from the family of Ahmed Hassan (H26) and his brothers. The eldest brother, Ali (H16), was much richer than the others, and as well as the shop he kept in the village, he had a flourishing transport business. He and his wife lived in a house which the other sisters-in-law regarded as pretentious, being newly built in the flat-roofed plains style, rather than in the style of the traditional old houses. Ali's wife was much older than her sisters-in-law and kept rather aloof from them, even though all four were related to each other as consanguines. Leila complained that her sisters-in-law Muna and Suhad, who were her cousins but real sisters to each other, were in league with each other against her. At the time when the household had been partitioned they had, she said, combined to cheat her and her husband of some of the land they were entitled to. She agreed with them both, however, that Ali and Assad (the eldest brothers) had done the best out of the partition and were probably not entitled to their present prosperity. Leila felt sorry for Suhad, who had suffered from poverty and overwork since her husband died, and she sometimes helped her by making small loans from her housekeeping money, although this almost always led to quarrels when she asked for the money back. It was Leila who had arranged for Suhad to do some domestic work for me when I first arrived in Shayfoun. I think that she derived a curious double satisfaction from this; she could feel both a righteous satisfaction that she had really helped to alleviate Suhad's financial distress and a mean satisfaction in seeing her perform menial work for another woman. The four sisters-in-laws' houses were very close together and all had to cross each other's courtyards to reach their fields and cattle sheds. In Suhad's weakened condition this general lack of privacy and the constant intrusions of the other women's small children caused her temper to flare up frequently and violently.

But if this shows the complexity and frequent ambivalence of relations among sisters-in-law, how far are these relations independent of the pattern of relationships among their respective husbands? It is known that the partition of a joint household will usually be attributed to the inability of the womenfolk to get along together. Some feminists have been critical of a tendency to accept uncritically the accounts of male informants who exaggerate the extent of women's quarrels and project the tensions in their own relationships onto their wives (Kandiyoti 1991). Sometimes personal incompatibilities between women do make it impossible for them to live together and these tensions have nothing to do with the relations among the brothers to whom they are married. But in other cases, women's quarrels have everything to do with matters like the division of property, and in their hostilities to each other they may be expressing solidarity with the interests of their husbands. For their husbands it may be harder to express these conflicts openly; brothers do quarrel, but it is less acceptable for them to indulge in public slanging matches than it would be for their wives. We can see in the example of Leila's family that personal antipathies interact with tensions over property and differential economic status to produce a particular pattern of unequal relationships among the women.

It seems to me that women's quarrels are neither more nor less trivial than those which erupt from time to time among men. The difference is that they erupt more easily because of the small irritations involved in sharing kitchens and courtyards, and are also made up more quickly because one cannot afford to sulk too long if one is looking to other women for practical help. Therefore these quarrels may appear both to male villagers and to outsiders as less rational and more spontaneous than men's quarrels, which are almost always over property and often lead to litigation. However, I would disagree with the informants, who regard men's quarrels as less frequent but more serious. Women's quarrels occur more frequently not because they are more petty but because they have chronic causes which women are not in a position to resolve on their own. Mernissi (1975) notes that men seldom champion women's quarrels with each other. This seems to me an abdication on the part of men of their real power to help women solve genuine disputes, and so it is no wonder that women's conflicts are more persistent.

A woman's relationship with her own sisters is often one of supportive affection, but because it has no recognised structural significance it has been neglected in the accounts of family relationships (Moghadam 1990). Sisters are depicted in popular culture as parting sorrowfully at marriage, but my data show that sisters often continue to have important contacts with each other after marriage, circumstances permitting. Munira (H19) had a younger sister, Aisha (H20), married but as yet childless, of whom she was very fond. Aisha visited Munira in Shayfoun several times a year, always bringing some little gift for the children. Huda (H22) was on particularly good terms with a sister married to a government official in Amman, and she and her children had often spent their holidays in Amman. Among the poorer families, the visit of a sister is often a welcome relief from routine. Women would make a fuss of a neighbour's visiting sister, especially if she were newly married or particularly amusing or good-looking. She was a guest whose company they could enjoy without any of the potential tensions already described in the relations of women with their husband's kin.

Whereas in high socioeconomic families women's parents will not accept a daughter's hospitality for fear of violating the principle that one does not receive where one has given a daughter in marriage, there is no such prohibition on a woman receiving hospitality if a sister's husband is agreeable. As we have seen, a woman will often take the responsibility for arranging her younger sister's marriage, or the marriage of one of her sister's children. The relationship between sisters is not marked by the formal and ritual celebration which attends the relationship between brother and sister, but it may still be a source of important emotional and practical support.

9.2 Relationships outside the family

So far we have been discussing relationships between women who are related as kin or affines. Is there such a thing as friendship between village women who are not kin? Friendship is distinguished from kinship among both men and women, although there are separate terms for a man's male friend (*sahib*) and a woman's female friend (*sadika*). In practice, though, the concept of friendship among men is more distinctly recognised than the idea of friendship among women. The term *sadika* is not used much among rural women except to express the relationship among unmarried girls of the same village. Among men we find a fairly free use of the term *sahib* to express a relationship formed with, for example, an associate at work, or a classmate at school or college. One of the reasons for this difference is that men are more mobile. They are more likely to leave the village to study or work, and hence to meet and make friends with people totally unrelated to them. Even men who are normally resident in the village have greater freedom to move about in public, with the opportunity to form friendships with people outside the immediate circle of neighbours and kin. Women are less likely to form friendships not already subsumed under some other category, such as kin or neighbour (Sharma 1980).

Kinship terms are widely used outside the family by members of both sexes as a matter of etiquette, even with people whose relationship to the speaker is only slight. So where women are concerned it is difficult to identify a category of friends within the wide range of people who will be addressed as though they were kin. There are at least three modes of fictive kinship noted by anthropologists: a) village kinship; b) courtesy kinship; and c) ritual kinship (Abu Lughod 1986).

Village kinship is the extension of kin terms or, for married women, affinal terms to all members of the same village, even to people of different *hamulas*. The actual terms used often refer to a fictive genealogical plan of the relationships between families in the village (Badran 1989), which is modified somewhat with respect to the relative status of speakers. Thus a married woman will refer to senior men in her husband's village as though they were her husband's uncles or older brothers, and will behave towards them much as she would to her husband's real uncles and older brothers, that is, she will veil her face from them. In this sense almost all the women in a village will be fictive 'sisters' or 'sisters-in-law' to each others' daughters, aunts or daughters-in-law, even where no known relationship can be traced between their families.

Courtesy kinship is the extension of kinship terms as a matter of politeness to any person whom one meets in the course of everyday activities. In her own village a woman will use terms appropriate to the village kinship system. But elsewhere, for instanceif she goes to live in a town or if she lives in a village where neither she nor her husband is a native, a woman has a good deal of choice as to how she addresses other women. Abu Lughod notes a tendency to prefer an appellation which makes the women 'sisters', provided they are of the same generation, since the relationship between real sisters is regarded as warmer and more relaxed than that of sisters-in-law (Abu Lughod 1986, p.266). Abu Lughod has also noted that in towns the systems of fictive kinship which develop among close neighbours are 'oriented around women and the type of role women prefer'. This may lead to inconsistencies so far as relationships among the men and among the women's children are concerned, which are less evident in the more formalised systems of 'village kinship' but commoner in smaller settlements. In communities with a population of six thousand or more, the system of fictive genealogical connections cannot so easily be sustained. No one can keep track of the generations, no one will even know and hence be able to place all the other inhabitants, and there will be too many immigrant families to be incorporated easily. In Shayfoun, women such as Aisha Ali's mother would address the other Ali women in accordance with a system of village kinship, that is, she would refer to women married in Ali families as sisters-in-law if they were of her own generation. But so far as non-Ali women were concerned she would use any convenient terminology, usually that of sisterhood.

So far as I myself was concerned, there was enormous inconsistency in my relations with others. Some women in Shayfoun preferred to assimilate me as an affine. Thus Aisha preferred to call me 'daughter-in-law'. Huda openly referred to me as 'daughter-in-law'. To Munira's children I was 'brother's wife'. Few of the women used my personal name.

The third type of fictive kinship, ritual kinship, is deliberately adopted by two individuals who want their relationship to be recognised as having more to it than the ordinary extension of kinship terms as a matter of courtesy. There are various ways of contracting such a relationship: one such is to become ritual brother or sister. It involves much the same obligations as real kinship, that is, ritual sisters or brothers will be expected to make gifts on all occasions when real brothers or sisters make gifts, although the value of gifts need not be so great. Many close friendships among women really fall between the categories of courtesy kinship and ritual kinship. Two women who live close together will start out by calling each other 'sister' as a matter of etiquette, but as their friendship develops it approaches ritual sisterhood since each feels obliged to make appropriate gifts at weddings and other family celebrations, even though there is no formal enactment of the transition of their affections as there would be in ritual kinship. Ritual kinship itself is not undertaken lightly. Most people have difficulty enough discharging all their obligations to their real kin and will not formalise a friendship beyond a certain point unless they have no siblings or children of their own (Moghadam 1990).

Women who wish to express feelings of friendship have few idioms other than that of kinship available to them, but the vocabulary is rich in possibilities. The difference between the system I have outlined above is mainly one of focus. The village kinship system is focused on relations among men; it supposes real or fictitious kinship between all men born in the same village, and women's relationships are structured accordingly. The system of courtesy kinship among neighbours may be focused upon men or upon women, but more usually upon women since, as Abu Lughod points out, among a group of unrelated neighbours it is the women who are likely to interact more – their husbands will probably work in different occupations or at different places. The women, therefore, are more likely to set the pace for relationships between their families (Abu Lughod 1986, p.268). Ritual kinship is focused on the personal choice of individuals, although obviously other members of those individuals' families will be affected.

There are two points which we need to note about the structuring of friendships among local women. Firstly, the more urbanised or complex a community, the more choice individual women have about how they address each other – they can express the friendships which develop among them in the terms which they prefer. On the other hand, they are still constrained to express their relationships with each other primarily in terms of kinship. Men also use fictive kinship to express friendship or regard, but they have other options as well. Even men of the same village are more likely to use each others' personal names than are women. There are more titles, occupational terms and nicknames available to men which they can use to strike the particular note they desire in their dealings with one another (Krieger 1986).

It is possible to become quite intimate with a woman without learning her personal name. The names of senior women were particularly hard to discover since there is a general taboo on hailing any senior person by name. But even if he is not called by it, the name of any man who is head of a household will be known to all, for it will serve as a tag for the whole family, who will then be referred to as 'so-and-so's wife', 'so-and-so's daughter', and so on; very few women's names were used in this way, however influential or respected their owners.[35] The individuality of women is suppressed far more than the individuality of men so far as the local community is concerned. A woman's social personality is communicated through her position in the systems of kinship, real and fictive, rather than through her name. This being so, it is possible to see why friendship among women receives less recognition than friendship among men even though it undoubtedly exists. There is no room for the concept in the local vocabulary, since women are primarily wives, mothers, daughters-in-law, sisters-in-law, and so forth from the point of view of the local community – that is, they are adjuncts or dependents of men. If they form independent relationships among themselves, these must be assimilated to fictive kin relationships of some appropriate type.

9.3 Women as neighbours

Women do not control substantial resources in the household and are therefore not in a position to provide much in the way of financial support to a friend or neighbour in need – or not without the knowledge and consent of others in their households. Women do loan sums of money among themselves, but friendships among women are as often cemented by small acts of cooperation and mutual aid. In Shayfoun, Aisha used to call upon Huda every morning to see if there was anything she wanted from the *suq*. Huda observed a degree of seclusion while Aisha did not, so her aid in shopping was of real help to Huda. Latifa (H6) used to supply Aida with milk when her goat

35 Said points out that it is quite possible for high socioeconomic women to be ignorant of the names of lower socioeconomic neighbours whom they see frequently; here status distance reinforces the tendency to identify women by reference to their husbands or fathers (Said 1982, p.62).

produced excess milk. Friends and neighbours will be called upon for special help where there is a wedding or birth ceremony, or any other occasion when the family expect to entertain large numbers of people. When Hisa (H11) sponsored a party, she borrowed utensils from her neighbours to cook food for her many guests. She asked her neighbour Fatima to allow the guests to use their courtyard since there was not enough room in her own. When Muna's daughter bore a son, Muna relied heavily on her friends and neighbours to help her cook food and entertain her daughters-in-law when they came to see the new baby. Women friends, kin or neighbours characteristically cooperate in domestic and ritual matters. However, agricultural work tends to be organised very much on a household basis. Men do sometimes lend agricultural implements and a widow may be obliged to ask a male neighbour to plough for her, but families do not ordinarily exchange agricultural labour as a form of mutual help (Boserup 1970).

With so much informal cooperation at the level of the village or neighbourhood, there is hardly any need for formal associations among women, and where social workers have tried to set up special circles, they have met with varying success. The ladies' circle is conceived by the political authorities as a grass roots movement among women, organised in the first place by the social workers who are responsible for rural development programmes among women, but eventually run by women themselves. They are intended to provide a means of furthering schemes for growing vegetables, raising poultry and disseminating knowledge of better nutrition and family planning. I formed the impression that ladies' circles were successful where they provided some activity through which women could earn money, or at any rate save money in some tangible way. One ladies' circle not far from the *suq* flourished when the women started to produce their own carpets through a modest cooperative setup to buy in bulk items such as cloth and wool. In Shayfoun, the social worker had tried to get a ladies' circle started. She proposed that Sara (H5) should be the first president. Sara agreed, but did nothing for several months on the grounds that the recent death of her husband had made it difficult for her to undertake much social activity. The social worker visited her several times and made suggestions as to how she could get the group started. For instance, she could hold a sewing class, and I accompanied her when she went to visit some of the women who had initially expressed an interest. But Sara always gave some reason why the sewing class would have to wait until next month, and I could see that she was reluctant to make the first move. The social worker saw this as just another example of the suspicious and unreliable nature of uneducated village women. From the point of view of the women, however, I think there was more to their unwillingness than this.

Some of the women were critical of the social worker behind her back. 'She sits on a chair and tells us that we should grow vegetables and rear poultry; but she is a college-educated woman. When did she ever dig a field or clean a chicken house?' Or as Sara said, 'Who wants to know about chickens?' The social worker was not as out of touch with the village women's attitudes as these comments might indicate, but her brief was to organise something which the women themselves were not convinced that they wanted. They saw the networks of kinship and neighbourly cooperation which they already had at their disposal as adequate for their practical and social needs. As well as this there was, I think, a real dislike among women of taking any role of leadership or authority over other women beyond the roles already written into the kinship structure of the household. A middle-aged woman might be prepared to order the activities of her daughters or daughters-in-law, but she would shy away from any role of formal authority over her neighbours and status equals. When I asked Aisha why women did not like to join circles, she did not answer as I had thought she might in terms of women's dislike of being seen in public, or their shyness in taking public roles, but in terms of their relations with each other and their inequality:

> If I join a circle, then I might have to judge a dispute among my own neighbours. If I gave judgment against a woman, do you think that she would help me when I needed help? I would have to make an enemy of one woman or the other. No one likes to be in that position.

A position of overt power over one's neighbours is incompatible with the friendly and informal reciprocity which women like to feel they can expect from neighbours. In Shayfoun, the indication from women is that they do not regard the public arena of formal social roles as appropriate or useful for themselves.

Anyone who has observed a village wedding or feast will know that women have extremely effective modes of informal organisation. When Aisha Husain's (H26) nephew got married, all the relatives and neighbours gathered in her brother's house, and I travelled with her to find a hired village woman, a poor widow, to spend the whole day cooking for her guests. The women assembled at her house were not a group who normally cooperated with one another, coming as they did from different villages. But with the minimum of directives the work somehow got done; I found myself with a knife in my hand and a pile of cauliflowers to cut.

9.4 Conclusion

Through the dominant use of kinship terms, women's relationships among themselves are defined as belonging to the private sphere of the domestic and familial. Women seem to prefer the private modality of these roles and resist attempts to transform women's forms of cooperation or leadership into systems of public roles. This means that men can either ignore or pretend to ignore women's relationships among themselves and can afford to be dismissive of women's conflicts or alliances as being too trivial for their serious attention. Yet it is the local team of friends, neighbours and female kin who assist a woman, not without conflict at times, in fulfilling her obligations as a wife. It is they who provide domestic help at weddings and other rituals, and who stand in for her as cook and child-minder if she is ill, confined or obliged to be away from home. Therefore a woman's capacity to maintain good relations with the local women has important consequences for all the members of her household, even though they do not recognise it.

10 Conclusions, suggestions and recommendations

This book is about women as unequal partners in the development process. The aim of the book is to elaborate on the various issues and problems women in Shayfoun village encounter socially and economically within their daily lives. I have attempted to show and elaborate on women's inequality as partners in the development process in connection with closely related factors such as the organisation of property and patterns of marriage. However, I should step back and consider whether I have discussed and analysed women's inequalities in Shayfoun village itself.

10.1 Women and property

The main kind of property which I considered in my book was land, or rights in land. This is because it is a major issue over which men and women differ in terms of its ownership. Land rights are transmitted through a thoroughly male inheritance system. Familial values are not merely congruent with this male property system, they are actually given over to maintaining its maleness. Sons must be produced at all costs. In spite of a general rise in age at marriage in the last fifty years, marriage still takes place at a relatively early age in rural families (few of the women in the sample households were married at later than 20 years old). Couples therefore have many years in which to produce a male heir. Those who do not produce sons at first will go to great lengths, both psychological and medical, to ensure that sons are conceived. As is well known, sons are given more importance than is given to daughters; the birth of a son is marked with much more elaborate ceremony than that of a daughter, and women who cannot produce sons are regarded with pity. Any woman of child-bearing age who has not already borne sons will constantly be reminded by others that she has not yet done her duty by her husband and his family, and this pressure is kept up until she either produces a male heir or resigns herself to failure. A man who fails to produce sons by his first wife may by custom marry again. Adoption, usually of a brother's son, is another solution. In this way, inequality in favour of sons prevails.

In short, while female children remain legally the residual heirs of male property, as far as it is within their power people see to it that there are male heirs to inherit.

Another point in my examination of inequality, is that, for reasons which I have made clear, I do not think that it is useful to regard dowry as it is practised in Shayfoun as a form of inheritance (although this might be a useful way of analysing dowry in other societies), or if we do use dowry as a form of inheritance, it is as much on behalf of the son-in-law as on behalf of the daughter. Dowry gifts go with the daughter to the son-in-law or his parents rather than to the daughter herself. Also dowries consist of particular types of property, and the chief difference between the kinds of property transferred at marriage and those given to sons at a man's death is that the former does not usually include wealth-generating forms of property. As far as I know, land is never gifted as dowry. I would therefore disagree with Goody (1976) in regarding dowry as a means by which daughters inherit in societies. If we want to understand the system of property and inheritance which obtains in Shayfoun today, it is necessary to look at practice rather than at legal codes alone. The statutes which allow for equal participation in inheritance on the part of daughters are not a dead letter by any means, but they are appealed to only in certain circumstances – in cases of disputes among siblings or where land ceiling legislation makes it expedient for large estates to be broken up 'on paper' among male and female heirs. Ordinarily daughters waive the rights which the law gives them and would be considered selfish sisters if they did not do so.

In addition to inheritance practices we need to look at the pattern of effective control, since it is clear that many women who do inherit land or who have land registered in their names have only minimal control over the land they officially own. This happens because norms governing women's movements in public inhibit them from taking an active part in the management and administration of estates and in all the legal business attendant upon land-holding. Usually a man – the husband or the brother in most cases – will act on the woman's behalf.

So what we actually find is a system of inheritance only slightly modified by modern legislation, in which daughters are certainly preferred to a man's more distant collateral heirs, but in which they do not actually inherit very often. Everything in the system of property which I have described tends to establish the primary control of income-generating property in the hands of men and augments the inequality which women face. Women may have a good deal to say in the way in which land is registered and farmed, and they may also have effective control of other forms of property – domestic goods, furniture, clothing and jewellery – as they reach positions of seniority in the household. But they have little direct control over wealth-generating forms of property.

Even those forms of property which do not of themselves generate new wealth – household equipment, agricultural implements, and so on – are passed on from father to son, with daughters entering only in the absence of sons. For many men, this is the only kind of property which they are likely to inherit since their fathers have no land to leave them. But even among labourers, once the tiniest plot of land is acquired, the property rules which I have just outlined assert themselves.

Diverging devolution remains a possibility within this system only as a last resort, and therefore does not seem to me to be a very useful term with which to characterise the system as a whole. Now it is possible to see such practices as *sharaf*, women's public invisibility, and so on, not so much as an antidote to misalliance, though they certainly do perform this function, so much as a system of practices which reinforce the male control of productive resources. Specifically they protect this control against modern attempts to modify it through legislation in favour of women. The ideology of the 'good sister' ensures that women do not claim land which their brothers might inherit, and the ideology of the deferential and dependent wife ensures that a woman will find it difficult to control land registered in her name independently of the assistance of her husband or some other male relative. The norms governing female roles by no means exclude women from an active role in agricultural and other productive work, but they limit the ways in which women can actually use whatever economic power they may derive from their role in production, whether collectively in the community or as individuals in the household.

These ideological constraints sustain the 'maleness' of the property system in a very direct way. We are not strictly obliged to appeal to the need for women to marry status equals in a class society in order to explain *sharaf* and associated practices, when a more direct connection between property and gender roles can be traced. However, this does not mean that these less direct paths of causation are irrelevant for all purposes. Those writers who have seen *sharaf* e.g. in relation to social differentiation are not incorrect in their views, only in their tendency to stress the dimension of 'status' or 'prestige'. The surveillance of women and the restriction of their movements and autonomy, especially as they affect the possibility of women marrying outside their own group, have an important function in relation to the organisation of property if we consider that, even if daughters rarely gain direct control of their fathers' estates, a son-in-law may well gain access to the household's productive resources in the absence of sons.

The subordination of women within the household also plays an important role in respect of class, which is not diminished by the fact that some assertive and strong-minded women exercise far more control within the household than the ideologies of the submissive daughter-in-law and the deferential wife allow to be recognised. I noted earlier that in rural households at all socio-economic levels it is quite usual to find a number of different class interests represented through the diverse activities and sources of livelihood of their members. The solid structure of the household lends authority to members' interests and may well explain why divergent interests do not tear such house-holds apart.

Sharaf, then, has a double ideological function. It favours the considera-tion of property-owning groups and the emulation of these groups' values and culture by others. It also favours the concentration of the direct control of property. I have stressed the latter aspect in my book, but the former is not necessarily less important.

But why should property be concentrated in the hands of men and not of women? Why should the distinction between the sexes constitute the water-shed for the definition of economic rights and duties in the household? It is not possible to suggest more than a few rather crude answers to this question here.

Any system of property and inheritance organises both the relations of people with each other and the relationship between people and resources. A system of inheritance which limits transmission in any way also limits the fragmentation of estates which can occur when large numbers of children are produced. The integrity or relative integrity of estates in a class society ensures that some members of the property-owning group maintain its posi-tion from generation to generation. Those who do not inherit may be provided for in ways which do not threaten the integrity of the landed estate, as when consumer durables are gifted as dowry to insure the good marriages of non-inheriting daughters. Or non-inheriting children may not be provided for at all – all but the youngest, all but the eldest or all but the elected heir among a couple's children may be left to fend for themselves or assigned inferior posi-tions within the dominant class (Kandiyoti 1991).

In the case of Shayfoun it is the daughters who are 'exported' to become wives in different, and often distant, households; the farther away they are married, the less of a threat they represent to the income and property of the natal group. Some household income is diverted in the form of dowry and other presentations to ensure that they marry status equals or superiors and that, having been married, they stay married and do not return – although we have seen in Chapter 8 that this arrangement is likely to backfire and in-directly make marriage breakdown more likely for some groups when dowry gifts become too lavish.

Within the propertied classes, the exclusion of daughters and the partition of the land among sons maintains a constant balance between people and land, or at least it does so in periods of demographic stability. In the past fifty years the population in Jordan has increased enormously and the fragmentation of holdings among some farmers is a serious problem. In fertile areas, the profitability of modern agriculture and the presence of accessible markets for agricultural produce has meant that those who already have land are even more likely to resist measures which encourage the further fragmentation of estates. In Shayfoun, the area studied, men who already have land usually feel that they would like to have more of it, and those who have no land wish to become landowners rather than divert resources into other kinds of property. Under these circumstances we should not expect measures designed to divide holdings further by admitting daughters as heirs to find much favour in practice. Both men and women rationalise the unwillingness of daughters to exercise their new rights to inherit quite differently, in terms of the mutual duties of brothers and sisters, but other rhetorics are available and are occasionally used with the same effect.

The women's position in inheritance of land can be seen as one of the various possible ways of controlling the relationship between people and resources in an agrarian society, although it is far easier to show why a 'male' property system stays 'male' than why it is 'male' rather than 'female' in the first place.

Much more work needs to be done on the relationship between property organisation and female gender roles, especially practices like seclusion and honour. Whilst Goody's contrast between African and Eurasian systems remains useful (Goody 1976), comparisons within the Eurasian group need to be made if we want to understand why and how the experiences of women in these societies differ. On recently re-reading Campbell's material on Greek peasants I was struck by many similarities to my work, especially by his accounts of ideas of female honour and the status of brides (Campbell 1964).

On the other hand, it may be possible that there are systems in which women have been even more thoroughly excluded from the control of property: pre-revolutionary China comes to mind as a possible example. Also, as yet there has been no analytical comparison between different peasant cultures in respect of the relationship of women's roles to property organisation. The tendency on the part of many anthropologists to stress the cultural distinctiveness of Jordanian society, either explicitly or implicitly, has inhibited such constructive comparisons between Jordan and other peasant societies, but there are signs that in the field of gender relations at least this isolationism is beginning to break down.

10.2 Capitalism, the cash economy and women

In theory, the right to work in general is not explicitly accorded to anyone in spite of being enshrined in the United Nations Universal Declaration of Human Rights, although trade unionists have sometimes asserted that it should be. Yet clearly some workers in Western societies have a status which is superior to others in this respect. Some, for instance, enjoy greater security of tenure, even in periods of unemployment, and if they do lose their jobs they are offered more substantial redundancy payments or better retraining opportunities. The right to work is explicitly denied to some children, but there may be other groups for whom it is very limited or offered only conditionally. These may include blacks, immigrants, the elderly or disabled, and the largest group, women.

These groups often constitute a reserve army of labour which can be drawn into production during times of boom or emergency (such as wartime) and excluded or relegated to marginal positions in the economy in times of recession. The historically prior domestic orientation of women made it easier to exclude them or offer them only marginal and insecure forms of employment. Indeed the domestic orientation of women has been accentuated since the Industrial Revolution with the development of the full-time 'housewife' role and the ideology of home-based consumerism. Should we expect the progress of capitalist production in Jordan to have different results so far as women are concerned?

On the whole, there seems reason to suppose that it will not. Existing modes of agrarian production and property already emphasise women's role as dependents of men. In some senses, peasant and labouring women were already a kind of rural reserve force, being drawn into or excluded from agricultural production as the need arose – honour (women are disgraced if they work in the fields) or necessity (women have to work in the fields because no one can afford to hire other labour) being appealed to, as the case might be.

On the whole the male head of the household retains some control over the labour of its female members. As we have seen, a girl can only train for paid work if her father wishes it and is prepared to pay for her education, and it will be difficult for a wife to work after her marriage without the goodwill of her husband and his parents. Women who do take paid employment cannot always find suitable work in the same place as their husbands, and Jordanian courts are now being asked to determine whether a wife has an independent right to decide where she should work, and, if necessary, to maintain a separate establishment from that of her husband – independent, that is, of her husband's consent. On the whole there has been a tendency to deny that right as an automatic entitlement.

Male control of female labour power continues. Although this control must be attenuated when the women are entering the industrial and bureaucratic workforce, the latter advancement is not on the same terms as men and it is under conditions which encourage their continued subordination to men in the household. So things seem set fair for a reproduction of the Western pattern of female dependence upon male wages, albeit for somewhat different historical reasons.

However, this is only a very general truth and it is important not to lose sight of the different ways in which these broad trends affect particular areas. Obviously there are considerable differences in the ways in which capitalist production and the cash economy have affected the area studied here.

The farmer households whose men go to the cities to work can only achieve the standard of living they enjoy – which is not always very high – because they depend on the double sources of agricultural production and waged work. The land is an important source of security against old age or unemployment and will not be abandoned lightly, but there is increasing specialisation within the household; thus working on the land becomes the concern of the women, and earning wages becomes the business of men. This specialisation in agriculture does not bring women any particular rewards, however, other than more work, and it certainly does not bring them an income of their own or any other kind of wealth which they could use on their own account. It does mean that their daily lives are relatively unsupervised by men and they have somewhat more freedom of movement than most Shayfoun women, but these are not necessarily seen as valuable assets. As one migrant's wife complained, 'It is all very well for people like my husband. We women stay at home and do back-breaking work even if we are feeling ill or if we are pregnant. There is no sick leave for us. But we do not have any money of our own and when the men come home we have to cast our eyes down and bow our heads, that is, act submissively before them.'

I am not sure whether it would be better to end with a call for the provision of more opportunities for rural women to gain access to independent sources of income, or with a rallying call to the defence of my original thesis that women's inequalities in the development process affect their role in production, and indeed explain much else about their social roles that has previously been explained in purely functionalist terms or in terms of the distinctive cultural features of the area.

I am aware that I have certainly over-simplified some local and class differences in order to accommodate the wide range of data which I was able to gather. I only hope that in doing this I have not done too much violence to the complexity of the social structure which I have studied.

But I have satisfied myself that the kinds of concerns which feminist researchers have demonstrated in studies of rural and urban societies are as valid in South Asia as anywhere else. Women's role in production does provide a useful starting point for an analysis of their general position, provided always that we interpret this phrase 'role in production' in a structural sense and not just as meaning the amount of work which women do, and provided that women's role in reproduction is considered also.

So far as the question of providing economic opportunities for women is concerned, the problem is a difficult one. I think that it is one which will only be tackled properly when rural women demand it themselves. A little well-meaning intervention from rural development experts, a few schemes to stimulate local crafts among village women – these are not going to change the structure of production, although they will undoubtedly be worthwhile for the women who benefit from them directly. Most of the women I knew did not experience their position as women as being oppressive, though they might express a sense of impotence as landless labourers, of insecurity as overworked peasants on tiny holdings, or of frustration as housewives making do on a husband's low salary in the face of rapid inflation. The female life cycle holds promise of greater power and prestige in the household with age; a woman knows that as she gets older and her sons bring brides into the household, her position there will be more privileged. Therefore, she is likely to accept the constraints and disabilities imposed on a young wife. The segregation of women means that they are less likely to compare themselves with men, but are more likely to see their prestige and standing as deriving from that of their menfolk. Also, the ethic of the female as the repository of family labour does not conflict with an ideology of individual achievement and self-fulfilment as it does in the West. Women tend to see their position as dependents as problematic only when the machinery of dependence breaks down – when the husband fails to provide, when he is sick or dies and the wife is left with no provider.

Women in Shayfoun certainly see themselves as divided by enormous differences: from my point of view it felt very different to be living among Shayfoun women after six months spent in Amman. Urban women 'come across' as more open and assertive in their personal manners than Shayfoun women, yet they also appear more housebound and more restricted in their movements and public activities. The contrast between the restrained public demeanour of Amman women and their spontaneity in the private company of other women is striking. Shayfoun women seemed to me more reserved at all times though less obliged to refer their behaviour and movements to men – if only because so many of their men folk were absent from the village for so much of the time.

Yet I concluded that while these differences were experienced as very important, when it came to analysis they were less significant than they seemed. The similarities in the underlying structure of the female situation turned out to be much greater than I had expected. In reality the chances for economic independence and the control over their own activities which this might bring are as limited for Shayfoun women as for urban women, even though the former are more actively involved in agricultural production. I found, for instance, that it was not automatically the case that women who perform such agricultural work have any greater say in agricultural decision-making than women who perform little agricultural work or none at all. Or if they do have a greater say, it is as likely to be due to the negative fact of their husbands' absence as migrant labourers as to the positive fact of their own productive activity. In other areas of social life, women's capacity to influence decisions and exert control was just as likely to depend on factors un-

related to the kind or amount of productive work which they do. One particular sphere which I examined in some detail (Chapter 8) was that of matchmaking; here the power which women wielded and their importance in
determining household policy depended on factors other than their capacity
to work or generate income. Their control in this field had much more to do
with their structural position as links between households in a system which
favours marriage among the *hamula*. If some women from low socioeconomic *hamulas* and some of the poorer higher *hamula* women seem to
have greater freedom to leave their husbands, this is not primarily because
they are economically more independent of men than other women. It is probably more closely related to factors such as the organisation of property and
patterns of marriage, especially the dowry (*mahr*) system with its associated
ideology. In theory we might certainly expect to find that women who work
for wages, and even women who work as family labourers, have a greater say
in household matters than women who perform domestic work only, and this
is an assumption that has often been made by anthropologists and others. But
the female labourer usually earns wages which are too small and sporadic to
lend her any special leverage in household politics, and the work of female
family labourers does not give women any particular control over the products of their labour.

As we have seen, there are variations in the internal structure of the household and its political machinery which are related to the kind of work which
its members do and especially to the sexual division of labour. But these are
not as conspicuous as the broad similarities in role patterns and the organisation of authority. A wife is a wife, in whatever kind of work she spends her
time, and a daughter-in-law a daughter-in-law. The subordination of female
to male and junior to senior pervades family life in the Shayfoun area and in
all classes, whatever modification we find in particular groups. I have not
dealt with women's participation in collective political processes in the
village, largely because it was difficult to make any worthwhile observations
in the short time available in Shayfoun. But here also, what I was able to
observe confirms the impression that there was much overall likeness at the
village level. Women's participation in community affairs is severely limited
by general standards of female behaviour in public which stress women's
invisibility and passivity and which circumscribe their movements, especially
their contacts with men. Their political effectiveness, whatever their role in
production, depends on their domestic power and their contacts with other
women; the direct routes to political influence are blocked, and for the most
part they have to exploit the opportunities offered by their situation within the
household.

This book considered, as a determinant of women's social power, their
participation in agricultural work, but this is only one variable among many.
It cannot on its own explain differences in marriage practices, dowry payments
and divorce arrangements, as has often been assumed by researchers.

There is a fund of common norms and images which all the women I studied recognised as bearing on their lives, a wrap of common values regarding women's special role which underlies all the differences due to class and regional culture. There are general similarities in the rules which govern women's public mobility, the organisation of marriage, kinship terminology and the domestic role system. There is likely to be even greater cultural convergence in future as the geographical isolation of some areas is broken down by modern communications.

So do we simply have a case of 'Ideology Rules OK'? Perhaps the traditional functionalist approaches which I criticised in the first chapter are valid after all. After all, why trouble to scrutinise the precise tasks which women perform to ascertain the exact degree of their control over production processes if we can explain everything that is important about female roles by appealing to the force of ideals of proper female conduct, which do not vary much for women of different groups?

I hope it will be clear that I do not think that this is the way out. If there is any explanatory key to women's position in Shayfoun it is more likely to be women's submission to men. Women depend on men because men may own land and hold tenancies and women on the whole cannot. The etiquette of public invisibility, the avoidance of male affines, the subordination of women within the household, the tendency to educate women to lower standards than men – all these practices elaborate secondary sources of dependence upon men – moral, practical and ritual – which feed and reinforce their primary economic dependence. Variations in the pressure and force of these practices can now be seen as responses to differences in the economic sources of women's dependence upon men, rather than as 'just' regional and cultural differences. The ideology of dependence is required by the material structure of production.

What, then, would development planning with female involvement look like? Here we can only sketch in a few of the necessary elements. First and foremost women would be integrated into the planning process from the beginning. They would not merely be consulted at an advanced stage of planning, when changes are virtually impossible to incorporate, to ensure their needs were being properly considered. Rather, women of different ages, social status and involvement in diverse economic activities would be able to articulate the diversity, and the similarity, of their interests and needs and these would form the central part of the considerations upon which planning would be based.

Secondly, given this, it would be self-evident that women as farmers, traders, food processors and so on need the same access to land, credit, training and inputs as other farmers, traders, and the like. They also need to be given the same incentives to produce more efficiently and effectively. Looking at production from a woman's point of view would result in much more attention being paid to ensuring the long-term viability of forms of production, the provision of more adequate storage to minimise in-field and on-farm crop wastage, and of more sensible distribution facilities to ensure local as well as national markets are supplied. Rather than looking to the quick-fix technical solution, planning with women would look to using the resources to hand in a more thorough and effective way, to work with the land and with nature and not merely to control them. Priority would be given to the rehabilitation of soils, the care and regeneration of woods and forests, and the better care management of water resources. Planning for production of a much wider range of crops so as to lessen the risk of climatic variation would require greater resources being spent on research into those crops which are widely eaten but not internationally tradeable – wheat, maize, olives or grapes are amongst some of the more obvious – as well as those forest or wild crops which are not nationally traded but widely consumed locally. More intensive research into traditional methods of intercropping, rotation, soil fertility and pest control would be married to modern organic farming knowledge. Intensive study would also be required on forms of draught power which would lessen a farmer's burden of work but which could also be used for water and wood haulage.

Thirdly, planning with women would look at the totality of what both men and women do in rural households, and look to see where men could be given better training or extension to support their roles as fathers, and where domestic technology is needed to lessen the burden of domestic chores for women and their daughters by a variety of tasks being taken on by men and their sons. The problem of most planning models, and even of some of the current rhetoric about including women in agricultural development planning, is the failure to predict conflict between the genders.

For development planning to be able to respond to the needs of rural women, a closer examination is needed of the social and economic relations between men and women, between men, and between women themselves. The different forms of household organisation and divisions of labour need to be understood in more detail, as do the division of and control over resources such as land and its products. But the ability to resolve such conflict must lie not in strengthening the resource base of the already stronger party, but rather in reducing the inequalities, to allow both to negotiate an acceptable solution.

Research methods, and approaches such as farming system research, would need a radical reorientation of focus which will take social relations within the household as much as beyond it into account, and look at how these are affected by gender and age. The variety of household forms and composition needs recognition, as does the different level of access of men and women to markets and inputs. Concepts such as household, production, reproduction and domestic will have to be opened out to reveal the diversity and complexity of the pattern of activity, decision-making, access and control which they hide.

Bibliography

Abdullah, Tahrunnessa and Zeidenstein, Sondra (1979) 'Women's Reality: Critical Issues for Program Design'. In Sondra Zeidenstein (ed.) *Learning about Rural Women*. Special Issue of *Studies in Family Planning*, 10:11/12, pp.344–52.

Abdullah, Tahrunnessa and Zeidenstein, Sondra (1982) *Village Women of Bangladesh: Prospects for Change*. Oxford: Pergamon for ILO.

Abu, Katherine (1983) 'The Separateness of Spouses: Conjugal Resources in an Ashanti Town'. In Christine Oppong (ed.) *Female and Male In West Africa*. London: George Allen and Unwin, pp.156–58.

Abu Lughod, Lila (1984) *Bedouin Ethnography – In a Different Voice*. Paper presented at the 18th Annual Meeting of the Middle East Studies Association, San Francisco.

Abu Lughod, Lila (1985) 'A Community of Secrets: The Separate World of Bedouin Women'. In *Signs*, 10:4, pp.637–57.

Abu Lughod, Lila (1986) *Veiled Sentiments: Honour and Poetry in a Bedouin Society*, Berkeley: University of California Press.

Abu Saud, Abeer (1984) *Qatari Women: Past and Present*. Burnt Mill, Harlow: Longman.

Adeyemo, Remi (1984) 'Women in Rural Areas: A Case Study of Southwestern Nigeria'. In *Canadian Journal of African Studies*, 18:3, pp.563–72.

Afshar, Haleh (1985) 'The Position of Women in an Iranian Village'. In Haleh Afshar (ed.) *Women, Work and Ideology in the Third World*. London: Tavistock, pp.66–82.

Afshar, Haleh (1987) 'Women, Marriage and the State in Iran'. In Haleh

Afshar (ed.) *Women, State and Ideology: Studies from Africa and Asia.* Basingstoke: Macmillan, pp.70–86.

Agarwal, Bini (1987) 'Gender Issues in the Agricultural Modernisation of India'. In Janet Momsen and Janet Townsend (eds) *Geography of Gender in the Third World.* London: Hutchinson, pp.334–36.

Ahmad, Zubeida and Loutfi, Martha (1985) *Women Workers in Rural Development.* Geneva: International Labour Office.

Ahmed, K. (1976) *Islam: Its Meaning and Message.* Leicester: The Islamic Foundation.

Al Masry (1992) *Jordanian Labour Force Structure.* Jordanian University Press.

Al Munjid Dictionary (1956). Beirut: Lebanon Press.

Al-Torki, S. (1986) *Women in Saudia Arabia: Ideology and Behaviour Among the Elite.* New York: Columbia University Press.

Arbery, A.J. (1955) *The Koran Interpreted.* London: Allen and Unwin.

Ardener, Edwin (1975a) 'Belief and the Problem of Women'. In Shirley Ardener (ed.) *Perceiving Women.* London: Dent, pp.1–18.

Ardener, Edwin (1975b) 'The "Problem" Revisited'. In Shirley Ardener (ed.) *Perceiving Women.* London: Dent, pp.19-28.

Ardener, S. (ed.) (1981) *Women and Space: Ground Rules and Social Maps.* London: Croom Helm.

Arizpe, Lourdes and Aranda, Josefina (1981) 'The Comparative Advantages of Women's Disadvantages: Women Workers in the Strawberry Export Agribusiness in Mexico'. In *Signs* 7:2, pp.453–73.

Asad, Talal (1975) *Anthropological Texts and Ideological Problems: an Analysis of Cohen on Arab Villages in Israel.* London: British Library.

Asia Partnership for Human Development (APHD) (1985) *Awake: Asian Women and their Struggle for Justice.* Sydney: APHD.

Badran, Adnan (1988) *The Political Economy of Jordan.* Cambridge: Cambridge University Press.

Badran, Adnan (1989) *Jordan's Economic Development.* London.

Badran (1989) London, George Allen and Unwin.

Ballard, Roger (1987) 'The Political Economy of Migration: Pakistan, Britain and the Middle East'. In Jeremy Eades (ed.) *Migrants, Workers and the Social Order.* Association of Social Anthropologists Monograph No.26, London: Tavistock, pp.17–41.

Beck, Lois and Nikki R. Keddie (eds) (1978) *Women in the Muslim World.* Cambridge, MA: Harvard University Press.

Beneria, Lourdes and Sen, Gita (1981) 'Accumulation, Reproduction and Women's Role in Economic Development'. In *Signs: Journal of Women in Culture and Society*, 7:2, pp.279–98.

Bhaduri, Amit and Rahman, Anisur Md. (eds) (1982) *Studies in Rural Participation.* New Delhi: Oxford and IBH Publishing Co. for ILO.

Bisharat, L. and Tewfik, M. (1985) 'Housing the Urban Poor in Amman: Can

Upgrading Improve Health?', In *Third World Planning Review*, Vol. 7, No.1, February.

Boserup, Ester (1970) *Woman's Role in Economic Development*. London: George Allen and Unwin. Reprinted 1986, Aldershot: Gower.

Bryceson, Deborah Fahy (1985) 'Women's Proletarianization and the Family Wage in Tanzania'. In Haleh Afshar (ed.) *Women, Work and Ideology in the Third World*. London: Tavistock, pp.128–52.

Butterworth, Douglas and Chance, John (1981) *Latin American Urbanization*. Cambridge: Cambridge University Press.

Campbell, J.K. (1964) *Honour, Family and Patronage*. Oxford: Oxford University Press.

Caplan, Patricia (1985) *Class and Gender in India: Women and their Organisations in a South Indian City*. London: Tavistock.

Casinader, Rex, Fernando, Sepalika and Gamage, Karuna (1987) 'Women's Issues and Men's Roles: Sri Lankan Village Experience'. In Janet Momsen and Janet Townsend (eds) *Geography of Gender in the Third World*. London: Hutchinson, pp.309–322.

Cecelski, Elizabeth (1985) *The Rural Energy Crisis, Women's Work and Basic Needs: Perspectives and Approaches to Action*. Geneva: Rural Employment Policy Research Programme, Technical Co-operation Report, International Labour Office.

Chambers, Robert (1983) *Rural Development: Putting the Last First*. London: Longman.

Chant, Sylvia (1987a) 'Family Structure and Female Labour in Queretaro, Mexico'. In Janet Momsen and Janet Townsend (eds) *Geography of Gender in the Third World*. London: Hutchinson, pp.277–93.

Chant, Sylvia (1987b) 'Domestic Labour, Decision-Making and Dwelling Construction: The Experience of Women in Queretaro, Mexico'. In Caroline Moser and Linda Peake (eds) *Women, Human Settlements and Housing*, London: Tavistock, pp.33–54.

Chant, Sylvia (1987c) 'Gender and Leadership in Low-Income Communities'. Paper presented at seminar 'Local Leaders and Community Development and Participation', Fitzwilliam College, Cambridge, 28–30 September.

Chant, Sylvia and Ward, Peter (1987) 'Family Structure and Low-Income Housing Policy'. In *Third World Planning Review*, 9:1, pp.5–19.

Chapman, Murray and Prothero, R. Mansell (eds) (1985) *Circulation in the Third World*. London: Routledge and Kegan Paul.

Charlton, Sue Ellen (1984) *Women in Third World Development*, Boulder, Colorado: Westview Press.

Chayanov, A.V. (1966) *The Theory of Peasant Economy*. Illinois: The American Economic Association.

Chimedza, Ruvimbo (1987) 'Women and Decision-Making: The Case of District Councils in Zimbabwe'. In Christine Qunta (ed.) *Women In*

Southern Africa. London: Allison and Busby, pp.135–45.

Clarke, Colin (1986) *Livelihood Systems, Settlements and Levels of Living in 'Los Valles Centrales de Oaxaca', Mexico*. Research Paper 37, School of Geography, University of Oxford.

Coontz, Stephanie and Henderson, Peta (1986) 'Introduction'. In Stephanie Coontz and Peta Henderson (eds) *Women's Work, Men's Property*. London: Verso, pp.1–42.

Cubitt, Tessa (1988) *Latin American Society*. London: Longman.

Cunningham, Susan (1987) 'Gender and Industrialisation in Brazil'. In Janet Momsen and Janet Townsend (eds) *Geography of Gender in the Third World*. London: Hutchinson, pp.294–308.

Dankelman, Irene and Davidson, Joan (1988) *Women and Environment in the Third World: Alliance for the Future*. London: Earthscan Publications.

Davies, Miranda (ed.) (1983) *Third World – Second Sex: Women's Struggle and National Liberation*. London: Zed.

Davis, Susan Schaefer (1978) 'Working Women in a Moroccan Village'. In Lois Beck and Nikki Keddie (eds) *Women in the Muslim World*. Cambridge, MA: Harvard University Press, pp.416–33.

de la Paz, Trinidad (1984) *The Katiwala: An Experience in Primary Health Care*. Paper presented to a joint UNICEF/WHO consultation on primary health care in urban areas, Guayaquil, Ecuador, 15–19 October, Geneva: World Health Organisation.

Deere, Carmen Diana (1977) 'Changing Social Relations of Production'. In *Latin American Perspectives,* 4:1/2, pp.48–69.

Deere, Carmen Diana (1986) 'Rural Women and Agrarian Reform in Peru, Chile and Cuba'. In June Nash and Helen Safa (eds) *Women and Change in Latin America*. Massachusetts: Bergin and Garvey, pp.189–207.

Deere, Carmen Diana and de Janvry, Alain (1979) 'A Conceptual Framework for the Empirical Analysis of Peasants'. In *American Journal of Agricultural Economics*, 61, pp.601–11.

Deere, Carmen Diana and Leon de Leal, Magdalena (1981) 'Peasant Production, Proletarianization and the Sexual Division of Labour in the Andes'. In *Signs: Journal of Women in Culture and Society*, 7:2, pp.338–60.

Deere, Carmen Diana and Leon de Leal, Magdalena (1982) *Women in Andean Agriculture*. Geneva: International Labour Office.

Dickenson, John *et al.* (1983) 'Sugar Daddies and Gold-diggers: The White Collar Single Women in Accra'. In Christine Oppong (ed.) *Female and Male in West Africa*. London: George Allen and Unwin, pp.344–66.

Dixon, Ruth (1983) 'Land, Labour and the Sex Composition of the Agricultural Labour Force: An International Comparison'. In *Development and Change*, 14, pp.347–72.

Dixon-Mueller, Ruth (1985) *Women's Work in Third World Agriculture: Concepts and Indicators*. Women, Work and Development 9, Geneva:

International Labour Office.

Durrani, Lorna Hawker (1976) 'Employment of Women and Social Change'. In Russell Stone and John Simmons (eds) *Change in Tunisia*. Albany: State University of New York Press, pp.57–72.

Dwyer, D. and Bruce, J. (1988) *A Home Divided: Women and Income in the Third World*, Stanford, CA: Stanford University Press.

Eakhurddin al Razi (1968) *Tafsir Kabir*. Beirut.

Ember, Carol R. (1983) 'The Relative Decline in Women's Contribution to Agriculture with Intensification'. In *American Anthropologist*, 85, pp.285–305.

Engels, Frederick (1972) *The Origin of the Family, Private Property and the State*, London: Lawrence and Wishart (Originally published in 1884).

Engracia, Luisa and Herrin, Alejandro (1984) 'Employment Structure of Female Migrants to the Cities in the Philippines'. In Gavin W. Jones (ed.) *Women in the Urban and Industrial Workforce: Southeast and East Asia*. Development Studies Centre Monograph No.33, Australian National University, Canberra, pp.293–304.

Ennew, Judith (1986) '*Mujercita* and *Mamacita*: Girls Growing Up in Lima'. In *Bulletin of Latin American Research*, 5:2, pp.49–66.

Fernandez-Kelly, Maria Patricia (1981) 'Development and the Sexual Division of Labour: An Introduction'. In *Signs: Journal of Women in Culture and Society*, 7:2, pp.268–78.

Fernea, E.W. and Bezirgan, B.P. (eds) (1977) *Middle Eastern Muslim Women Speak*. Austin: University of Texas Press.

Fernea, E.W. and Fernea, R.A. *The Arab World: Personal Encounters*. Garden City, NY: Anchor Press.

Firestone, Y. (1975) *Crop Sharing Economics in Mandatory Palestine*. *Middle Easten Studies* XI.

Friedl, E. (1967) '*The Position of Women, Appearance and Reality*'. *Anthropological Quarterly*, 40:3 pp.97–108.

Friedman, G. (1993) *Women's Empowerment*. Oxford: Oxford University Press.

Ghai, Dharam and Radwan, Samir (1983) *Agrarian Policies and Rural Poverty in Africa*. Geneva: International Labour Office.

Gilbert, Alan and Gugler, Josef (1982) *Cities, Poverty and Development: Urbanisation in the Third World*. Oxford: Oxford University Press.

Goody, Jack (1976) *Production and Reproduction: A Comparative Study of the Domestic Domain*. Cambridge: Cambridge University Press.

Gore, M.S. (1968) *Urbanisation and Family Change*. Combay: Popular Prakashan.

Granot, T.A. (1952) *The Land System in Palestine* (Trans). London.

Guyer, Jane and Peters, Pauline (1987) 'Introduction'. In *Conceptualising the Household: Issues of Theory and Policy in Africa*. Special issue of *Development and Change*, 18:2, pp.197–214.

Hagan, George Panyin (1983) 'Marriage, Divorce and Polygyny in Winneba'. In Christine Oppong (ed.) *Female and Male in West Africa*. London: George Allen and Unwin, pp.192–203.

Hariss, Barbara and Watson, Elizabeth (1987) 'The Sex Ratio in South Asia'. In Janet Momsen and Janet Townsend (eds) *Geography of Gender in the Third World*. London: Hutchinson, pp.85–115.

Harris, Olivia (1981) 'Households as Natural Units'. In Kate Young, Carol Wolkowitz and Roslyn McCullagh (eds) *Of Marriage and the Market*. London: CSE Books, pp.48–67.

Heyzer, Noleen (1986) *Working Women in South East Asia: Development: Subordination and Emancipation*. Milton Keynes: Open University Press.

Hijab, Nadia (1988) *Womenpower: the Arab Debate on Women at Work,* Cambridge: Cambridge University Press.

Hirashima, S. (ed.) (1977) *Hired Labour in Rural Asia*. Tokyo: Institute for Developing Economies.

Horowitz, Berny and Kishwar, Madhu (1984) 'Family Life: The Unequal Deal'. In Madhu Kishwar and Ruth Vanita (eds) *In Search of Answers: Indian Women's Voices from Manushi,* London: Zed, pp.69–103.

Humphrey, John (1985) 'Gender, Pay and Skill: Manual Workers in Brazilian Industry'. In Haleh Afshar (ed.) *Women, Work and Ideology in the Third World*. London: Tavistock, pp.214–31.

Hunt, Pauline (1980) *Gender and Class Consciousness*. Basingstoke: Macmillan.

Huston, Perdita (1979) *Third World Women Speak Out*. New York: Praeger.

Hyden, Goran (1986) 'The Invisible Economy of Smallholder Agriculture in Africa'. In Joyce Lewinger Moock (ed.) *Understanding Africa's Rural Households and Farming Systems*. Boulder, Colorado: Westview Press, pp.11–35.

Ibn Al-Hajj (1929) *An Introduction to the Development of Deeds*. Cairo.

Ingrams, Doreen (1983) *The Awakened: Women in Iraq*. London: Third World Center for Research and Publishing.

Institute of British Geographers Women and Geography Study Group (IBG) (1984) *Geography and Gender: An Introduction to Feminist Geography*. London: Hutchinson.

Inter-American Development Bank (IDB) (1987) *Economic and Social Progress in Latin America: Special Section – Labour Force and Employment*. New York: IDB.

International Labour Office (ILO) (1977) *Poverty and Landlessness in Rural Asia*. Geneva: ILO.

International Labour Office (ILO) (1982) *Rural Development and Women in Asia*. Geneva: ILO.

International Labour Office (ILO) (1984) *Rural Development and Women in Africa*. Geneva: ILO.

International Planned Parenthood Federation (IPPF), Evaluation Department (1982) *Planned Parenthood – Women's Development.* London: IPPF.

Isiugo-Abanihe, Uche C. (1985) 'Child Fosterage in West Africa'. In *Population and Development Report,* 11:1, pp.53–73.

Issawi, C. (1966) *The Economic History of the Middle East.* Chicago: Jacobson.

Jacobson, J. (1977) *The Women of North and Central India.* Columbia: South Asia Books.

Jain, Devaki (1980) *Women's Quest for Power.* Sahibabad, India: Vikas.

Jayawardena, Kumari (1986) *Feminism and Nationalism in the Third World.* London: Zed.

Jeffrey, Patricia (1979) *Frogs in a Well: Indian Women in Purdah.* London: Zed.

Jelin, Elizabeth (1977) 'Migration and Labour Force Participation of Latin American Women: The Domestic Servants in the Cities'. In Wellesley Editorial Committee (eds) *Women and National Development: the Complexities of Change.* Chicago: University of Chicago, pp.129–41.

Jelin, Elizabeth (1980) 'The Bahiana in the Labour Force of Salvador, Brazil'. In June Nash and Helen Safa (eds) *Sex and Class in Latin America.* New York: Bergin, pp.129–46.

Jelin, Elizabeth (1982) 'A Micro-Social Indictment of Life-Style: The Organization of Expenditures Among Domestic Units of the Popular Sectors'. Paper presented at a seminar on Demographic Research in Latin America, Mexico City.

Jones, Gavin W. (ed.) (1984) *Women in the Urban and Industrial Workforce: Southeast and East Asia.* Development Studies Centre Monograph No.33, Australian National University, Canberra.

Jules-Rosete, Benetta (1985) 'The Women Potters of Lusaka: Urban Migration and Socioeconomic Adjustment'. In Beverly Lindsay (ed.) *African Migration and National Development.* Pennsylvania: Pennsylvania State University, pp.82–112.

Kabeer, Naila (1985) 'Do Women Gain from High Fertility?' In Haleh Afshar (ed.) *Women, Work and Ideology in the Third World.* London: Tavistock, pp.83–106.

Kabeer, Naila (1994) *Reversed Realities: Gender Hierarchies in Development Thought.* London: Verso.

Kamugisha, Stephanie (1986) 'Violence Agianst Women'. In Pat Ellis (ed.) *Women of the Caribbean.* London: Zed, pp.74–9.

Kandiyoti, D. (1980) 'Urban Change and Women's Roles: An Overview and Evaluation'. In Helen Anne B. Rivlin and Katherine Helmer (eds) *The Changing Middle Eastern City,* New York: Center for Social Analysis Program in Southwest Asian and North African Studies, State University of New York at Binghamton.

Kandiyoti, Deniz (1988) *Women in Rural Production Systems: Problems and Policies.* Paris: UNESCO.

Kandiyoti, Deniz (ed.) (1991) *Women, Islam and the State:* London: Macmillan.

Katakura, M. (1982) *Bedouin Village: A Study of a Saudi Arabian People in Transition.* Tokyo.

Keddie, N.R. (1979) 'Problems in the Study of Middle Eastern Women'. In *International Journal of Middle Eastern Studies,* 10, pp.225–40.

Keddie, Nikki. (1990) 'The Past and the Present of Women in the Muslim World'. In *Journal of World History* 1:1, pp.77–108.

Keesing, R.M. (1975) *Kin Groups and Social Structure.* New York: Holt, Rinehart and Winston.

Khoo, Siew-Ean (1984) *Urbanward Migration and Employment of Women in Southeast and East Asia.* Development Studies Centre Monograph No.33, Australian National University, Canberra, pp.277–92.

Khouri, R.G. (1981) *The Jordan Valley: Life and Society Below Sea Level,* London: Longman.

Kidron, Michael and Segal, Ronald (1984) *The New State of the World Atlas.* London: Pan.

Kishwar, Madhu and Vanita, Ruth (eds) (1984) *In Search of Answers: Indian Women's Voices from Manushi.* London: Zed.

Krieger, L (1986) 'Negotiating Gender Role Expectations in Cairo'. In T.L. Whitehead and M.E. Connoway (eds) *Self, Sex and Gender in Cross-Cultural Fieldwork.* Urbana and Chicago: University of Illinois Press.

Lenin, V.I. (1965) *A Great Beginning, Collected Works,* Vol. 29, London: Lawrence and Wishart.

Lenin, V.I. (1967) *The Development of Capitalism in Russia.* Moscow: Foreign Publishing House.

Lerner, Gerda (1986) *The Creation of Patriarchy.* New York and London: Oxford University Press.

Levi-Strauss, Claude (1969) *The Elementary Structures of Kinship.* London: Eyre and Spottiswoode.

Lewis, N. (1987) *Nomads and Settlers in Syria and Jordan 1800–1980,* NY: Cambridge University Press.

Lewis, Oscar (1966) 'The Culture of Poverty'. In *Scientific American,* October, pp.19–25.

Lewis, W.A. (1977): 'The Evolution of the International Economic Order'. Discussion paper 74, Princeton University, NJ, Woodrow Wilson Research Program in Development Studies.

Lim, Linda (1983) 'Capitalism, Imperialism, and Patriarchy: The Dilemma of Third-World Women Workers in Multinational Factories'. In June Nash and Maria Patricia Fernandez-Kelly (eds) *Women, Men and the International Division of Labour,* Albany: Sunny Press, pp.70–91.

London Iranian Women's Liberation Group (LIWLG) (1983) 'Iranian Women: The Struggle Since the Revolution'. In Miranda Davies (ed.) *Third World – Second Sex: Women's Struggle and National Liberation.* London: Zed, pp.143–58.

MacCormack, Carol (1983) *Minimum Planning and Evaluation Guidelines for Women, Health and Development*. Report prepared for World Health Organisation, Division of Family Health. Evaluation and Planning Centre, London School of Hygiene and Tropical Medicine.

Machado, Leda (1983) 'Low-Income Housing in Brazil and Women: Evaluation of the PROFILURB Project in Terms of its Capacity to Define and Reach Female-Headed Households as a Target Group'. Masters Dissertation, Development Planning Unit, University College, London.

Madelelbaum, D. (1970) *Society in India*. Berkeley and Los Angeles: University of California Press.

Madi, M. & Musa (1984) *The History of Jordan in the Twentieth Century* Amman, Jordan (in Arabic).

Maher, Vanessa (1974) *Women and Property in Morocco*. Cambridge: Cambridge University Press.

Maher, Vanessa (1978) 'Women and Social Change in Morocco'. In Lois Beck and Nikki Keddie (eds) *Women in the Muslim World*. Cambridge, MA: Harvard University Press, pp.100–123.

Mahmood, Tahir (1972) *Family Law Reform in the Muslim World*. Delhi: Delhi Press.

Mahmood, Tahir (1987) *Personal Laws in Islamic Countries*. Delhi: Delhi Press.

Maloney, K. (1986) 'More than a Parley'. In *Community Development Journal*, 21:1, pp.52–58.

Mandelbaum, David (1972) *Women's Seclusion and Men's Honour*. Tucson: University of Arizona Press.

Manushi (1983) 'Indian Women Speak Out Against Dowry'. In Miranda Davies (ed.) *Third World – Second Sex: Women's Struggle and National Liberation*. London: Zed, pp.201–13.

Masri, M. and Abu Jaber, K. (1983) 'Education and Training of Women'. In K. Abu Jaber (ed.) *Major Issues in Jordanian Development*, Amman: The Queen Alia Jordan Social Welfare Fund, 9:45.

Massey, Doreen (1987) *Nicaragua*. Milton Keynes: Open University Press.

Massiah, Joycelin (1986a) 'Women in the Caribbean Project: An Overview'. In *Social and Economic Studies*, 35:2. Institute of Social and Economic Research, University of the West Indies, pp.1–29.

Massiah, Joycelin (1986b) 'Work in the Lives of Caribbean Women'. In *Social and Economic Studies*, 35:2. Institute of Social and Economic Research, University of the West Indies.

Maududi, S.A. (1975) *Finality of Prophethood*. Lahore: Islamic Publications Ltd.

Mazumdar, Vina (1979) 'From Research to Policy: Rural Women in India'. In Sondra Zeidenstein (ed.) *Learning About Rural Women*. Special issue of *Studies in Family Planning*, 10:11/12, pp.353–58.

McCall, Michael (1987) 'Carrying Heavier Burdens but Carrying Less

Weight: Some Implications of Villagization for Women in Tanzania'. In Janet Momsen and Janet Townsend (eds) *Geography of Gender in the Third World*. London: Hutchinson, pp.192–214.

McLean, Scilla (ed.) (1985) *Female Circumcison and Infibulation: The Facts and Proposals for Change*. London: Minority Rights Group.

Mernissi, Fatima (1985) *Beyond the Veil: Male–Female Dynamics in Modern Muslim Society*. London: Al Saqi Books.

See Fatima Mernissi, *Beyond the Veil: Male–Female Dynamics in a Modern Muslim Society*, Cambridge: Schenkman, 1975.

Mernissi, F. (1991) *Women and Islam: A Historical and Theological Enquiry*.

Merrick, Thomas and Schmink, Marianne (1983) 'Households Headed by Women and Urban Poverty in Brazil'. In Mayra Buvinic, Margaret Lycette and William McGreevey (eds) *Women and Poverty in the Third World*. Baltimore: John Hopkins, pp.244–71.

Midgely, James with Hall, Anthony, Hardiman, Margaret and Dhanpaul, Narine (1986) *Community Participation, Social Development and the State*. London and New York: Methuen.

Mies, Maria (1980) *Capitalist Development and Subsistence Production: Rural Women in India*. Bulletin of Concerned Asian Scholars, Vol. 12, No.1, pp.2–14.

Mies, Maria (1982) 'The Dynamics of the Sexual Division of Labour and Integration of Rural Women into the World Market'. In Lourdes Beneria (ed.) *Women and Development*. New York: Praeger, pp.1–28.

Mies, Maria (assisted by Lalita K. and Krishna Kumari) (1986) *Indian Women in Subsistence and Agricultural Labour*. Geneva: International Labour Office.

Mikell, Gwendolyn (1984) 'Filiation, Economic Crisis and the Status of Women in Rural Ghana'. In *Canadian Journal of African Studies*, 18:1, pp.195–218.

Minces, Juliette (1982) *The House of Obedience: Women in Arab Society*. London: Zed.

Ministry of Jordanian Agriculture Report 1991.

Ministry of Jordanian Agriculture Report 1992.

Ministry of Jordanian Agriculture Report 1993.

Moghadam, V.M. (1990) *Gender Development and Policy: Toward Equity and Empowerment*. Helsinki: World Institute for Development Economics Research of the UN University.

Molyneux, Maxine (1985) 'Women'. In Thomas Walker (ed.) *Nicaragua: The First Five Years*. New York: Praeger, pp.145–62.

Momsen, Janet Henshall (1987) 'The Feminisation of Agriculture in the Caribbean'. In Janet Momsen and Janet Townsend (eds) *Geography of Gender in the Third World*. London: Hutchinson, pp.192–214.

Momsen, Janet and Townsend, Janet (eds) (1987) *Geography of Gender in the Third World*. London: Hutchinson.

Moock, Joyce Lewinger (ed.) (1986) *Understanding Africa's Rural Households and Farming Systems*. Boulder, Colorado: Westview Press.

Morsy, S.A. (1990) *Rural Women, Work and Gender Ideology*. New York and Oxford: Berg Publishers and UNESCO.

Moser, Caroline (1987) 'Gender: The Experience of Poor Women in Guayaquil'. In Eduardo Archetti, Paul Cammack and Bryan Roberts (eds) *Sociology of Developing Societies: Latin America*. Basingstoke: Macmillan, pp.305–20.

Mujahid, G.B.S. (1985) 'Female Labour Force Participation in Jordan'. In J. Abu Nasr *et al.* (eds) *Women, Employment and Development in the Arab World,* Berlin: Mouton.

Murray, Colin (1987) 'Class, Gender and the Household: The Developmental Cycle in Southern Africa'. In *Development and Change,* 18, pp.235–49.

Myrdal, G. (1968) *Asian Drama*. London: Pelican Books.

Nath, Kamla (1985) *Women and Vegetable Gardens in the Gambia: Action Aid and Rural Development*. Boston University African Studies Center Working Paper No. 109, Boston.

Nazir, P. (1991) *Local Development in the Global Economy: The Case of Pakistan*. Aldershot: Avebury.

Nelson, Nici (1979) *Why Has Development Neglected Rural Women? A Review of the South Asian Literature*. Oxford: Pergamon.

Nelson, Nicki (1981) 'Mobilizing Village Women: Some Organisational and Management Considerations'. In Nicki Nelson (ed.) *African Women in the Development Process*. London: Frank Cass, pp.47–58.

Nelson, Nicki (1987) 'Rural–Urban Child Fostering in Kenya: Migration, Kinship Ideology and Class'. In Jeremy Eades (ed.) *Migrants, Workers and the Social Order*. Association of Social Anthropologists Monograph No.26, London: Tavistock, pp.181–98.

Neustatter, Angela (1988) 'The Co-operative Way Ahead'. In *The Guardian,* 23 February.

Nimpuno-Parente, Paula (1987) 'The Struggle for Shelter: Women in Site and Service Project in Nairobi, Kenya'. In Caroline Moser and Linda Peake (eds) *Women, Human Settlements and Housing*. London: Tavistock, pp.70–87.

Oakley, P. and Marsden, D. (1984) *Approaches to Participation in Rural Development*. Geneva: International Labour Organisation.

Oberai, A.S. and Singh, H.K. (1983) *Causes and Consequences of Internal Migration*. Delhi: Oxford University Press for International Labour Office.

Odie-Alie, Stella (1986) 'Women in Agriculture: The Case of Guyana'. In *Social and Economic Studies,* 35:2. Institute of Social and Economic Research, University of the West Indies, pp.241–85.

Olesen, Adolf (1984) *A Study of Slums and Slum Improvement in Madras*. Report of a study period in Madras. Institute of Development and Planning, Aalborg, Denmark (mimeo).

Oppong, Christine (1980) *A Synopis of Seven Roles and Statuses of Women: An Outline of a Conceptual and Methodological Approach*. Geneva: International Labour Office Working Paper No. 94.

Oppong, Christine (ed.) (1983) *Female and Male in West Africa*. London: George Allen and Unwin.

Oppong, Christine and Abu, Katherine (1985) *A Handbook for Data Collection of Seven Roles and Statuses of Women*. Geneva: International Labour Office.

Oppong, Christine and Abu, Katherine (1987) *Seven Roles of Women: Impact of Education, Migration and Employment of Ghanaian Mothers*. Geneva: International Labour Office.

Organization of Angolan Women (OAW) (1984) *Angolan Women: Building the Future*. London: Zed.

Ortner, Sherry (1974) 'Is Female to Male as Nature is to Culture?' In Michelle Zimbalist Rosaldo and Louise Lamphere (eds) *Woman, Culture and Society*. Stanford, California: Stanford University Press, pp.67–88.

Ortner, Sherry and Whitehead, Harriet (1981) 'Introduction: Accounting for Sexual Meanings'. In Sherry Ortner and Harriet Whitehead (eds) *Sexual Meanings*. Cambridge: Cambridge University Press, pp.1–28.

Ottenberg, Simon (1955) 'Improvement Associations among the Afikpo Ibo'. In *Africa*, 25:1, pp.1–28.

Owen, R. (1983) 'Government and Economy in Jordan: Progress, Problems and Prospects'. In P. Seale (ed.) *The Shaping of an Arab Statesman: Sharif Abd al-Hamid Sharaf and the Modern Arab World*, London: Quartet Books.

Page, Hilary J. (1986) *Child Bearing Versus Child Rearing: Co-residence of Mothers and Children in Sub-Saharan Africa*. Working Paper 1986–2, Interuniversity Programme in Demography, Brussels.

Pakizegi, Behnaz (1978) 'Legal and Social Positions of Iranian Women'. In Lois Beck and Nikki Keddie (eds) *Women in the Muslim World*. Cambridge, MA: Harvard University Press, pp.216–26.

Palmer, Ingrid (1979) 'New Official Ideas on Women and Development'. In *Bulletin*. Institute of Development Studies, University of Sussex, 10:3, pp.42–52.

Papanek, Hanna (1973) 'Purdahi Separate Worlds and Symbolic Shelter'. *Comparative Studies in Society and History*. 15(3): pp.289–325.

Papanek, Hanna (1976) 'Women in Cities: Problems and Perspectives'. In Irene Tinker, Michele Bo Bramsen and Mayra Buvinic (eds) *Women and World Development*. Chicago: University of Chicago, pp.14–21.

Papanek, Hanna (1977) 'Development Planning For Women'. In Wellesley Editorial Committee (ed.) *Women and National Development: The Complexities of Change*. Chicago: University of Chicago, pp. 14–21.

Papola, T.S. (1986) 'Women Workers in the Formal Sector of Lucknow, India'. In Richard Anker and Catherine Hein (eds) *Sex Inequalities in Urban*

Employment in the Third World. Basingstoke: Macmillan, pp.171–212.

Peake, Linda (1987) 'Government Housing Policy in Guyana and its Implications for Women'. In Caroline Moser and Linda Peake (eds) *Women, Human Settlements and Housing.* London: Tavistock, pp.113–38.

Pearson, Maggie (1987) 'Old Wives or Young Midwives? Women as Caretakers of Health: The Case of Nepal'. In Janet Momsen and Janet Townsend (eds) *Geography of Gender in the Third World.* London: Hutchinson, pp.116–30.

Pearson, Ruth (1986) 'Latin American Women and the New International Division of Labour: A Reassessment'. In *Bulletin of Latin American Research,* 5:2, pp.67–79.

Phongpaichit, Pasuk (1984) 'The Bangkok Masseuses: Origins, Status and Prospects'. In Gavin Jones (ed.) *Women in the Urban and Industrial Workforce: Southeast and East Asia.* Development Studies Centre Monograph No.33, Australian National University, Canberra, pp.251–57.

Radcliffe, Sarah (1986) 'Gender Relations, Peasant Livelihood Strategies and Migration: A Case Study from Cuzco, Peru'. In *Bulletin of Latin American Research,* 5:2, pp.29–47.

Radwan, S. (1977) *Agrarian Reform and Rural Poverty 1952–1975.* Geneva: International Labour Office.

Ragib, E. (1979) *Islam.* Chicago and London.

Rechini de Lattes, Zulma and Wainermann, Catalina (1986) 'Unreliable Accounts of Women's Work'. In *Signs: Journal of Women in Culture and Society,* 11:4, pp.740–50.

Redcliffe, Nanneke and M. Thea Sinclair (eds) (1991) *Working Women: International Perspectives on Labour and Gender Ideology.* London and New York: Routledge.

Rees, Judith and Odell, Peter (eds) (1987) *The International Oil Industry: An Interdisciplinary Perspective.* Basingstoke: Macmillan.

Rifkin, Susan (1984) *Community Participation in MCH/CP Programmes: An Analysis Based on Case Study Materials.* Geneva: World Health Organisation.

Roberts, Pepe (1979) 'The Integration of Women into the Development Process: Some Conceptual Problems'. In *Bulletin,* Institute of Development Studies, University of Sussex, 10:3, pp.60–6.

Roberts, Pepe (1984) 'Feminism *in* Africa: Feminism *and* Africa'. In *Review of African Political Economy,* 27/28, pp.175–84.

Robertson, Claire (1987) 'Developing Economic Awareness: Changing Perspectives in Studies of African Women 1976-85'. In *Feminist Studies,* 13:1, pp.97–135.

Rogers, Barbara (1980) *The Domestication of Women: Discrimination in Developing Societies.* London: Tavistock.

Rosenzweig, M.R. (1986) 'Program Interventions, Intrahousehold Distribution and the Welfare of Individuals: Modelling Household Behaviour'. In

World Development, Vol. 14, No. 2, pp.233–43.

Ross, Marc Howard (1986) 'Female Political Participation: A Cross-Cultural Explanation'. In *American Anthropologist,* 88, pp.843–58.

Sacks, Karen (1974) 'Engels Revisited: Women, the Organisation of Production, and Private Property'. In Michelle Rosaldo and Loise Lamphere (eds) *Women, Culture and Society.* Stanford, California: Stanford University Press, pp.207–22.

Sacks, Karen (1979) *Sisters and Wives.* Westport, Connecticut: Greenwood Press.

Said, E. (1982) *The Question of Palestine*, London: Routledge and Kegan Paul.

Salman, Magida (1987) 'The Arab Woman'. In Khamsin (ed.) *Women in the Middle East.* London: Zed, pp.6–11.

Savara, Mira (1983) 'A Report of a Workshop on Women, Health and Reproduction'. In Miranda Davies (ed.) *Third World – Second Sex: Women's Struggle and National Liberation.* London: Zed, pp.220–27.

Schildkrout, Enid (1983) 'Dependence and Autonomy: The Economic Activities of Secluded Hausa Women in Kano'. In Christine Oppong (ed.) *Female and Male in West Africa.* London: George Allen and Unwin, pp.107–26.

Schmink, Marianne (1986) 'Women and Urban Industrial Development in Brazil'. In June Nash and Helen Safa (eds) *Women and Change in Latin America.* Massachusetts: Bergin and Garvey, pp.136–64.

Scott, Alison MacEwen (1986a) 'Industrialization, Gender Segregation and Stratification Theory'. In Rosemary Compton amd Michael Mann (eds) *Gender and Stratification.* Cambridge: Polity Press, pp.154–89.

Scott, Alison MacEwen (1986b) 'Women and Industrialization: Examining the "Female Marginalisation" Thesis'. In *Journal of Development Studies,* 22:4, pp.649–80.

Scott, Alison MacEwen (1988) 'Capitalist Development and Woman's Marginalisation from Production: Theoretical and Methodological Problems'. In *Gender and Society* (forthcoming).

Seager, Joni and Olson, Ann (1986) *Women in the World: An International Atlas.* London: Pan.

Sen, Amartyak (1990) 'Gender and Cooperative Conflicts'. In I. Tinker (ed.) *Persistent Inequalities: Women and World Development.* Oxford: Oxford University Press.

Sen, Gita and Grown, Caren, for Development Alternatives with Women for a New Era (DAWN) (1988) *Development, Crises and Alternative Visions: Third World Women's Perspectives.* London: Earthscan Publications.

Sharma, Ursula (1978) 'Segregation and its Consequences in India'. In Patricia Caplan and Janet Bujra (eds) *Women United, Women Divided: Cross-cultural Perspectives on Female Solidarity.* London: Tavistock, pp.259–82.

Sharma, Ursula (1980) *Women, Work and Property*. London: Tavistock.

Sharma, Ursula (1984) 'Dowry in North India: Its Consequences for Women'. In Renee Hirschon (ed.) *Women and Property – Women as Property*. London/New York: Croom Helm/St Martins, pp.62–74.

Sharma, Ursula (1986) *Women's Work, Class and the Urban Household: A Study of Shimla, North India*. London: Tavistock.

Simon, David (1984) 'Responding to Third World Urban Poverty: Women and Men in the "Informal" Sector in Windhoek, Namibia'. In Janet Momsen and Janet Townsend (eds) *Women's Role in Changing the Face of the Developing World*. Papers, Women and Geography Study Group Session, Annual Conference of the Institute of British Geographers, Durham, January 1984, pp.95–130.

Siraj, Mehrun (1984) 'Islamic Attitudes to Female Employment in Industrializing Countries: Some Notes from Malaysia'. In Gavin Jones (ed.) *Women in the Urban and Industrial Workforce: Southeast and East Asia*. Development Studies Centre Monograph No.33, Australian National University, Canberra, pp.163–73.

Spiro, Heather (1987) 'Women Farmers and Traders in Oyo State, Nigeria: A Case Study of their Changing Roles'. In Janet Momsen and Janet Townsend (eds) *Geography of Gender in the Third World*. London: Hutchinson, pp.173–91.

Standing, Hilary (1985) 'Resources, Wages and Power: The Impact of Women's Employment on the Urban Bengali Household'. In Haleh Afshar (ed.) *Women, Work and Ideology in the Third World*. London: Tavistock, pp.232–57.

Stewart, Frances (1985) *Planning to Meet Basic Needs*. London: Macmillan.

Stivens, Maila (1985) 'The Fate of Women's Land Rights: Gender, Matriliny and Capitalism in Rembau, Negeri Sembilan, Malaysia'. In Haleh Afshar (ed.) *Women, Work and Ideology in the Third World*. London: Tavistock, pp.3–36.

Stivens, Maila (1987) 'Family and State in Malaysian Industrialisation: The Case of Rembau, Negeri Sembilan, Malaysia'. In Haleh Afshar (ed.) *Women, State and Ideology: Studies from Africa and Asia*. Basingstoke: Macmillan, pp.89–110.

Tessler, Mark with Rogers, Janet and Schneider, Daniel (1978) 'Women's Emancipation in Tunisia'. In Lois Beck and Nikki Keddie (eds) *Women in the Muslim World*. Cambridge, MA: Harvard University Press, pp.141–58.

The Jordanian Institute for Social Services (1978) *The Conditions of Working Women in Factories in Amman City*, a report submitted to the Women's Department, Ministry of Labour, Amman.

Thiam, Awa (1986) *Black Sisters Speak Out: Feminism and Oppression in Black Africa*. London: Pluto.

Tilly, Louise, and Scott, Joan (1978) *Women, Work and Family*, New York and London: Holt, Rinehart and Winston.

Tilly, Louise and Scott, Joan (1987) *Women, Work and Family.* London: Methuen.

Tinker, Irene (ed.) (1990) *Persistent Inequalities: Women and World Development.* New York: Oxford University Press.

Tipple, A. Graham and Helen, J.A. (1986) *Priorities for Public Utilities and Housing Improvements in Kumasi, Ghana: An Empirical Assessment Based on Six Variables.* Seminar Paper No.44, Department of Geography, University of Newcastle upon Tyne.

Townsend, Janet (1987) 'Rural Change: Progress for Whom?' In David Preston (ed.) *Latin American Development: Geographical Perspectives. Harlow:* Longman, pp.199–228.

Townsend, Janet and Momsen, Janet (1987) 'Towards a Geography of Gender in the Third World'. In Janet Momsen and Janet Townsend (eds) *Geography of Gender in the Third World.* London: Hutchinson, pp.27–81.

Tucker, J. (1986) *Women in Nineteenth-Century Egypt.* Cambridge: Cambridge University Press.

Tucker, Judith (1993) *Arab Women: Old Boundaries, New Frontiers.* Indiana: Indiana University Press.

United Nations Centre for Human Settlements (UNCHS) (1985) *Women and Human Settlements.* Nairobi: UNCHS (HABITAT).

United Nations Children's Fund (UNICEF) (1984) *Reaching Children and Women of the Urban Poor.* Occasional Papers Series No. 3. New York: UNICEF.

United Nations Development Programme (UNDP) (1994). Oxford: Oxford University Press.

United Nations (UN) (1989) 'World Population Prospects as Assessed in 1980'. New York: Department of International Economic and Social Affairs, *Population Studies No. 78*, United Nations.

United Nations (1992) *World Investment Report*, New York: UN.

Vance, Irene (1985) *Women's Participation in Self-Help Housing: The San Judas Barrio Project, Managua, Nicaragua.* Gender and Planning Working Paper No.4, Development Planning Unit, University College, London.

Vellenga, Dorothy Dee (1983) 'Who is a Wife? Legal Expressions of Heterosexual Conflicts in Ghana'. In Christine Oppong (ed.) *Female and Male in West Africa.* London: George Allen and Unwin, pp.144–55.

Verdon, Michel (1979) 'African Apprentice Workshops: A Case of Ethnocentric Reductionism'. In *American Ethnologist,* 6:3, pp.531–42.

Ward, Peter (1986) *Welfare Politics in Mexico: Papering over the Cracks.* London: Allen and Unwin.

Ward, Peter (1987) 'Reproduction of Social Inequality: Access to Health Services in Mexico City'. In *Health Policy and Planning,* 2:1, pp.44–57.

Ward, Peter and Chant, Sylvia (1987) 'Community Leadership and Self-Help Housing'. In *Progress in Planning,* Vol. 27, Part 2, pp.69–136.

Webster, Andrew (1984) *Introduction to the Sociology of Development*. Basingstoke and London: Macmillan.

Weiss, Ruth (1986) *The Women of Zimbabwe*. London: Kesho Publications.

Wells, Troth and Sim, Foo Gaik (1987) *Till They Have Faces: Women as Consumers*. International Organisation of Consumer Unions, Regional Office for Asia and the Pacific/ISIS International, Penang/Rome.

Westwood, Sallie (1984) '"Fear Woman": Property and Modes of Production in Urban Ghana'. In Renee Hirschon (ed.) *Women and Property – Women as Property*. London/New York: Croom Helm/St Martins, pp.140–57.

Weulersse, J. (1946) *Paysans de Syrie et du Porch Orient*, Paris.

White, Christine (1981) 'Women's Employment and the Family: Report on a Colloquium Comparing the Women's Movement and Government Legislation in Britain and Vietnam'. In *Bulletin*, 15:1, Institute of Development Studies, University of Sussex, pp.57–61.

White, Douglas R., Burton, Michael and Dow, Malcolm (1981) 'Sexual Division of Labour in African Agriculture: A Network Autocorrelation Analysis'. In *American Anthropolist*, 83, pp.824–49.

Whyte, Robert Orr and Whyte, Pauline (1978) *Rural Asian Women: Status and Environment*. Notes and Discussion Papers No. 9, Institute of Southeast Asian Studies, Singapore.

Wikan, Unni (1980) *Life Among the Poor in Cairo*. London: Tavistock.

Wilkinson, Clive (1987) 'Women, Work and Migration in Lesotho'. In Janet Momsen and Janet Townsend (eds) *Geography of Gender in the Third World*. London: Hutchinson, pp.225–39.

Williams, Cheryl (1986) 'The Role of Women in Caribbean Culture'. In Pat Ellis (ed.) *Women of the Caribbean*. London: Zed, pp.109–14.

Wilson, Adrian (1985) *Family*. London: Tavistock.

World Bank Report, 1993. Oxford: Oxford University Press.

Young, Kate (1978) 'Modes of Appropriation and the Sexual Division of Labour: A Case Study from Oaxaca'. In Annette Kuhn and Anne Marie Wolpe (eds) *Feminism and Materialism*. London: Routledge and Kegan Paul, pp.124–54.

Young, Kate (1993) *Planning Development with Women*. Basingstoke: Macmillan.

Young, Kate, Wolkowitz, Carol and McCullagh, Roslyn (eds) (1981) *Of Marriage and the Market*. London: CSE Books.

Young, Mei Ling and Salih, Kamal (1987) 'The Malay Family: Structural Change and Transformation – A Research Proposal?' In Janet Momsen and Janet Townsend (eds) *Geography of Gender in the Third World*. London: Hutchinson, pp.348–54.

Youssef, Nadia (1972) 'Differential Labour Force Participation of Women in Latin American and Middle Eastern Countries'. In *Social Forces*, 51, pp.135–53.

Youssef, Nadia and Hetler, Carol (1983) 'Establishing the Economic Condition of Women-Headed Households in the Third World: A New Approach'. In Mayra Buvinic, Margaret Lycette and William McGreevey (eds) *Women and Poverty in the Third World*. Baltimore: John Hopkins, pp.216–43.

Zabaleta, Marta (1986) 'Research on Latin American Women: In Search of Our Political Independence'. In *Bulletin of Latin American Research*, 5:2, pp.97–103.

Zack-Williams, A.B. (1985) 'Female Urban Employment'. In Editorial Committee *Women in Nigeria* (WIN) (eds) *Women in Nigeria*, London: Zed Press, pp.104–13.

Zagha, H. (1987) 'Housing Problems, Policies and Solutions in Jordan'. In R. Keles and H. Kano (eds) *Housing and the Urban Poor in the Middle East – Turkey, Egypt, Morocco and Jordan,* Tokyo: Institute of Developing Economies, pp.178–96.

Zeidenstein, Sondra (ed.) (1979) *Learning about Rural Women*. Special issue of *Studies in Family Planning,* 10:11/12 November/December.

Zosa-Feranil, Imelda (1984) 'Female Employment and the Family: A Case Study of the Bataan Export Processing Zone'. In Gavin Jones (ed.) *Women in the Urban and Industrial Workforce: Southeast and East Asia.* Development Studies Centre Monograph No.33, Australian National University, Canberra, pp.387–403.

Index

percentage of production of wet land 78

productive season 78

thyme 146

tomatoes, crop labour requirements 82

wheat, cost, outcome and income per acre 81

dalals 84

decision-making in agricultural production 126–9

divorce 161–6
consequences for women 16–17
dowry and 154
innovatory 16
involuntary 16
laws 165–6
return to parental family 164
women's right to (*khula'*) 154, 166–7

dowry (*mahr*) 71, 153, 154–5, 189
composition 156
divorce and 154
expectations of 153
as property 66–7, 182
role of women and 153–6

earnings *see* income

economy 82–4
development of, women and 10–12
strata 89

education 9, 94, 116, 121, 145–6, 147

elderly people, work done by 120

employment
benefits of 118
outside their own village 115
professional 115
in rich families 115–18
right to 186
seasonal 114
wage labour 85–7
women in 10–11, 14, 114–18
see also agricultural work; household work

Engels, F.: *Origin of the Family, Private Property and the State* 5, 69

European Union (EU) 26

extra-household responsibilities 123

farm systems research 32

faskh 166

fertility rates of Muslem women 9, 17
divorce and 16

field research
household budgets 35–8
land and property 35
methodology 33–9
qualitative data 38–9

food expenditure 43, 126

furniture, expenditure on 131

gandu system 29

Hadiths 15

hamula 113, 114
traditions of 143

Hired Labour in Rural Asia 33

hma (mother-in-law) 16, 171–2

household
composition 108–11
definition 109–11
self-sufficiency 12
typologies of structure in Shayfoun 36
as unit of diversified economic activity 111–14

household budgeting, control of 130–4

household commodities 90, 91

household work 5
female work teams 122, 123–4
organisation of 118–24
relation between agricultural work and 147–50
sexual division of labour 118–24
women's perceptions of 144–7

Ibn Al-Hajj 60

income
control over 134–7
multiple sources 113
women's 82, 114, 117–18

India, women's participation 23

infanticide, female 155

inheritance
divorce and right to 166–7